Reclaiming a Lost Heritage

JOHN R. CAMPBELL

Reclaiming a Lost Heritage

Land-Grant and Other Higher Education Initiatives for the Twenty-first Century

IOWA STATE UNIVERSITY PRESS / AMES

John R. Campbell has undergraduate and graduate degrees in dairy science from the University of Missouri–Columbia, the land-grant university of his native state. Although engaged in research and outreach, he emphasized teaching while serving on the faculty of his alma mater from 1960 through 1977. He authored *In Touch with Students: A Philosophy for Teachers* (1972) and co-authored *The Science of Animals that Serve Humanity* (third edition, 1985) and *The Science of Providing Milk for Man* (1975). In 1973 he was honored as a distinguished teacher by both the National Association of Colleges and Teachers of Agriculture and the American Dairy Science Association (ADSA). He was elected president of ADSA in 1980.

In 1977 Dr. Campbell became associate dean for resident instruction and in 1983 dean of the College of Agriculture at the University of Illinois at Urbana-Champaign. He served as president of Oklahoma State University from 1988 to 1993. As an administrator, Dr. Campbell became widely respected as an energetic and visionary leader. He continues to participate actively on several facets of the work of the National Association of State Universities and Land-Grant Colleges and enjoys the emeritus status three land-grant institutions have conferred upon him—professor emeritus at Missouri, dean emeritus at Illinois, and president emeritus at Oklahoma State.

© 1995 Iowa State University Press, Ames, Iowa 50014

♾ Printed on acid-free paper in the United States of America

First edition, 1995

Library of Congress Cataloging-in-Publication Data

Campbell, John R.
    Reclaiming a lost heritage: land-grant and other higher education initiatives for the twenty-first century / John R. Campbell.—1st ed.
        p.   cm.
    ISBN 0-8138-2159-2
    1. State universities and colleges—United States. 2. Education, Higher—United States—Aims and objectives. 3. State universities and colleges—United States—Public services. 4. State universities and colleges—United States—Planning.   I. Title.
LB2329.5.C35   1995
378'.053—dc20   95-30989

This book is respectfully dedicated

to all who share a passion for and commitment to the concept and philosophy of democratized education and

to the marvelous men and women who, through their signal public service in discharging the responsibilities associated with the well-conceived, publicly mandated teaching, research, and outreach missions of the land-grant college and university system, have made an important difference in the lives and pursuits of others.

We thank, commend, and salute you!

Contents

Foreword

When the history of the twenty-first century is written it will document that education was a central element of those societies that succeeded in improving the lives of their people. And that history (still in the future) also will reveal that higher education—and especially the state and land-grant universities—was the creative fuel for the social engine. The value and virtue of John Campbell's book is that it puts these universities into clear perspective in context of both their history and of their future. The author—having served higher education the past four decades as teacher-researcher, college dean, and university president—is extraordinarily well-qualified to do this job.

The specific merit of this book is twofold. First, it honors education. Oliver Wendell Holmes, Jr., once remarked, "We need education in the obvious more than elucidation of the obscure." This book reminds us over and again, through sharp and telling anecdotes, why these people-serving universities have been essential to the fulfillment of the signal ideals of American democracy. If some of the points are obvious, they are not always as well appreciated and understood as they should be. *Reclaiming a Lost Heritage: Land-Grant and Other Higher Education Initiatives for the Twenty-first Century,* written in compelling and lively fashion, serves a fundamental educational purpose.

Second, this book, while drawing on the past and explaining the present, forthrightly speaks to the future. It is a future in which the state and land-grant university must play a revitalized central role. We must continuously remind ourselves not only of the history but also of the promise of a tomorrow founded on the concept of education as an absolutely essential element of continuing progress as a nation.

The historic 1862 Morrill Act had one overriding purpose: to directly serve the people's fundamental needs. The premise of Senator Justin Morrill's magnificent legislative accomplishment was profoundly democratic: education would be extraordinarily valuable to all of America if there were universities open to all—to the daughters and sons of farmers, mechanics, and other workers, not only to the rich, the well-born, the privileged. These universities were to promote education in the liberal arts and the pursuit of general knowledge. But they also were to promote education that would be practically applied to meet the economic development needs of that era, primarily agriculture and engineering. We should make no mistake: this was a radical, populist concept. In effect, universities were to be chartered by the people (through their representatives) to serve the people.

We must never forget that food will always be an essential need of every human being and therefore the agricultural front will always be a critical part of these universities. But today and tomorrow the state and land-grant universities need to be redefined not in terms of a particular activity, whether it be agriculture or engineering, but in terms of the concept—the core land-grant concept—of making the knowledge that we discover useful to and usable by every citizen, for we serve all citizens. Moreover, this concept—which was always intended to undergird an inclusive, people-serving enterprise—must be expanded and promoted as a philosophy appropriate to all of America's great public universities, regardless of whether they have colleges of agriculture and engineering and regardless of where they are located. Indeed, location should be considered in terms of the entire state and region—the larger community—for this is at the core of the public-service mission of land-grant universities, which is their defining feature.

In concept and in purpose, then, the state and land-grant university of tomorrow will be the same as it is today. But the way its faculty and staff go about their people-serving mission will not be the same as it was twenty years ago, or even as it is today. Ours is now an incredibly international and technological world, and unless state and land-grant universities change so as to adapt, they run the risk of becoming marginalized. Then much of their work would be taken over by other generators of knowledge and information and providers of education who will not have the base of knowledge, understanding, and selfless devotion to public service that remains the irreducible core of the land-grant mission.

As one reads and ponders John Campbell's wisdom, ideas will be clarified as to the role the state and land-grant university can and should play in the years ahead. I suspect every reader will think about how these universities can serve the nation's future.

My own vision of our state and land-grant universities in the twenty-first century goes something like this. We will be doing our work of education in a world in which technology massively affects teaching and learning and the way we go about our responsibilities as agents of critical thinking and providers of useful information. In this world our nation will flower as one of diverse cultures, one in which majorities and minorities will become indistinguishable—but not in any false way. They will be indistinguishable by virtue of being united through lifelong learning and an understanding of our complex world and of being dedicated to making our society better for all of our people.

The state and land-grant university of the next century will still be hugely engaged in matters of nutrition and food and agriculture. Its research and outreach activities will still be serving these compelling needs. But, as John Campbell too predicts, they will be just as engaged in new and exciting partnerships in engineering and technology and industry and business. These universities will also be participating front and center in matters of elementary and secondary education—our public schools—as an obligation of the academy. They will also have moved forward, even beyond their current activities, to significant reform in the ways they provide undergraduate education and how they reward faculty members for their efforts. Moreover, the state and land-grant university of tomorrow will go forward on its commitment to access for citizens of all circumstances and from all positions. It will do so because a commitment to all citizens is not only the moral thing to do; it is the smart thing to do. These universities will stand in the forefront of making sure that our society does not waste the stunning array of talent possessed by our citizenry, the rich talent inherent in every individual.

Finally, the state and land-grant university of the twenty-first century will be profoundly involved in international education, not only in its outreach and research programs but also in its work of providing understanding about the world and the complex interrelationships it involves. The reason must be obvious: unless our colleges and universities lead in internationalizing their curricula, in fostering relationships with people of other nations, in promoting study and research on international interconnections and issues, the United States of America as a nation simply will be unequipped to meet the challenges of the next century in ways that will ensure a continuing high standard of living for its citizens.

Idealistic as these prescriptions may seem—perhaps they really are dreams and hopes—they also are grounded in realism and the proven track record of the American state and land-grant university, one of the truly great educational wonders of the world. John Campbell's extensive tour of the land-grant university—its history, its workings, its accomplishments in the face of a barrage of challenges—provides reassurance that this dream, this idealistic yet practical vision of how land-grant academe can serve the total society, can come to fruition again in the new environments of the twenty-first century.

John Campbell's work, in short, is both a sourcebook and a guidebook to the exciting future of the American state and land-grant university in its continuing mission of service to this democracy and, indeed, to the world. This book could hardly be more timely, coming as it does when numerous entities across the spectrum of activities in our nation are needing just such inspiration and just such a resource as they plan for coping with the challenges higher education will face in the next millennium. With no reservation whatsoever, I commend *Reclaiming a Lost Heritage: Land-Grant and Other Higher Education Initiatives for the Twenty-first Century* to your attention. I expect you will find it, as I did, stimulating, valuable, and profoundly encouraging.

C. Peter Magrath

PRESIDENT
NATIONAL ASSOCIATION OF STATE UNIVERSITIES
AND LAND-GRANT COLLEGES

Preface

Virtually every great chapter in our nation's history began by an expansion of educational opportunities for the citizenry. The land-grant college and university system is a marvelous example. Novel in form, noble in purpose, the land-grant system has from the start had no equal. We owe much to our Republic's early visionaries who saw the need and seized the opportunity to conceptualize, legislate, and implement what has become the world's most successful system of higher education—one that has made provisions for essentially all to have access to a college education.

In his June 1904 inaugural address as president of The University of Wisconsin, Charles R. Van Hise said:

> A state university can only permanently succeed ... where its doors are open to all ... who possess sufficient intellectual endowment, where the financial terms are so easy that the industrious poor may find the way. ... This is a state university ideal, and this is a new thing in the world.

A nation preserves that which it treasures. I share the view with many academic colleagues that too few Americans treasure our rich land-grant heritage. As often is the case, this state of affairs probably exists because the land-grant legacy has not been effectively communicated. This book is intended to reflect on the sound philosophy espoused by those who conceptualized and implemented the land-grant college and university system as well as on subsequent successes emanating from the "land-grant" Morrill Acts of 1862 and 1890. This approach has worked wonders in the United States. The book is further intended to serve as a challenge to return to the basics that undergird the land-grant system as we prepare to move into the twenty-first century.

We must keep our root system in the people. Land-grant institutions should take a much more active outreach in the state's

public education system, and at the same time serve as an engine
of economic growth.

WILLIAM FRIDAY

My overarching purpose in this book is to revisit the truism that the course of human events is ultimately determined not by a select few—important though they may be—but it is determined rather by those in the mainstream of society. The Russian reformer Count Leo Tolstoy observed more than a century ago that the hopes and dreams, doubts and fears, courage and tenacity, and quiet commitments of ordinary people determine human destiny in the long run. Moreover, Thomas Jefferson's belief in the common people led him to vigorously espouse the notion that a democracy works best when its citizens are well-educated. He recognized that ultimately democracy cannot succeed without the benefits of education and that education cannot fulfill its potential without democracy. The land-grant college and university system has contributed immeasurably to providing greater educational access to the citizens of the United States.

The people's university is an epitome of the people's revolu-
tion. Once universities were chartered by the king—now by the
people; once they were supported mainly by devoted sects, pri-
vate gifts, and endowments—now, in addition, by all the people;
once they provided curricula only for a few learned professions—
now increasingly for all professions, vocations, and human needs
as deep as life and as wide as the world; once they served mainly
the privileged classes—now increasingly all groups and all peo-
ple.

FRANK P. GRAHAM

Land-grant colleges and universities are on the hinge of history. While closely connected with the past, many are swinging in other directions. This book revisits their historical past. It examines the public mandate that served so well as the guiding compass. It describes and attempts to evaluate significant new developments. Finally and importantly, it proposes new initiatives for the twenty-first century. If implemented, these new directions could help garner greater public support as land-grant institutions respond to crucial public issues and needs. It is my hope that the proposed initiatives will provide a starting point for constructive dialogue and evolutionary process. They are essential to the land-grant system in recapturing the public support it so clearly needs and so rightly deserves.

To stimulate thought, each chapter and subsection begins with a philosophical quotation.

Quotations preserve for humanity not only the beauty of literature, but also the wisdom of philosophy, the counsel of experience, and the inspiration of achievement.
LEWIS COPELAND

I quote others only in order the better to express myself.
MICHEL DE MONTAIGNE

Preparation of this book was a self-imposed task inspired by a profound interest in, a deep respect for, and a strong commitment to the land-grant college and university system. The system gave me an opportunity to earn undergraduate and graduate degrees and to participate in the teaching, research, outreach, and administration of three land-grant universities.

The project depended heavily upon the encouragement, cooperation, support, and assistance of many people contacted during research and preparation phases. Space does not permit a listing of the names of all contributors. Suffice it to say that the assistance of each and every one enriched the manuscript. They provided references, shared articles, papers, historical tidbits, anecdotes, personal experiences and philosophies, and offered invaluable comments, suggestions, and recommendations on early drafts.

Notwithstanding the above, special appreciation is expressed to Eunice Campbell for her various contributions to manuscript preparation, to Dr. Stanley E. Curtis of The Pennsylvania State University for his editorial efforts with later drafts, to my presidential executive assistant Sheila Harp for her research and overall support, and to my fellow associates in The Hannah Group, an organization headquartered at Michigan State University that is dedicated to revitalizing the land-grant university system. My special thanks also to Benita Bale for her fast and efficient clerical assistance. In addition, I gratefully acknowledge the excellent editorial assistance, including many important contributions to clarity and consistency, by the staff of Iowa State University Press. We hope readers will enjoy the fruits of our collective efforts.

I have somewhere seen it observed that we should make the same use of a book that the bee does of a flower; she steals sweets from it, but does not injure it.
C.C. COLTON

A person intent upon a book may be marginally aware of the temperature of the room and the ticking of the clock.

ROBERT M. BLACKBURN

Finally, considering the following words of Alfred North Whitehead, I believe the importance of "reclaiming a lost heritage" is such a critical part of revitalizing the land-grant spirit needed to appropriately serve students and the public in the twenty-first century that any treatment of the subject would be inadequate. Yet few ideas or ideals are actualized until they have been verbalized.

The trouble is not with what the author does say, but rather with what one does not say. It is not what one knows has been assumed, but rather with what one has unconsciously assumed.

John R. Campbell
PRESIDENT EMERITUS
OKLAHOMA STATE UNIVERSITY

Reclaiming a Lost Heritage

A Historical Perspective of the Land-Grant University System

Open the doors to all. ... Let the children of the rich and the poor take their seats together and know of no distinction save that of industry, good conduct, and intellect.

TOWNSEND HARRIS

1.1 Introduction

That which is honored in a country will be cultivated there.

PLATO

When Columbus first visited America more than five centuries ago, an estimated 370,000 Native Americans inhabited this vast country. It was a land of abundant natural resources—oil, coal, forests, minerals, water, wildlife, and woodlands. But most of all, it had rich soil and a climate favorable to the growth of food crops; yet these natural resources lay largely untapped.

The first European settlers who entered these marvelous lands encountered many hardships and dangers. They sometimes found harsh weather, new diseases, and a shortage of food. They brought little experience that fitted them for the struggle with Nature that followed. It is not surprising, then, that progress in agricultural and industrial development was slow in early America.

But here, quilted across the sweeping landscape of this wonderful country, an ocean of golden prairie and blue sky promised abundant opportunities for families craving a better way of life. Frequently discouraged but rarely defeated, these determined early settlers found great strength and inspiration in their love for fellow human beings and their appreciation of challenging frontiers.

As soon as they started a new settlement, these stalwart pioneers typi-

3

cally demonstrated their abiding faith in community life by building a school and a church. They sincerely believed that a firm foundation in education and religious values would enable their children and grandchildren to live happier, healthier, more productive lives.

The spirit of this common faith in and commitment to education is clearly evident in records of this emerging culture. A frontier historian, reflecting more than a century ago on early pioneer families on the Illinois prairie, wrote of their fervent faith in the inherent power of education:

> As the royal monogram on the clothing of the infant prince marks him as belonging to the royal family, so the rough schoolhouse in each settlement was the royal mark, telling that it belonged to the people foreordained by Almighty God to be the royal nation of the world. The bulk of the nation might be far away toward the eastern ocean, and the settlement might consist of but six scattered cabins—whose occupants were struggling for daily bread—yet the humble, log-ribbed schoolhouse was the rough-robed prophet of a future time, when on these shores, the grateful world shall see what it has never seen before—the national power of education.

Fortunately, this national vision of the power of education has been perpetuated by each subsequent generation. The dreams and aspirations of our founders in this respect happily did not end with the one-room schoolhouse. Regardless of ethnic heritage or personal interests, the early pioneers quickly moved to add higher education and later vocational education to the spectrum of educational opportunities.

I can only say that I view education as the most important subject which we as a people can be engaged in.
ABRAHAM LINCOLN

It is difficult to understand and fully appreciate the land-grant college and university system without first understanding the conditions that led to its creation. These important events and developments include:

The Declaration of Independence. This document gave us important freedoms, including the freedom to think, discuss issues, and express views openly; the freedom to dream of how we would prefer things to be; and the freedom to pursue changes needed to achieve our dreams and ambitions.

A representative form of democracy. Our democracy is one that permits individual and collective needs to surface and that requires decision-making and rule by consensus.

A commitment to education of the masses. The nation's earliest settlers—largely European in ethnic origin—firmly believed in the merits of education. Although many were unable to pursue their own educational goals, they struggled to ensure ample opportunities were available to their children. They persevered and they succeeded.

> *I consider a human soul without education like marble in the quarry, which shows none of its inherent beauty until the skill of the polisher brings out the colors, makes the surface shine, and discovers every ornamental cloud, spot and vein that runs through the body of it.*
>
> **JOSEPH ADDISON**

Education legislation enacted by Congress. This provided for the establishment of elementary schools through the use of federal grants of public land, and is the origin of the term "land-grant."

This early land-grant movement was driven by a national consensus that higher education should be available to the poor as well as the rich, to women as well as men, to people of color as well as European Americans. Indeed, from the very beginning, the land-grant college and university system has had a common objective, that of extending to working people as well as others practical education based on scientific knowledge.

> *For me, it goes back to what the land-grant college is. It is an extraordinary achievement when you think of it—that the government had an obligation to make higher education available to people whether they had any scratch or not. And this was during the Civil War. So, today, when the federal government says it has no business dealing in education, I have to say that Mr. Lincoln thought it did, even when he was in midst of a great national crisis. … If it had not been for land-grant colleges, I would never have gone to a university at all; … this affected my life and career a great deal.*
>
> **JAMES RESTON**
> Columnist, *New York Times*

The population of the United States was predominantly rural during the first half of the nineteenth century. Despite their apparent isolation, farmers were not immune to the growing spirit of democracy and freedom. Wherever possible—in speeches, letters, editorials, and elsewhere—they voiced dissatisfaction with their economic plight, the social inequity they experienced, and their political infirmity. When crops failed in 1838, agricultural needs became a pressing issue not only to farmers but to everyone in this young nation. Fortunately, this period was followed by strong economic recovery, but the ups and downs of agriculture had been brought to the attention of all.

> *It will not be doubted that with reference either to individual or national welfare, agriculture is of primary importance. In proportion as nations advance in population and other circumstances of maturity this truth becomes more apparent, and renders the cultivation of the soil more and more an object of public patronage. Institutions for promoting it grow up, supported by the public purse; and to what object can it be dedicated with greater propriety?*
>
> **GEORGE WASHINGTON**
> Presidential Address to the U.S. Congress, December 7, 1796

Interest in improving agriculture was evidenced by the organization of numerous local, state, and national agricultural associations and societies during the first half of the nineteenth century. These organizations encouraged experiments, essays, and reports of improvements in farming practices. In 1852, the United States Agricultural Society was established, with headquarters in Washington. It counted among its members some 300 societies in thirty-one states and five territories. The concerted support of these entities greatly influenced the eventual success of the impending attempt to secure congressional support of educational programs in agriculture and the mechanical arts (engineering).

By about 1850, consensus had developed throughout the nation favoring the establishment of colleges that would offer practical education for the young people of the agricultural and industrial classes. Although many people were involved in this movement, it was Jonathan Baldwin Turner, a visionary academic in Illinois, who conceptualized the end-product, crystallized the ideas of many people into a workable plan, and then promoted the plan through frequent speeches, published articles, and extensive travel, mostly on horseback.

> *Ideas are like babies, they are born small, immature and shapeless. They are promise rather than fulfillment.*
>
> **PETER DRUCKER**

Advocates of the movement to make technical college education available to people of all economic and social backgrounds were motivated by the belief that education benefits not only each individual participant but the entire society as well.

> *Let us in education dream of an aristocracy of achievement rising out of a democracy of opportunity. Preach, my dear sir, a crusade against ignorance; establish and improve the law for educating the common people. Let our countrymen know that the people alone can protect us against these evils, and that the tax which will be paid for this purpose is not more than the thousandth of what will be paid ... if we leave people in ignorance.*
>
> **THOMAS JEFFERSON**

The ultimate success of virtually all movements and programs is directly related to the will of those involved—that is, how determined they are to make things happen. The working classes were determined to have their own colleges and universities. They gave tremendous momentum to the land-grant movement. Generated by inspired individuals and encouraged groups, this spirit has not been paralleled in the succeeding history of higher education.

> *When the souls of men are fired up, the money will not be wanting.*
>
> **JONATHAN BALDWIN TURNER**

1.2   Federal Grants of Land

> *They can conquer who believe they can.*
>
> **VIRGIL**

The Northwest Ordinances of 1785 and 1787 over the next 150 years set aside more than 80 million acres of land and hundreds of millions of dollars from land leases and sales to support elementary schools, secondary schools, and colleges and universities.

The Northwest Ordinance of 1787—one of the truly monumental documents developed during the history of our Republic—espouses some of the liberties most cherished by Americans to this day: freedom of religion, the right to trial by jury, the repudiation of human slavery. While extending the principles of republican government to frontier territories, it also—with a simple declaration—laid the foundation for a national system of free education: "Religion, morality, and knowledge being necessary to good government and the happiness of mankind, schools and the means of education shall forever be encouraged."

The Northwest Ordinance was passed by the U.S. Congress on July 13, 1787, approximately two months before the Constitution of the United States was signed on September 17, 1787. This demonstrated very early federal interest in higher education. The Northwest Ordinance included provisions for the states that were carved from the Northwest Territory to set aside two or more townships of government-owned land per state for the support of higher education.

During the history of our Republic, there have been three types of "grants of land" designed to aid and encourage education: (1) *Section grants* in the early 1800s, when Horace Mann said, "A free and comprehensive education is the birthright of every child." As a strong proponent of that view, he pushed for passage of legislation that would give four sections of land per township to establish a one-room school for grades one through eight in each township. (2) In 1836, the U.S. Congress authorized the granting of two townships (46,080 acres) "to establish (a) a state university, and (b) a seminary in any state." With this came "grants of land" to establish, for example, the University of Michigan in 1837 and The University of Wisconsin in 1848. Then throughout the 1850s, Jonathan Baldwin Turner of Illinois pushed for federal "grants of land" to establish colleges of agriculture and the mechanical arts for the "sons and daughters of the industrial classes." (3) In 1862, the world-renowned land-grant act, providing grants of federal land to help establish land-grant colleges and universities, was signed into law.

During the first half of the nineteenth century, several pieces of legislation were passed that authorized the "granting of publicly held land" for various purposes. For example, in 1819 the U.S. Senate passed a bill donating federal land to the state of Connecticut for a seminary of learning for the "deaf and dumb." In 1827, Congress donated land to Kentucky for the same purpose. In 1838, a township in Florida was granted to Dr. Henry Perrine to "promote the cultivation of tropical plants." In 1841, each of the new states received 500,000 acres of land. Then in 1846, Congress donated 300,000 acres to the state of Tennessee, on the condition that the state would endow and establish a college (at an expense of not less than $40,000).

1.3 Conceptualization and Passage of the Land-Grant Act of 1862

Dreams can be fulfilled only when they are defined.

ERNEST L. BOYER

Occasionally, there is a person whose views and philosophies, whose vision and leadership, whose courage and tenacity change the course of history. Jonathan Baldwin Turner certainly was one such person. Turner was born on a rocky farm near Templeton, Massachusetts. He went to New Haven, Connecticut, at the age of twenty-two, spent two years in preparatory study, then entered Yale College (now Yale University), where he took a traditional classical education. It was fortunate for the land-grant college and university movement when, in 1833, Turner accepted a teaching position at Illinois College in Jacksonville, Illinois. There he taught rhetoric, Latin, Greek, and nearly every subject in the humanities. Illinois College had been founded in 1827 under Presbyterian auspices. Yale President Jeremiah Day personally encouraged Turner to accept the teaching position at Illinois, and promised to award him a diploma, even though Turner would leave before graduation.

Jonathan Baldwin Turner was a unique combination of classical scholar, educator, farmer, amateur scientist, orator, religionist, social reformer, entrepreneur, and rugged individualist. But most importantly he was a restless visionary, abundantly imbued with a strong missionary spirit. Throughout his life, he was a proselytizer in the three areas that consumed his interest and energy—religion, politics, and education. In all three, Turner's ideas often were unorthodox, and this fact made him the subject of considerable criticism. In the church, he attacked many of the conventional views of his denomination. In politics, he was among the first in Illinois to speak out publicly against slavery. And in the 1830s, he plunged headlong into the crusade for universal education for those who normally did not have that opportunity—the sons and daughters of what he called "the working class."

In each of these areas of public debate, Turner brought vigor, passion, eloquence, and imagination. He was so much the center of public turmoil that finally, in 1848, under pressure, he gave up his professorship at Illinois College. He returned to his first love—agriculture.

Jonathan Baldwin Turner's thinking, talking, and planning for education ultimately led to concrete proposals for the creation of an industrial university. His speech before the Illinois Teachers Institute in Griggsville, Illinois, on May 13, 1850, entitled "A Plan of our State University for the Industrial Class" was a blueprint for what followed in the organization of public higher education in the United States. He proposed not only the foundation of a state university for the agricultural and general industrial classes in Illinois, but such a system in every state of the Union.

Turner's plan was influenced and guided by Jeffersonian ideals. He sought to develop young people's reasoning faculties, enlarge their minds, and cultivate their morals so that commerce, agriculture, and manufacturing could prosper to the benefit of every American. Education was truly in the public interest. The plan included three basic goals: (1) to establish colleges that would be open, at minimum cost, to laborers in agriculture, commerce, and the arts who needed educational assistance; (2) to develop curricula that would include instruction in practical and vocational subjects for the benefit of the working classes; and (3) to endow these colleges by grants of land from the enormous holdings of the federal government.

There is debate as to the extent of Jonathan Baldwin Turner's influence upon Justin Smith Morrill, who later sponsored the legislation that gave impetus to the unique land-grant college and university system. Although the legislation carries Morrill's name, many have claimed for Turner the original definition of the idea and its transmission to Morrill. Turner's personal sincerity and profound conviction for the importance of his cause is well known. He is remembered as the "John the Baptist" of a great national movement in education—a prophet of democracy who, like Thomas Jefferson before him, recognized an educated electorate as prerequisite to a sustained, successful democracy. He was long on ideas and enthusiasm, and his philosophy and concepts remain valid today. Listen to the words and fervor of his creed, as expressed to a large audience in Monmouth, Illinois:

> The sun never shown on such a nation, and such a power, as this soon would be, with such facilities of public advancement and improvement put into full and vigorous operation. Set the millions of eyes in this great Republic to watching, and intelligently observing and thinking, and there is no secret of Nature or art we cannot find out; no disease of man or beast we cannot understand; no evil we cannot remedy; no obstacle we cannot surmount; nothing lies in the power of man to do or to understand, that cannot be understood and done.

The second major group Jonathan Baldwin Turner targeted for support of his plan for the establishment and maintenance of an industrial university was the Illinois farmers. In response to a passionate plea for their support of his plan, the following resolutions were adopted by the Convention of Illinois Farmers, held November 18, 1851, at Granville, Illinois:

> Resolved, that we greatly rejoice in the degree of perfection to which our various institutions, for the education of our brethren engaged in professional, scientific, and literary pursuits have already attained, and in the mental and moral elevation which those institutions have given them, and their consequent preparation and capacity for the great duties ... of life in which they are engaged. ...
> Resolved, that as representatives of the industrial classes, including cultivators of the soil, artisans, mechanics and merchants, we desire the same privileges and advantages for ourselves, our fellows and our posterity ... as our professional brethren enjoy in theirs. ...
> Resolved, that we take immediate measures for the establishment of a university ... expressly to provide a means of applying knowledge or science to the several pursuits of the industrial classes of our state ... as well as to teach them

how to read, observe and think, and act so as to derive the same needful and wholesome mental discipline from their pursuits in life, which the professional and military classes are taught to derive, from theirs.

Turner's plan was printed and widely distributed, and it was reprinted in many newspapers, including *The New York Tribune,* the nation's most widely circulated newspaper at the time. The newspaper's editors responded in their September 4, 1852, issue:

The greatest idea of a higher or thorough education for the sons and daughters of farmers, mechanics and laborers, is everywhere forcing itself on the public attention. Our race needs instruction and discipline to qualify them for working, as well as for thinking and talking. It may now be ten years since a few poor and inconsiderate persons began to "agitate" in favor of a more practical system of thorough education, whereby youth without distinction of sex should be trained for eminent usefulness in all the departments of industry. It is worthy of note that one of the most extensive of the public land states proposes a magnificent donation of public lands to each of the states. In furtherance of this idea, Illinois has taken a noble step forward, in a most liberal and patriotic spirit, for which its members will be heartily thanked by thousands throughout the Union. We feel that this step has materially hastened the scientific and practical education for all who desire and are willing to work for it. It cannot come too soon.

And the editor of the *Southern Cultivator* wrote in his Augusta, Georgia, newspaper:

We have been gratified by the perusal of an address delivered by Professor J. B. Turner of Jacksonville, Illinois, before a convention of farmers held in that state, in support of the establishment of a university, in which agriculture and the sciences shall be made a special branch of study. His suggestions are urged with zeal and ability, and his arguments are convincing, as to the need and importance of such institutions. There is no subject more worthy of the highest effort of the human intellect, nor one which has been, until recently, so culpably disregarded, if not condemned. The triumph of a Republic can only be successfully achieved and permanently enjoyed by a people, the mass of whom are an enlightened yeomanry, the proprietors of the land, too independent to be bought, too enlightened to be cheated, and too powerful to be crushed. There is not a good agricultural school in the United States. The truth is, the American people have yet to commence the study of agriculture as the combination of many sciences. Agriculture is the most profound and extensive profession that the progress of society and the accumulation of knowledge have developed. Whether we consider the solid earth under our feet, the invisible atmosphere which we breathe, the wonderful growth and decay of all plants and animals, or the light, the cold, or the electricity of heaven, we contemplate but the elements of rural science. The careful investigation of the Laws that govern all ponderable and imponderable agents, is the first step in the young farmer's education. This subject is beginning to take a strong hold on the minds of the people, and we are glad to see gentlemen of the talents and influence of Professor Turner lending a hand to put the ball in motion which, ultimately, will sweep down all opposition.

The third group to which Turner turned for support of his plan for educational reform was the Illinois Industrial League. He told those attending their 1851 convention in Chicago:

> ... All of society is divided into two classes—the professional class and the working class. Colleges of this day provide a good liberal education for the professional class, which constitutes only a small fraction of the population. Nowhere are there colleges for the great mass of people. Society has become wise enough to know that its teachers need to be educated, but it has not become wise enough to know that its workers, too, need an education. We need a system of education adapted to the needs of the common man, which would elevate him to his rightful place in society. Education should be practical, as well as academic, and it should not be the monopoly of the privileged few, but rather the right of everyone who has the desire and the ability to learn.

From then on, influential groups in Illinois reaffirmed their endorsement of the plan at their annual conventions. Most groups focused on the U.S. Congress. The following resolution was adopted at the third Convention of Illinois Farmers on November 24, 1852:

> Resolved, that this convention memorialize Congress for the purpose of obtaining a grant of public lands to establish and endow industrial institutions in each and every state in the Union.

Other groups directed their resolutions and petitions to the Illinois Senate and House of Representatives. The fourth Convention of the Industrial League of Illinois, held in Springfield on January 8, 1853, adopted the following resolution:

> ... We would, therefore, respectfully petition the honorable Senate and House of Representatives of the State of Illinois, that they present a united memorial to the Congress now assembled at Washington to appropriate to each state in the Union an amount of public lands not less in value than $500,000, for the liberal endowment of a system of Industrial Universities, one in each state in the Union, to cooperate with each other, and with the Smithsonian Institution at Washington, for the more liberal and practical education of our industrial classes and their teachers, in their various pursuits, for the production of knowledge and literature needful in those pursuits, and development to the fullest and most perfect extent the resources of our soil and our arts, the virtue and intelligence of our people, and the true glory of our common country.

> We further petition that the executive and legislature of our sister states be invited to cooperate with us in this enterprise, and that a copy of the memorial of this legislature be forwarded by the Governors and Senates of the several states.

This petition was unanimously adopted February 8, 1853, with the following preamble and resolutions:

> Of the General Assembly of the State of Illinois, relative to the establishment of industrial universities, and for the encouragement of practical and general education among the people.
>
> Whereas, the spirit and progress of this age and country demand the culture of the highest order of intellectual attainment in the theoretical and industrial science: and whereas, it is impossible that our commerce and prosperity will continue to increase without calling into requisition all the elements of internal thrift arising from the labors of the farmer, the mechanic, and the manufacturer, by every fostering effort within the reach of the government: and whereas, a system of industrial universities, liberally endowed in each state of the Union, cooperative with each other and the Smithsonian Institution at Washington, would develop a more liberal and practical education among the people, tend the more to intellectualize the rising generation, and eminently conduce to the virtue, intelligence, and true glory of our common country; therefore, be it:
>
> Resolved, by the House of Representatives, the Senate concurring herein, that our Senators in Congress be instructed, and our Representatives be requested, to use their best exertions to procure the passage of a Law of Congress donating to each State in the Union an amount of public lands not less in value than five hundred thousand dollars, for liberal endowment of a system of Industrial Universities, one in each state in the Union, to cooperate with each other, and with the Smithsonian Institution at Washington, for the more liberal and practical education of our industrial classes and their teachers; a liberal and varied education adapted to the manifold want of a practical and enterprising people, and a provision for such educational facilities, being in the manifest concurrence with the intimations of the popular will, it urgently demands the united efforts of our national strength.
>
> Resolved, that the Governor is hereby authorized to forward a copy of the foregoing resolutions to our Senators and Representatives in Congress, and to the Executive and Legislature of each of our sister states, inviting them to cooperate with us in this meritorious enterprise.

Now, Turner's campaign for educational reform had become truly national in scope. He and his fellow crusaders around the country recognized that they had to rely on the united efforts of like-minded groups across the nation if they were to gain congressional support for their plan.

Although Illinois was the first state to advocate a national appropriation to establish an industrial university for every state and territory, New York and other states soon asked Congress for appropriations of land to establish institutions in their respective states. For example, on April 2, 1850, the legislature of Michigan petitioned Congress for 350,000 acres of public land to establish an "Agricultural College." And in February 1855 the Congress enacted a law that created the first college in the United States to offer agricultural courses for credit. That institution was an important forerunner of the national network of land-grant colleges and universities made possible by the Morrill Act of 1862. This victory represented the outcome of many years of agitation by various groups throughout the country for a new kind of higher education made possible by the creation of what were respectfully—even reverently— referred to as "people's colleges" and "people's universities."

Other states, some by recommendation, others by petition, asked Congress to appropriate U.S. Treasury funds to establish both an Agricultural Bureau and a national institution similar to those at West Point and Annapolis for the teaching of agriculture. For example, on April 20, 1852, the state of Massachusetts asked for a grant of public land in aid of a "National Normal Agricultural College, which should be to the rural sciences what the West Point Academy is to the military, for the purpose of educating teachers and professors for service in all the States of the Republic."

The New York Senate, in response to the invitation to support the Illinois Plan, passed a resolution on March 30, 1852, which was endorsed by the New York House of Representatives on April 17, 1852, asking Congress "to make grants of land to all the States for the purpose of education and for other useful public purposes."

Throughout the 1850s, Jonathan Baldwin Turner corresponded with members of the Illinois delegation in Congress, providing philosophical and conceptual information. He shared his own correspondence, speeches, and related materials, and entreated the delegates to introduce a bill supporting establishment of an "Industrial University" in each state of the Union.

Among Turner's voluminous correspondence, later organized and reviewed by his daughter Mary Turner Carriel, were two letters of special historical significance. The first, dated June 1852, was a letter from Richard Yates, member of the U.S. House of Representatives from Illinois. In it, Yates acknowledged receipt of Turner's plan and stated that he had presented it to the National Agricultural Association, then in session in the city of Washington. This and its publication in the "Report of the U.S. Patent Office" gave Turner's plan wide publicity among people interested in the progress of agricultural education.

At the request of Congressman Yates, Professor Turner prepared a bill on the subject of industrial universities. But Yates concluded that it would not be politically prudent to push the matter in that session. The following fall, Yates was not re-elected to Congress, so the bill, unfortunately, was again delayed.

... Further thought and discussion will suggest valuable amendments, so that the compulsory delay will not be wholly lost. Two years, or ten years, are nothing in the life of an institution such as this, compared with the importance of giving it a substantial basis and right direction.

JONATHAN BALDWIN TURNER

On October 7, 1857, Turner wrote Lyman Trumbull, U.S. senator from Illinois, respectfully asking him to introduce the bill. The senator was supportive of the concept but, because he sensed a feeling of opposition in Congress against further major grants of federal land, expressed reluctance to comply. He believed the bill would more likely pass if it were sponsored by members of Congress from "some of the old States."

On December 4, 1855—some eighteen months after the Illinois resolution had been introduced—Justin Smith Morrill of Vermont entered the U.S. House of Representatives. The Illinois members, following the reasoning of Senator Trumbull, believed introduction of their bill could be entrusted to him. Representative Morrill was able, had a pleasing personality, and was a staunch friend of agriculture. He represented Vermont in the House from 1855 to 1866 and in the Senate from 1866 to 1898. In addition to the Morrill Acts of 1862 and 1890, he introduced the Morrill Tariff Act in 1861. Additionally, he helped to found the Republican Party and to pass the legislation that established the Library of Congress.

Just three months into his first term in Congress, Representative Morrill introduced a resolution authorizing "the Committee on Agriculture to inquire into the expediency of establishing one or more National Schools upon the basis of the naval and military schools, in order that one scholar from each Congressional District and two from each State at large may receive a scientific and practical education at the public expense." The resolution was rejected.

Senator Trumbull's October 19, 1857, letter had embraced Turner's plan, but recommended it be presented by a member from one of the old states. Trumbull noted that "Congress had given so much toward educational interests in the new states that they were in no frame of mind to do more, not even for Turner's plan, which embraced all the states, new and old." After considering the various strategies, Turner decided to send all documents, papers, speeches, pertinent correspondence, and pamphlets to Representative Morrill, along with the request that he introduce the bill. At first, Morrill was reluctant to do this. But after much persuasion, he consented.

The bill was introduced on December 14, 1857, but it was reported back unfavorably by the Committee on Public Lands. Morrill submitted it again, omitting the proposed grant of land to the territories (these were later reinstated), in a spirited speech on April 20, 1858. He said, "There has been no measure for years which has received so much attention in the various parts of the country as the one now under consideration, so far as the fact can be proved by petitions which have been received here from the various states, north and south, from State sessions, from county sessions and from memorials" (*Congressional Globe,* 35th Congress, p. 1692).

It did not pass the House, but it was introduced again the next year, when it passed the House but failed in the Senate. Finally, in 1859, it was introduced again and passed both the House and Senate. In spite of its considerable congressional support, President James Buchanan, an independently wealthy graduate of Dickinson College in Carlisle, Pennsylvania, vetoed the measure.

Disappointed but not discouraged, Turner conferred with his anti-slavery colleague and friend, Abraham Lincoln, about the bill President Buchanan had vetoed. Through two of his former students at Illinois College, Turner had indirectly helped Abraham Lincoln learn grammar when the future president was but a harvest hand. Before the Republican Convention of 1860, Turner told Lincoln that he believed the lawyer from the Illinois prairie would be nominated for president and then elected. To this Lincoln responded, "If I am, I will sign your bill for State Universities."

Later Turner met with Lincoln's presidential opponent, Illinois Democratic Senator Stephen A. Douglas, from whom he extracted the commitment: "If I am elected I will sign your bill." So regardless of how the people voted, Jonathan Baldwin Turner knew that, after more than a decade of arduous effort, the world's greatest plan for education of the masses was assured passage.

In June 1861, Senator Douglas wrote Turner requesting a copy of his plan and the historical background of the proposed Industrial University System. He wished to personally introduce it in the next session of Congress. Senator Douglas had long before declared, "This educational scheme of Professor Turner's is the most democratic ... ever proposed to the mind of man!"

Turner responded with a full and complete account, and sent it to the post office with his oldest son. To Turner's surprise and dismay, Rhodolphus Turner returned with the letter, saying a telegram had just been received announcing the death of Senator Douglas in Chicago.

When Justin Smith Morrill again introduced the bill, it passed both the House and the Senate (the Senate sponsor was Ohio's Benjamin Franklin Wade), and it was the first civil bill signed into law by President Lincoln on July 2, 1862. Representative Morrill cited two principal reasons for introducing the now famous land-grant act:

(1) ... the loud demand for more scientific instruction in the colleges, and (2)

so much of the abundant public lands of the United States were being given away to local corporations, railroads, and other entities that he thought it very desirable for a portion of the proceeds from such lands be directed in some way to the good of the whole people ... and that the thoroughly educated, being most sure to educate their sons, appeared to be perpetuating a monopoly of education inconsistent with the welfare and complete prosperity of American institutions.

Although 1862 was a year of national crisis, the U.S. Congress, with commendable foresight, enacted three visionary laws—laws that have had profound impact upon the economic and social development of our nation.

First, on May 15, 1862, President Abraham Lincoln signed the act that established the U.S. Department of Agriculture. This legislation provided important footing for the development of a scientific American agriculture, upon which would rest our nation's enormously productive food and agricultural enterprise.

Second, on May 20, 1862, Lincoln signed the Homestead Act, which greatly encouraged westward expansion by opening some 200 million acres of land for agricultural settlement and development.

Third, on July 2, 1862, Lincoln signed the first Morrill Act:

> An Act donating public lands to the several states and territories which may provide colleges for the benefit of agriculture and the mechanic arts: Be it enacted by the Senate and House of Representatives of the United States of America, in Congress assembled, that there be granted to the several states, for the purpose hereinafter mentioned, an amount of public land, to be apportioned to each state, in quality equal to 30,000 acres, for each Senator and Representative in Congress to which the States are respectfully entitled by apportionment under the census of 1860; ... And be it further enacted, that all monies derived from the sale of lands aforesaid ... shall be invested in stocks of the United States, or of the States, or some other safe stocks, yielding not less than five percent, upon the par value of said stock; and that the money so invested shall constitute a perpetual fund, the capital of which shall remain forever undiminished, and the interest of which shall be inviolably appropriated ... to the endowment, support, and maintenance of, at least, one college where the leading object shall be, without excluding other scientific and classical studies, and including military tactics, to teach such branches of learning as are related to agriculture and the mechanic arts, in such manner as the legislatures of the states may respectively prescribe, in order to promote the liberal and practical education of the industrial classes in the several pursuits and professions in life.

Altogether, by 1890, the states and territories had received 11,367,832 acres of land. There were certain states, particularly in the Northeast (where the federal government did not own much land), that were empowered by the Morrill Act to select land in the West, then sell it. Money derived from the sale of this land was to be invested and the interest used in perpetuity to establish and maintain in each state and territory at least one college where the principal object would be training "in agriculture and the mechanic arts."

Some of the institutions that benefitted from the Morrill Act of 1862 had already been established by the states. For example, Michigan had established an agricultural college in February 1855, and admitted its first seventy-three students in May 1857. In other cases, proceeds from the 1862 land-grant act were given to pre-existing institutions on condition that they would provide instruction in agriculture and the mechanic arts. Some of these were state-supported, others were private institutions. In Massachusetts, the money was allocated partly to the Massachusetts Institute of Technology and partly to an institution in Amherst (now the University of Massachusetts) created for the express purpose of providing agricultural education. In Connecticut, the money went first to Yale College, but later to a special institution organized to take advantage of the act. In other states, notably Minnesota and Wisconsin, the money was given to the state universities that had already been established.

The land-grant act of 1862 proved to be an emancipation proclamation for those of modest financial circumstances who were striving for a college education. Federal provisions for the land-grant institutions were made in an era when fewer than 2 percent of the U.S. population continued their formal education beyond the twelfth grade. For the first time, colleges were accessible to the people, and the idea of equality of educational opportunity became reality. The land-grant act of 1862 has indeed appropriately been described as our nation's "Bill of Educational Rights."

The land-grant university system is being built on behalf of the people, who have invested in these public universities their hopes, their support, and their confidence.

ABRAHAM LINCOLN

1.4 Passage of the Land-Grant Act of 1890

Although the problems are complex ... we must continue to strengthen our ability to nurture the minds and lives of the people we serve. The story of the black land-grant system is the story of ideals and industry. ...

WILLIAM P. HYTCHE

The first Morrill Act (1862), in its attempt to democratize higher education, did not exclude African Americans. However, Southern customs, traditions, and laws requiring racial segregation prevented these newly emancipated citizens from becoming full participants in the new educational venture.

Before emancipation, some 90 percent of the approximately 4 million African Americans in this country were in slavery. Moreover, the approximately 250,000 "free blacks" were circumscribed in their social interaction with whites. Hence, the early land-grant colleges became white bastions, barring blacks from admission by custom, by law, or both. Congressman Morrill wanted these new colleges to be accessible to all of the nation's citizens, thus democratizing higher education. But as a Whig from Vermont, he probably gave minimal thought to the plight of African Americans in the Southern and border states.

Before passage of the second Morrill Act (1890), Booker T. Washington, president of Tuskegee University, made an important observation about the circumstances and mobility of the African American population. He said, "Something must be done to stem the swelling tide which each year sweeps thousands of black men and women and children from the sunlit monotony of the plantation to the sunless inequity of the slums: from a drudgery that is not quite cheerless to competition that is altogether merciless."

Twenty-eight years after the passage of the Morrill Act of 1862, Justin Smith Morrill—by then serving in the U.S. Senate—introduced the bill that was to become popularly known as the second Morrill Act. It was presented twelve times before becoming law. Because the act stated that funds should be "equitably divided" between white and black colleges, there was strong opposition from white Southern congressmen. Specifically, the Morrill Act provided "that no money shall be paid out under this Act to any State or Territory for the support and maintenance of a college where a distinction of race or color is made in the admission of students, but the establishment and maintenance of such colleges separately for white and colored students shall be held to be a compliance with the provisions of the Act, if the funds received in such State or Territory be equitably divided as hereinafter set forth."

The Morrill College Aid Act, passed on August 30, 1890, provided for a permanent appropriation of $15,000 per annum (to be increased by $1,000 per year until it reached $25,000 annually) to every state in the Union for the more complete endowment and support of these colleges and for the benefit of agriculture and the mechanic arts as established under the act of 1862.

Under the provision that became known as the "separate-but-equal" policy, the so-called 1890 institutions began their federally mandated mission. Tuskegee University and seventeen other institutions were funded through the 1890 Morrill Act.

Today, all fifty states, Guam, Puerto Rico, and the Virgin Islands receive federal grants supporting land-grant colleges and universities.

1.5 Passage of the Hatch Act

The goal of education is the advancement of knowledge and the dissemination of truth.

JOHN F. KENNEDY

The early private colleges did not emphasize research, but rather they focused on teaching and the preservation of knowledge and traditions. Neither faculty nor students were particularly interested in creating new understandings in either the realm of human experience or that of the natural world. They focused on reinforcing the cultural traditions they served.

The first federal call for adding a research dimension to higher education's mission—indirect though it was—came from George Washington. In his 1796 presidential message to Congress, he requested a Board of Agriculture, with one of its purposes to be the encouragement of experimentation. This is not surprising since George Washington's Mount Vernon estate was a veritable experimental farm on which the owner sought ways to conserve soil, diversify cropping, and use new machinery. By careful seed selection, Washington developed an improved strain of wheat; he obtained one of the first patents on seed-sowing devices; his sheep produced nearly three times as much wool as those of his neighbors; and he was the first American to raise mules.

Thomas Jefferson, who served as a member of President Washington's cabinet and then as the third president of the United States, had an inventive mind as well as a flair for scientific experimentation. He worked out the mathematical principle of least soil resistance for an all-metal moldboard plow. He also invented a seed drill, a hemp brake, and improvements for the threshing machine. He tested varieties of at least thirty-two different vegetables at Monticello and practiced horizontal plowing for soil-erosion control.

There was no agricultural research literature in the eighteenth century. Washington, Jefferson, and other early visionaries created it by conducting experiments on their own farms, then sharing the results by exchanging correspondence with interested persons in this country and abroad. They sought new seeds, new machines, improved foundation stocks, and better ways of farming. Indeed, Washington and Jefferson established a rich legacy for scientific experimentation.

Just six years after Thomas Jefferson saw the University of Virginia open with forty students enrolled in 1825, Cyrus McCormick demonstrated his newly perfected reaper to a skeptical audience on a farm in Rockbridge County, Virginia. McCormick had at long last solved a problem that, for thousands of years, had plagued farmers. New developments followed quickly, producing rapid agricultural progress that would relieve some of the drudgery for farm families.

Norman J. Colman, a Missouri farm magazine editor, was in 1885 appointed the first U.S. Commissioner of Agriculture (now Secretary of Agriculture). Colman was committed to passage of legislation that would provide funding for state agricultural experiment stations. A legislative committee comprised of three land-grant university presidents worked with Commissioner Colman in these efforts, which were endorsed by Congressman William Henry Hatch of Missouri and Senator James Z. George of Mississippi, who agreed to sponsor the proposed legislation. After considerable debate and compromise, the bill known as the "Hatch Act" was passed on March 2, 1887. It provided $15,000 per annum to establish agricultural experiment stations in connection with the land-grant colleges and universities established in the several states and territories under the provisions of the Morrill Act approved July 2, 1862, "to aid in acquiring and diffusing among the people of the United States useful and practical information on subjects connected with agriculture, and to promote scientific investigations and experiments respecting the principles and applications of agricultural science."

Congressman Hatch's own farm on the outskirts of Hannibal, Missouri, was later quite appropriately acquired by the Missouri Agricultural Experiment Station. This author and many others over the years conducted research on the Hatch farm.

The Hatch Act of 1887 was a sort of "second growth" from the seed sown first by Jonathan Baldwin Turner, who also conducted experiments related to agriculture on his own farm near Butler, Illinois.

Another major contributor to passage of the Hatch Act of 1887 was Wilbur Olin Atwater, who directed the Storrs (Connecticut) Agricultural Experiment Station from 1887 to 1902. Dr. Atwater served for thirty-four years as professor of chemistry at Wesleyan University, Middletown, Connecticut. The first agricultural experiment station in the United States was established at Middletown under his direction in 1875. It was later moved to New Haven. Atwater also served as the first chief of the Office of Experiment Stations of the U.S. Department of Agriculture.

In 1892, with the assistance of Dr. E. B. Rosa, professor of physics at Wesleyan, Atwater constructed the first human-respiration calorimeter. Atwater conducted classic research on the energy value of various food materials a century ago. The "Atwater factors" for carbohydrates, fats, and protein were derived from the heats of combustion of the three classes of nutrients as they occur in foods comprising average human and animal diets.

1.6 Passage of the Smith-Lever Act

What a man hears, he may doubt; what he sees, he may possibly doubt; but what he does, he cannot doubt.

SEAMAN A. KNAPP

Agriculture is this nation's oldest and largest primary industry. It is the oldest industry because the most basic ingredients for the necessities of life—food, clothing, and shelter—are supplied by people on the land. It is largest because progressive people worked together in the spirit of a free-enterprise system and in concert with the men and women of the land-grant college and university system to create a globally competitive industry, all the while improving their own lot in life. Using less than 1 percent of the world's agricultural labor force, U.S. farmers and ranchers produce over 8 percent of the world's food grains, 27 percent of the feed grains, 21 percent of the beef, and 28 percent of the poultry. On average, each U.S. producer provides food for more than 130 people in the world. For healthy, safe, convenient foods, U.S. consumers spend only about 11 percent of their total personal disposable income—the best food bargain, by far, in the world.

But this has not always been the case. For nearly three centuries this nation's agriculture expanded horizontally across the continent. New land was the frontier of agriculture in the United States prior to the twentieth century. Then farsighted supporters of agriculture in Congress and elsewhere realized that population pressures and soil depletion would eventually lead to the need for more productive plants and animals. Believing that research leading to new knowledge would show the way, they enacted the Hatch Act in 1887 (Section 1.5), which authorized establishment of agricultural experiment stations. During the twentieth century, research has determined the frontiers of agriculture. Increased food and fiber production no longer depends on new acres. Now it depends upon vertical expansion—greater productivity per acre and unit of input.

When Alexis de Tocqueville of France toured the United States in 1831, he could not have foreseen the potential power of research in general and the high-impact changes agricultural research in particular could bring about in a democratic society. If he had, he would not have made this statement in his book *Democracy in America*: "Agriculture is perhaps, of all the useful arts, that which improves most slowly among democratic nations."

All over the world, the words "American agriculture" evoke an image of abundance and economic success. Agriculture is highly important—economically and strategically—to the United States and to the world. The strategic importance of our food, agriculture, and natural resource system will increase as we enter the twenty-first century.

The developments already reviewed rightfully serve as a source of pride for all Americans, especially those associated with the land-grant college and university system. But there remains one additional link in the chain of progress to be noted. It was this link, added twenty-seven years after the Hatch Act was passed into law, that made it possible for the earlier legislation to pay enormous dividends. The coupling of research with a workable way to disseminate and popularize the knowledge generated through the aegis of the Hatch Act was the key that unlocked the full potential of the visionaries from Turner to Morrill to Hatch. That key was the Smith-Lever Act of 1914, which Secretary of Agriculture David F. Houston called "one of the most striking educational measures ever adopted by any government."

Houston believed that nothing short of a comprehensive attempt to make rural life attractive, comfortable, and profitable would solve the chronic problems of agriculture and rural life. He viewed the Smith-Lever Act as the mechanism through which the intellectual and social aspects of rural life could be improved. Specifically, the Smith-Lever Act facilitated the distribution of information on research results to the user group. The act provided for cooperative financing of the present-day county extension agent system under the direction of land-grant colleges and universities. Not only does this system communicate new research findings from the agricultural experiment station staff to farmers and others, it encourages problems identified on farms and ranches and other areas to be brought to the attention of the station staff for research, study, and resolution.

The purpose of the Smith-Lever Act, as stated by Congress, was "to aid in diffusing among the people of the United States useful and practical information on subjects relating to agriculture and home economics and to encourage the application of the same." To assure that the appropriated funds were used for outreach purposes, the act stipulated further that agricultural extension was to "consist of the giving of instruction and practical demonstrations in agriculture and home economics to persons not attending or residents in said colleges in the several communities, and imparting to such persons information on said subjects through field demonstrations, publications, and otherwise."

Beginning with an initial appropriation of $600,000, each state was to receive $10,000 annually. Federal funds were to be available in amounts not to exceed 50 percent of the cost of extension; the rest was to be provided by state, county, and local authorities, as well as by other contributions from within the state. This mechanism of joint funding is in keeping with the term "cooperative extension"—a *cooperative* venture among federal, state, local, and individual funding support—a system of adult and youth education that has become a model for the rest of the world (Sections 8.2 and 8.3).

1.7   The Tribal Colleges

*Teach the children. The Grandfathers and the Grandmothers
are in the children. If we educate them, our children tomorrow
will be wiser than we are today. They're the Grandfathers and
Grandmothers of tomorrow.*

EDDIE BENTON-BANAI

Just as the original land-grant act of 1862 and the second Morrill Act of 1890 were attempts to democratize higher education, so too was the initiative to secure land-grant status for the nation's tribal colleges. The Tribally Controlled Community College Act of 1978 stimulated development of the variety of technical two-year, four-year, and graduate schools presently located in or near tribal reservations. Their success in meeting community needs, coupled with a prevailing climate of strong self-determination, led the American Indian Higher Education Consortium (AIHEC) to approach the National Association of State Universities and Land-Grant Colleges (NASULGC) to consider the potential of a cooperative effort to secure land-grant status for their twenty-nine tribal colleges. Employing the same argument used during the successful campaign by the University of the District of Columbia, the Pacific Islands territories, and the Virgin Islands to achieve land-grant status, the Native Americans noted that their reservations, held in trust for American Indian tribes, were the only areas under the U.S. flag that had not participated in the land-grant college program.

During the spring of 1993, the leadership of AIHEC and NASULGC met to discuss opportunities that the granting of land-grant status to the tribal colleges would provide the members of both organizations. At the onset of the meetings, NASULGC President C. Peter Magrath pledged full support of the effort to achieve land-grant status for the Native American-controlled colleges when he emphatically stated, "It is simply the right thing to do." Shortly thereafter, the Board of Directors of NASULGC approved a resolution "endorsing the quest by this nation's tribal colleges for federal legislation conferring land-grant status upon these colleges."

In November 1993, the AIHEC and NASULGC jointly testified before the U.S. Senate Select Committee on Indian Affairs in favor of land-grant status for the tribal colleges. In January 1994, Magrath created a special task force on tribal colleges and land-grant status to strengthen cooperation between the present NASULGC member schools and the tribal colleges. Task force chairman Michael P. Malone (president of Montana State University) and other NASULGC member institution presidents met with their tribal college counterparts in Kansas City, Missouri, to discuss issues of mutual interest.

In October 1994, Congress passed legislation conferring land-grant status on the twenty-nine Native American tribal colleges as a provision of the Elementary and Secondary Reauthorization Act. The bill authorized a $23 million endowment over a period of five years. The colleges will receive annual interest payments from this endowment. Additionally, the legislation authorized a $1.7 million challenge grant program for higher education initiatives in agriculture and natural resources and $50,000 per school for higher education in agriculture and natural resources. The legislation also provided $5 million that will go to the Cooperative Extension Service of the 1862 land-grant institutions in states that have tribal colleges. The 1862 institutions are to cooperate with the tribal colleges in setting up joint agricultural extension programs focused on the needs of Native Americans.

A month after passage of the bill granting land-grant status to the tribal colleges, the NASULGC board voted to admit the AIHEC as a member of the National Association. Thus, in January 1995 the AIHEC became the newest member of NASULGC, the nation's oldest higher education association (Section 14.2).

The twenty-nine tribal colleges are located in twelve states. Most are two-year colleges and technical schools, but three are four-year institutions and one offers a master's degree. While some of the tribal colleges may differ in scope and nature from most other NASULGC institutions, they have an outstanding record in providing educational opportunities to American Indian and other students as well as in providing important services to Native American people. Therefore, their role and mission are highly compatible with the legendary land-grant mission of providing and promoting educational opportunities where they are needed.

The land-grant college and university movement that began so nobly in 1862 in providing "democracy's colleges" is now in the present era demonstrating once again its ability to adapt and change to meet new educational challenges and contingencies for a new century.

1.8 Summary

> *Sow a thought, reap an action;*
> *Sow an action, reap a habit;*
> *Sow a habit, reap a character;*
> *Sow a character, reap a destiny.*
>
> **CHINESE PROVERB**

The history related in this chapter emphasizes the fact that sound ideas are not always implemented in a timely manner. Twelve years passed from the time Jonathan Baldwin Turner first publicly disclosed his plan for the "Industrial University" and the passage of his plan in 1862. The land-grant act of 1890 was presented twelve times before it passed and was signed into law. Although good ideas may be suppressed for a long time, with the determination, leadership, and tenacity of visionary individuals they are finally embraced by enough people to come to fruition. Indeed, in a democracy, a good idea does not die. The person who spawned and espoused it may be ridiculed and even destroyed, but if the idea is sound, it cannot be killed. In time, some one will see that it resurfaces.

The federal land-grant act of 1862 marked the beginning of one of the most comprehensive and far-reaching provisions for the endowment of higher education ever devised and adopted. It enabled higher education in this great nation to evolve from being a privilege of a minority to a right of the masses. The "land-grant" institutions quickly came to be recognized as "the people's colleges."

Land-grant colleges and universities made all human endeavors legitimate subject matter for scholarship and scientific investigation. Prior to their establishment, academic endeavors were confined largely to history, theology, the arts and letters, the law, and medicine. This stupendous paradigm shift in the character of academe was profoundly democratic. It meant that research could provide scientific insights into—and answers to—people's everyday problems. Then, with the advents of the Hatch Act of 1887 and the Smith-Lever Act of 1914, federally funded provisions were made to support not only organized research in agriculture and engineering but also to distribute new knowledge directly to the public through the Cooperative Extension Service as well.

From their inception, the land-grant universities developed in accord with the intentional philosophical bent of service to the public. As these respective institutions have grown and expanded over the years to serve more and more people, groups, business firms, and industry and trade organizations of the entire states in which they are located, new alliances and contracts have been forged with the community, and these have engendered essential public support. This has represented a dramatic shift from the early American tradition in higher education.

Land-grant institutions truly created a new social force in world history. Never before had universities been so closely linked with the daily lives of their clients and constituents. The university campus came to be recognized as one of the most heavily traveled crossroads in America—an intersection traversed by farmers and ranchers, by homemakers, by persons in other businesses and industries, and by politicians as well as by students from every part of every state, not to mention many other states and nations. The cloister and the ivory tower, largely male-dominated, were replaced by academic and practical opportunities open to all.

Supporting the land-grant movement was a contribution of the German model to American universities. The German model gave academic respectability to the "land-grant" concept, as German intellectualism and American populism were merged in the new land-grant universities. Pure intellect and raw pragmatism made a successful alliance. In the new land-grant institutions, emphasis was on the application of learning in the service of the best interests of the people.

Again, the unique and most lasting legacy of the land-grant college and university system has been service to the public. That public service is what has forged and maintained the strong partnership between land-grant institutions and the citizens who support them.

Inscribed on a plaque honoring John Milton Gregory, the first president of the University of Illinois, are the following words: "If you seek his monument look about you!" The University of Illinois, one of this nation's premier land-grant institutions, is a monument not only to President Gregory but to other pioneer educators as well whose aim it has been to make higher education accessible by all people. For it is the people—the entities who matter most in a democratic, free-enterprise society—whose lives and professional pursuits have been touched in often remarkable ways by these special land-grant institutions. Indeed, the very course of this great nation for over a century has been determined in large part by the fruits of our marvelous land-grant system of higher education.

It seemed to me that when a person gets old and looks back over his life, what is important in it is not prestige or the amount of money in the bank, but rather whether or not he feels that his life has been useful. If he has been able to contribute, even in some small way, to making it possible for people to live lives that are more satisfying to them than they might otherwise have been, that, it seems to me, is probably the most meaningful of all life's satisfactions.

JOHN A. HANNAH
President (1941-1969), Michigan State University

Prevailing Public Perceptions of Higher Education

Universities never like to be challenged. They want our money, but they want to be autonomous. You can't have both.

B. PATRICK BAUER

Indiana State Representative

2.1 Introduction

We must all hang together, or most assuredly we shall all hang separately.

BENJAMIN FRANKLIN

Traditionally colleges and universities have been accorded special status by the public as places of idealism and integrity. Those who teach have historically been revered by society. But, in the minds of many main street and back road Americans, things have changed in higher education. As reported in an article, "Planning to Get Real" (March 1992 by James Harvey), public pollster Lou Harris found that in the 1960s an estimated 61 percent of all Americans placed a high degree of confidence in the "people running higher education." Today only about 25 percent feel the same.

Over the past three decades, the value of higher education has been questioned as never before in American history. Much criticism has come from persons who appear to have only a minimal concept of, or appreciation for, the values of advanced education. Perhaps this results partly from the fact that people tend to mistrust the most those whom they understand the least. Yet in a democracy such as the United States, public attitude, understanding, and perceptions directly affect decisions in both public and private sectors.

In her recent book, *Stealing into Print* (University of California Press,

29

1992), Marcel LaFollette of George Washington University noted a problem in the reluctance of members of the scientific community to take its public constituency seriously enough:

> To them, the word public is a dirty word. To them, their financial support just happens to come. Taxpayers are never really seen as the source. If you look at the rhetoric, everyone talks about these issues as though funding just happened. It has been keeping them in a nice, middle-class life. The notion that the money came from people next door was a notion the community couldn't grapple with. They were like politicians losing touch with their constituency. A sense of service just doesn't fit into what they perceive is their reason for being.

Society needs facts and reliable judgments about the benefits of higher education. If this need is not fulfilled by educators, decisions concerning the allocation of resources to higher education will be made on the basis of incomplete criteria that are biased toward the tangible, the quantifiable—and perhaps the least relevant for the long-term public good.

For many years higher education existed as an independent arm of society, secure in its isolation from such concerns as balance sheets, management audits, and budgetary oversights. Those were the days of autonomy that were only rarely visited by a call for accountability. Those days are over for higher education, as they should be.

Recently the general public, legislators, and others have become increasingly skeptical of higher education's argument that the huge and costly enterprise is overextended, and that the value of its outcomes justifies—indeed exceeds—the amount of fiscal resources being expended. Many are calling for greater accountability, seeking the intelligible reporting of specific outcomes as well as formal accounting for expenditures. It makes extraordinary common sense that, when public money is provided, public scrutiny and input into decision making will inevitably prevail. Governments cannot and will not ignore what is done with public money.

As the need to trim governmental budgets has forced reconsideration of public priorities, governments are learning to differentiate between not only the teaching and research missions of institutions but between higher education and other public services—including public schools, social welfare, correctional facilities, and health care—as well. Increasingly, the legislative mindset is regarding higher education as more a private benefit than a public good. The message that a college degree translates into the higher earnings that traditionally come with a good job notwithstanding, the conclusion being drawn more and more often is that a college education contributes to individual advancement more than to the nation's social fabric. The result: students enrolled in public institutions are being required to pay an ever greater share of the cost of a college education. This places increased financial pressure on low- and middle-income families at a time when a sluggish economy, employment uncertainties, global trade deficits, and other economic pressures are becoming increasingly apparent. The result is that public concern is mounting that rising costs have made a college education much like health care—inaccessible to a growing number of Americans.

Recent studies conducted by the California Higher Education Policy Center and the American Council on Education indicate that a major public concern with higher education is the cost of a college education and the consequent prospect of diminished access for many. As the college degree becomes increasingly important to a young person competing for a job, there is concern that the means of advancement will be lessened for those less capable of paying their own way. Public fear of reduced access to higher education parallels public fear about eroding health-care coverage.

Some legislatures are considering "high tuition-high aid" policies which distribute public money (in the form of student financial aid) principally to students from economically disadvantaged families attending public institutions and to targeted programs encouraging students from underrepresented groups to enroll in science, engineering, and other high-need career fields. Such approaches would leave most other students to pay nearly the full cost of tuition and fees.

2.2 Why the Public Displeasure with Higher Education?

Higher education is too resistant to change. Too often, public colleges want to keep doing things the way they have always been done. They need a "wake-up call." Everything is changing around us, and they have to change, too. It is for their own good.

RAY C. ALBRIGHT
Tennessee State Representative

The most fundamental challenge facing higher education is to reverse the significant decline in public trust. Unfortunately, there is a growing perception that higher education is not responding effectively to the problems being faced by society. What the public hears and reads about—exorbitant tuition increases, research overcharges, athletic scandals, political correctness, coaches being paid more than professors and presidents, ineffective teaching, lumbering obsolescence, self-serving attitudes, failure to focus and make changes, among others—contribute directly to erosion of public trust. Adding to this, the mass media tend to characterize higher education as an industry that is exhausting itself attempting to escape a morass of its own making. The consensus quickly emerging is that colleges and universities have high consumption patterns but low output rates. The conventional wisdom holds that this results from their being inefficient, outmoded, incapable of securing their own survival.

Ironically, land-grant institutions have helped solve complex societal problems by providing moral, scientific, medical, social, economic, and educational leadership and by building the character, courage, and integrity of our nation's most valued resource—people. The charge that higher education is not meeting the needs of society is particularly galling to those of us imbued by the land-grant spirit because it cuts to the very core of the land-grant mission.

If land-grant institutions are to enjoy a high level of public support, it is imperative that they stay close to their basic constituencies—those who need and use their services. The relationship between land-grant institutions and their constituents might be compared with a stream-fed lake. The lake's level is related to the rate of water inflow; if high, lake level will be high. Similarly, if the inflow of public support is high, colleges and universities are enabled to grow, to be more productive, to render expanded services to the public. When institutions fail to respond to public concerns, needs, and problems, they cannot reasonably expect to continue receiving the same level of public support. We can expect the public to continue communicating its expectations of—and disappointments in—higher education.

> *The university must not stand apart from its society and its immediate environment but must be an integral part of that society. The university best serves itself and society by assuming an active leadership role, as opposed to its traditional stance of somewhat passive responsiveness.*
>
> **CHARLES E. HATHAWAY**

The greatest anxiety about higher education resides in the shapers of public policy—those close to their constituents. These include governors, legislators, regulators, heads of public agencies, and an increasing number involved with private philanthropy. Many of those responsible for higher education's funding believe public colleges and universities have become too isolated from the economic pressures that are forcing most other American enterprises to revisit their purpose and mission, to rightsize, often to reduce scope and function. As the instinct to impose punitive regulation has expanded, so too has the impulse to teach higher education a lesson, to make it less smug and insular.

Policy makers have expressed in specific terms several serious concerns. First there is the perception that higher education has not fulfilled promises that served as the basis of increased funding over the past three decades. These include at least three unfulfilled promises. The first has to do with entry access for underrepresented segments of the population. Another is the failure to foster notable economic development for states and regions. Finally, there is widespread criticism that too often we have failed to assure an appropriately educated citizenry—graduates with sufficient skills to be effective workers and informed citizens. Even the best and brightest, they argue, often exhibit a self-centered aggressiveness that renders them incapable of working effectively with others in a spirit of teamwork. Lacking such workplace skills, they fail to interact with and earn the support of their various publics as well.

More to the point is the public perception that many institutions are havens for a privileged class that has forgotten its societal responsibilities. Higher education is perceived as looking after its own interests first, the needs of society last. Increasingly, those responsible for public policy and appropriated public money describe higher education's faculty as a self-perpetuating oligarchy openly disdainful of the opinions of others. They perceive most academicians as persons who have rarely if ever been outside the ivied halls and therefore know little about the real world for which they supposedly are preparing students. Time after time, academic tenure (approximately two-thirds of the full-time faculty members in the United States are tenured) is the common touchstone for these critics. "Why," they ask, "should college and university professors, who rarely work hard enough anyway, enjoy not merely greater job security but better pay than most taxpayers (and more than most state legislators as well)? Why sustain them in their accustomed privileges and lifestyles?"

The general public is much more supportive of increased compensation for laborers than for professors. An Oklahoma state senator noted that legislators having no higher education institution in their district rarely hear from faculty members, but they hear frequently from working women and men. Also, legislators rarely hear from the higher education community with regard to important public issues such as workers compensation. Yet, higher education could provide important, useful information concerning safety in the workplace, healthy lifestyles, and other related matters.

The result is that many makers of public policy are inclined to impose restrictive regulations even as they reduce public funding for higher education. Several state legislators are pursuing work-rule changes through laws to force faculty members to "work harder by teaching more." A major concern is that the future could yield not only a greater number of such ill-advised regulations but that the discussion and debate likely to accompany them could further solidify strongly negative feelings among policy makers and the public. Many already believe that faculty members are more concerned about their own well-being than that of those they are supposed to be serving.

It is important to note that legislative bodies cannot legislate academic productivity anymore than they can legislate fair weather. Forcing faculty into the classroom a given number of hours each week does not force teachers to engage the imagination of students. Real faculty productivity and student learning requires a voluntary commitment, as well as a strong interaction among students and teachers.

2.3 Communicating the Purpose, Contributions, and Merits of Higher Education

The whole history of education ... shows that we must begin with the higher institutions, or we can never succeed with the lower; for the plain reason, that neither knowledge nor water runs up hill. No people ever had, or ever can have, any system of common schools or lower seminaries worth anything, until they first founded their higher institutions and foundation of knowledge from which they could draw supplies of teachers ... for the lower.

JONATHAN BALDWIN TURNER
(1851)

The Law of the Harvest governs. We shall reap what we sow. Moreover, the Law of Justice also is immutable, and the closer we align ourselves with the purposes of higher education, the better our judgment will be in assuring a progressive future.

No compassionate nation can long neglect the educational plight of its young people without paying a big price. When public trust declines and complacency for education prevails, the need for improved communication mounts dramatically. This is exactly the situation in which we now find ourselves.

The underlying purpose of education is to provide opportunities for people to gain the knowledge and understanding required to recognize and discharge personal and social responsibilities to the fullest extent possible. Education serves people of varying backgrounds and talents, helps them discover their interests, and assists them in developing along lines compatible with their individual abilities. It can serve as an instrument for widening human expression and reducing inequalities among people. It is through extending the cultural arc, through broadening the dimensions of human worth, that higher education can best help reconcile equality with excellence.

In our rapidly changing world, institutions of higher education serve as custodians of the intellectual capital of humanity. They also serve as centers of innovation and change. Both involve an investigation of the application of knowledge to current needs and opportunities, and the examination and criticism of society itself. These are tasks for which higher education bears primary responsibility in our society—but for which it is impossible to assign a monetary value. They include interpreting and preserving the artifacts of the past, discovering and defining the meaning of human life, appraising and explaining social trends, formulating carefully considered recommendations for public policy, and fostering the fine arts. These tasks are carried on quietly and steadily, year in and year out, yet they generally go unnoticed and not fully appreciated by the general public and even by many in the wider academic family. But if these activities were to stop, their absence would soon be noticed. When asked, Why are we fighting this war? Winston Churchill replied, "If we were to stop, you would soon know why." So it is with much of higher education. To avoid cultural deterioration, society would be obligated (at substantial expense) to find substitute institutions for carrying on these various important functions.

Higher education's role as transmitter of civilization's values is worthy of note. If not colleges and universities, who would acquaint each generation with what has been known, said, and accomplished in the world? Indeed, higher education is a major component of the sizing that strengthens the fabric of society. It also is important to appreciate the connections between higher education and economic growth, higher education and social progress, higher education and a responsible citizenry, higher education and the nation's future.

The modern land-grant university has frequently been a center for a creative tension among varying and even conflicting values and viewpoints. Many have noted that universities are among the most conservative of social institutions. They are especially slow to embrace innovation (Chapter 11). At the same time, they also are widely perceived as catalysts for change on the basis of the new knowledge and understanding they generate. Similarly, we expect universities to preserve and transmit society's historical self-understanding and cultural artifacts, yet we also increasingly expect them to assist in society's progressive transformations and to provide the creative impetus for contemporary cultural artifacts.

The wisdom of expending public money on education cannot be measured solely by its direct fruits. Education enables people to take advantage of many new opportunities that otherwise would not have come their way. And how does one measure the economic value of the educated industrial genius whose expertise, innovativeness, and business prowess create hundreds of jobs? And how does one measure the societal benefits of the medical discoveries of Jenner, Pasteur, or Salk? Such discoveries not only save lives, but also enable people to be more productive and to enjoy life without the fear of many heretofore deadly diseases.

Indeed, the myriad public criticisms of higher education notwithstanding, the public benefits of higher education far exceed the costs. The monetary returns, in the form of enhanced earnings, increased taxes, and improved technology are sufficient to offset the costs. In addition to the monetary returns are the personal development and life enrichment enjoyed by millions of people, the preservation of our rich cultural heritage, the advancement of knowledge in the arts, the major contribution to the nation's power and prestige, and the direct satisfaction derived from attending college and from living in a society where knowledge is honored and the arts can flourish. These non-monetary benefits probably exceed the monetary benefits, but they are difficult to quantify.

At no time in American history have individuals and hence higher education faced more urgent demands and challenges than in the present. Scientific advancements and rapid expansion of the knowledge base foretell major changes. The increasing complexity of today's social, political, scientific, and economic structure requires of educated persons such knowledge and understanding as could not have been imagined even a generation ago. Particularly significant is the demand for research and development programs. These are urgently needed to promote understanding, advance knowledge, and hasten the application of new discoveries during a period of growing populations and increasing global competition and tension. The scope of higher education extends beyond the college years to include continuing education and international educational exchanges as well as technical assistance to business, government, and other sectors of society. In short, proper investments in higher education involve those adequate to an enterprise that increasingly undergirds both our dynamic national economy and our free society as a whole.

Defending the integrity of the land-grant college and university system is crucial for this nation. This extensive system can greatly aid society in meeting the needs and challenges of the twenty-first century. Lack of public support would soon leave this an intellectually impoverished, uncompetitive society, and—because many land-grant institutions have done so much for the creative arts—an artistically impoverished society as well.

Public support of university research and education is based in large part on the notion that generation of new knowledge and education of a skilled workforce are necessary investments to achieve our national goals of a high quality of life based on a productive, competitive, growing economy.

Institutions of higher education must invest more in public perception. The public needs to know more about the merits and contributions of higher education to our nation. Napoleon once said, "Ten people who speak make more noise than 10,000 who are silent." The time is ripe for land-grant colleges and universities to work more closely with the various media to increase public awareness of the handsome dividends being paid on public investments in the education, research, and outreach programs of land-grant institutions. This awareness then must be used to spur the collective efforts of concerned citizens, business and governmental leaders, and professional groups. Only then will we maximize the widespread benefits we seek from higher education.

> *Public sentiment is everything. With public sentiment, nothing can fail. Without it, nothing can succeed.*
>
> **ABRAHAM LINCOLN**

2.4 Restoring Public Trust in Higher Education

> *I am concerned that in recent years, higher education's historic commitment to service seems to have diminished. I am troubled that, to put it simply, many now view the campus as a place where professors get tenured and students get credentialed, but what goes on there is not seen as relevant to many of our social problems. The overall efforts of the academy are not considered to be at the vital center of the nation's work. And what I find most disturbing is the growing feeling in this country that higher education is a private benefit, not a public good. I think we are paying a price for that!*
>
> **ERNEST L. BOYER**
> Executive Director,
> Carnegie Foundation for the Advancement of Teaching

The end of the Cold War removed a major anxiety fueling political support for higher education. Virtually all academic programs—not only those in the sciences—benefited from the post-Sputnik panic that fostered the rapid growth of research universities and led to such programs as the National Defense Education Act Humanities Fellowships. Indeed, post-war enthusiasm for higher education now appears to have been a relatively short-lived aberration in American cultural politics. Elementary and secondary schools, which indeed face complex new social responsibilities, are now expected to absorb most of the new public monies available for education over the next several years.

Other economic and social needs—such as health care, correctional facilities, the decay of highways—seem to have more visibility and more politically potent constituencies than does higher education. Further, continuing public attacks discourage legislators from allocating new monies to higher education. Sparked by "scandals" over low faculty teaching loads, misused public research funds, outspoken tenured faculty, and controversies over "hate speech" and sexual harassment, these attacks have stimulated additional anger in taxpayers and thereby galvanized resistance to tuition increases. In this climate of hostility, public college and university budgets can be reduced at little or no political cost to the legislator.

In his book *Impostors in the Temple: American Intellectuals Are Destroying Our Universities and Cheating Our Students of Their Future* (Simon and Schuster, New York, 1992), Martin Anderson wrote of today's universities: "There is nothing comparable to stockholders to whom corporate boards and executives must ultimately answer. No one "owns" a university. Virtually all the major universities and colleges in America are minisocialist states in which trustees, administrators and faculty answer only to themselves."

Higher education's lackluster public image is based in part on the public's lack of appreciation of the accountability, relevance, and impact of many of higher education's functions and programs. Comprehensive public universities are responsible for providing high-quality professional, technical, and liberal education of today's young people for tomorrow's increasingly sophisticated careers; for conducting basic, strategic, and applied research that will enlarge our body of useful knowledge; for assisting businesses, industries, governmental agencies, and local communities through effective technology-transfer programs; and for meeting the important continuing education needs of individuals, families, and other specialized clientele through timely extension outreach initiatives. A greatly improved public image—and particularly a fuller understanding by the citizenry of the impact higher education programs have on the economic well-being of and quality of life in our society—is clearly needed if we are to gain essential support for the high-priority work of our nation's public colleges and universities.

Feedback from alumni, business leaders, legislators, and others indicates that our institutions of higher education must work more aggressively to shed an "ivory tower" image and, working with supporters in both public and private sectors, to acknowledge and underscore their accountability to and favorable impact on society as a whole.

Former Oklahoma A&M College (now Oklahoma State University) President Henry G. Bennett once said that our nation's publicly supported institutions of higher education represent "gateways of opportunity for our democratic society—serving as the watchtowers and service stations of applied knowledge and providing assertive leadership in the progressive reconstruction of society." An enhanced public image and greater credibility among our various constituencies will be critical factors in garnering needed public support as higher education faces the complex challenges coming in the twenty-first century. Simply put, we in higher education must not only reassert our leadership in discovery, dissemination, and application of useful knowledge; we also must work to build clear, positive public recognition of these key roles. Higher education should pursue opportunities to reach large audiences of future opinion leaders through electronic communications such as Internet. Every college and university should assign a high priority to the development of an effective Speakers Bureau. This requires preparing a list of topics and speakers and sharing it with various organizations and groups in the institution's area of influence. Invitations to share positive information about institutional contributions and public services with all citizens should be actively solicited.

If we are to restore public confidence in—and thereby garner increased public support for—higher education, we must better control the cost of a college education. Administrative cost-cutting and restructuring are crucial. So are improving the quality and efficiency of our basic educational and service functions. We must redeploy, restructure, and downsize our faculties and staffs to free funds for quality improvements and new investments in areas of greatest need and promise.

Measuring and then reporting educational progress by students to the American people also are important aspects of recapturing public support for higher education. This includes better defining what students need to know, better assessing whether they know it, and ascertaining that the measurements are accurate and appropriate. Achievement tests should not simply measure minimum competencies. They also should measure higher levels of reading, writing, speaking, critical-thinking, and problem-solving skills. The primary emphasis in higher education should be on academic achievement and meeting well-defined standards rather than on credit hours, class schedules, and examination scores.

Public demand for greater efficiency and accountability in higher education is legitimate. Higher education has a clear responsibility to operate as efficiently as possible and to report its costs and benefits to the taxpayers. But the demand for accountability will be practically impossible to fulfill if it be reduced to absolute quantitative terms. Higher education also must be concerned with matters of intellect, personality, and values. These are not readily quantifiable as we evaluate our diverse outcomes. They are interrelated, often subtle, sometimes unexpected, frequently difficult to document, and judged differently by various observers in a pluralistic society.

2.5 Summary

The corrals are getting smaller, and the barbed wire is getting higher.

CLARK KERR

Higher education is facing more than temporary budgetary restraints. It is undergoing a critical test of public trust. Members of the public—directly and through their elected officials—are asking legitimate, pertinent questions about the costs, pricing, productivity, access, outcomes, effectiveness, and efficiency of higher education. Up to now, we have rather arrogantly ignored these questions. By our reactions, it often seems as if these questions are insults to our integrity. A typical response by many in higher education, when questioned by the public, is to talk and talk, explain and explain, defend and defend. Perhaps a wiser course of action would be to listen and listen. And then try to understand what is being asked and why.

Another lesson that seems to be difficult for those in higher education to learn is that there is little to be gained but much to be lost in arguing with members of our various publics or their legislative representatives. The rhetorical firepower of institutions of higher education notwithstanding, neither the public at large nor legislative critics of higher education are pleased to hear detailed explanations of why scholarly initiatives cost so much, why the processes of research and discovery are so important and expensive, and why it is best to do things in the future much the same as in the past. These people are even less interested in being reminded of the special values higher education claims to enshrine.

Reducing financial support is perhaps the most effective way the public can express its dissatisfaction with higher education. We can expect more popular backlash against colleges and universities in the foreseeable future. Fiscal constraints are likely to tighten more before they loosen appreciably. Appropriated state and federal monies will be insufficient to "save the day." These institutions must retrench even further. They must re-examine their missions, roles, and scopes; set goals and priorities (including timely new programs); then implement a strategic plan to achieve them (Chapter 13).

Institutions of higher learning must emphasize substitution and subtraction instead of addition. When budgets tighten, the instinctive thing to do is protect individual interests, and this stifles an institution's capacity to change. Universities must purposefully recast their set of functions. In considering courses of change, they must balance the need to maintain a high level of collegiality with the awareness that deferring painful steps is not an acceptable option. It is important to purposefully consider alternative changes as well as to discuss openly the consequences of not changing at all.

To gain greater flexibility in setting priorities for new needs and opportunities, it will be necessary to decrease the proportion of Expense and General (E&G) monies consumed by salaries and benefits from the common 80-percent level to a target of perhaps as little as 50 to 60 percent. Such a significant change would require a planned reduction in the size of faculty and staff, some of which could be achieved through attrition and early retirements.

But what is further required is a conscious fundamental decision—which to be acceptable within academe means a fully debated decision—to allocate human resources in more effective ways and to abandon the goal of employment entitlements. Such savings need to be invested in new high-priority programs and opportunities, in improved technologies, and in greater outreach to a clientele that will increasingly have at its disposal educational opportunities already being offered by the new information superhighways (Chapter 4).

Such redesigning will mean challenging the conventional wisdom that educational quality is linked to class size and the student:faculty ratio. It will require hands-on management as well as the courage and willingness to demystify bureaucracies—academic and administrative—that preserve turf largely by sustaining procedures that are sufficiently idiosyncratic to defy combination (and hence reduction). Such restructuring must embrace an unshakable commitment to major changes and show a willingness—indeed a determination—to make do with smaller staffs, simplified policies and procedures, and reduced paper work. It will stress technology as a signal measure of efficiency and progress. Such monumental change, of course, will require the unwavering support of governing boards.

Multicultural Diversity Initiative

Cast down your bucket where you are—cast down by making friends in every manly way with the people of all races by whom you are surrounded. Cast it down in agriculture, in mechanics, in commerce, in domestic science, and in the professions.

BOOKER T. WASHINGTON

3.1 Introduction

The American economy, and thus American society, has been built around the idea that tomorrow's generation will do better than today's. The poor believed that, too. But if those at the bottom of the economic ladder stop believing the child's future holds more promise than the parent's past, we will be in serious trouble.

WILLIAM S. WOODSIDE

The nature of the American free-enterprise system of the future will be planned and achieved by people. New discoveries are brought about by people. Teaching and public service are rendered by people. Technology transfer and applications are accomplished by people. Management is performed by people. In the equation where the viability of our democracy and free-enterprise system is the dependent variable, the most important independent variable is human capital—people! Any plan for ensuring the strength and competitiveness of America's agricultural, industrial, and technological complexes necessarily includes a critical aspect: the development of human capital.

43

To provide state, national, and global leadership for all entities of our free-enterprise system—including the assurance of new information and systems that preserve and enhance the environment, expand and enhance the quality of life for all groups of rural and urban Americans alike—bright young minds in sufficient numbers and from all segments of the populace must be developed. Because all of these needs are for the public good, it makes sense that they be fulfilled by means of public money.

As we prepare to begin the twenty-first century, achieving multicultural diversity is especially important to higher education, as it is to our society. Unfortunately, American higher education is losing ground in terms of practical accessibility to citizens in minority sectors (Section 3.4). This has resulted in part from the fact that recently there has been a major shift of emphasis in federal student aid from grants to loans. This poses a tremendous access barrier for many minority students. These accessibility problems come at a time when absolute minority matriculation rate at our nation's colleges and universities is declining proportionately, and when a shortage of university graduates is developing in certain technical and professional fields.

We must move forward with unwavering resolve to increase the participation of underrepresented groups in higher education. We must aspire to engage the full range of talents of all people, and this of course begins with equalizing educational opportunities. Achieving multicultural diversity clearly is in keeping with the spirit of providing this equality, which was affirmed and mandated by the land-grant acts of 1862 and 1890. Addressing the critical and growing need of making higher education more accessible to students of underrepresented groups should not be viewed simply as a matter of social justice. It is one way to enhance the overall level of excellence in institutions of higher education, as well as in corporate America. People in underrepresented groups—including women—are expected to fill more than 70 percent of our nation's new and vacant technical and professional career positions between now and the year 2000. It is therefore imperative that providing advanced education to underrepresented groups immediately be given high priority.

We seek an educational community in which intellectual diversity and human diversity enlarge mutual goals and strengthen fundamental purposes. We seek an enlarged vision of diversity that celebrates differences and cherishes commonalities. Diversity should be woven thoroughly into the fabric of the academic life and purpose of all institutions of higher education. It should be highly valued by faculty and staff, completely expressed through curricular and academic service programs, consistently sustained through opportunities for cultural expression and extracurricular life.

The real issue on campus and in the classroom is not

whether there will be multiculturalism, but rather what kind of multiculturalism will there be?

DIANE RAVITCH

Although human diversity and multiculturalism are highly important, they remain one of the most intractable problems facing this nation. Cultural patterns are built on shared beliefs, behaviors, and assumptions. Beliefs are value statements as to what we hold true or false, relevant or irrelevant, good or bad. Behaviors are observable actions that reflect beliefs. Assumptions are the unconscious rationales for applying beliefs and behaviors. Multiculturalism is a powerful tool that can either reinforce change or impede it.

America is a land that from its very beginning was marked by heterogeneity. And although we share the same films, television programs, sporting events, and fast-service restaurants, we remain a diverse people. In a democratic, free-enterprise society, diversity is an asset—an important part of the wonder of this nation—a way of life of which we rightly can be proud.

America is not a melting pot, but rather a salad bowl, each piece distinct and diverse.

SHIRLEY CHISHOLM

Why do people marvel at variation in leaf color among trees in the fall and drive hundreds of miles to enjoy this wonder of Nature, but then resist appreciating and accepting variation in skin color among humans? What makes some leaves red, some yellow, others brown? The same biological phenomena that impart black, brown, red, white, or yellow skin to individual humans. Genetically determined pigments.

The beauties of Nature come in all colors. The strengths of humankind come in many forms. Every human being is a precious individual, wonderfully unique. We all contribute to our fellow travelers and all of society in different ways. When we learn to honor the differences and fully appreciate the mixtures, we will soon find harmony and peace.

The first step on this journey is to pay attention to abilities and potential contributions but not the color of skin. The spirit of intercollegiate and professional athletics is a leader in embracing multicultural diversity. There is no other enterprise in American life where various ethnic and multicultural groups have better learned to work together and mutually support one another.

3.2   One Nation, Many Peoples

The metaphor of the melting pot is unfortunate and mislead-

ing. A more accurate analogy would be a salad bowl, for, though the salad is an entity, the lettuce can still be distinguished from the chicory, the tomatoes from the cabbage.

CARL N. DEGLER

Multiculturalism as an ideal has flourished mainly in the Western Hemisphere. As a society, the United States of America represents a rich melding of peoples from every part of the globe, each with its own cultural roots and proud heritage.

History is replete with examples of nation states that failed to combine diverse ethnic/linguistic/religious groups to form a single sovereignty. For many if not most societies, attempts to promote multiculturalism, to celebrate differences, have resulted in fomenting prejudice, persecution, fratricide, tribal war, even anarchy. The United States is more nearly an exception; Yugoslavia more nearly the rule.

Refugees from many multicultural conflagrations have sought in the United States a unique brand of political comity they believed was accorded by a constitutional system devolved in the ideal to universal equality, universal human rights. The fundamental ideals that encourage culturally rooted differences to co-exist and cooperate rather than to persecute and annihilate, that afford celebration of difference without leading to discrimination and internecine warfare, must be regarded as precious and rare. Moreover, these noteworthy ideals and covenants must be perpetuated.

In 1994 there were approximately 500,000 international students enrolled in institutions of higher education in the United States. These people aim to develop their knowledge and abilities in their respective disciplines. Along the way, they observe how Americans have merged the skills and expertise of peoples of hundreds of cultures to form one nation, a nation where democratic principles respect the rich heritage associated with multicultural diversity.

3.3 Demographic and Philosophical Aspects

The United States is on the verge of revolution. And like most, this revolution is a mix of promise and peril. Simply put, in the next decade, blacks and hispanics are going to reshape the American work force. From now until the year 2000, new minority and immigrant entrants to the labor markets will outnumber new white entrants by three to two.

CLIFTON R. WHARTON, JR.

Normal trends and changes in demographics, socioeconomics, and the political character of the people will dramatically affect higher education in the years ahead. By the year 2050, the United States will reflect the cultures of the world. If current trends continue, in approximately fifty years, America's population will have no majority ethnic or racial group. Most of the increase in America's population over the next fifty years will come from immigrants, and nine of ten of these are expected to be present-day "minorities."

By 2010, Hispanic Americans will be the nation's largest ethnic minority, increasing from about 25 million in 1993 to a projected 40 million. The high school graduation rate for Hispanics is about 50 percent, compared with approximately 80 percent for non-Hispanic whites. And less than 10 percent of Hispanics complete college, compared with 22 percent for non-Hispanic whites.

According to Bureau of the Census projections, during the forty-year period 1990 to 2030, the white population of the United States will increase by an estimated 25 percent, while the African American population will increase by 68 percent; the Asian American, Pacific Island American, and Native American populations by 79 percent; and the Hispanic population by 187 percent. This will bring about a multicultural diversity revolution. Multicultural research, teaching, and engagement in the public arena will move from the wings to center stage.

In the next twenty years the United States will add a net 4.4 million African American, Hispanic, Asian, Native American, Alaskan natives, and Middle Eastern young people to its population, while the number of white youth will drop by a net 3.8 million. Already, from 1980 to 1990, post-secondary enrollments of Asian and Hispanic Americans increased 94 and 61 percent, respectively. Projections indicate that by the year 2001, the majority of students attending college in California and Texas—our two most populous states—will be African Americans and Hispanics.

According to census data, minority students represent about 30 percent of all public school enrollments. By the year 2010 they will amount to about 40 percent. Nearly half now are from low-income families, and the fraction is increasing. Some 46 percent of African Americans under age eighteen live in poverty, including 50 percent under age six and 53 percent under three years. This comes at a time when financial assistance for college students in general is becoming increasingly difficult to obtain.

This dramatic shift in demographics will reflect low fertility and in-migration rates in whites, out-migration from largely white rural areas to urban areas, and high fertility rates among minority populations. Many states will experience an increasing proportion of university-eligible high-school graduates from historically underrepresented racial and ethnic groups. A large number will represent the first generation of their families to attend college. It can therefore be predicted that they will have minimal knowledge of the complex delivery systems for scholarships, student financial aid, and other student services. Moreover, faculty and administrators will need to become more aware of the cultural features of fast-growing minority populations and more sensitive to addressing concerns among many minority families with regard to their daughters and sons "staying near home" as opposed to living at a residential university campus.

A great challenge facing all of education is knowing how best to prepare this multicultural group for the future. The influx of underrepresented students will exacerbate a problem that already exists on many campuses: racial and cultural conflict. How well we respond to this profound change in the cultural mix on our campuses will be important.

Simple pledges of nondiscrimination will not suffice. The public will not tolerate a system of higher education that serves the economically privileged but leaves second- and third-generation minority "have-nots" to fend for themselves. Indeed, demographic changes and racial tensions will occur within a context of any such economic constraint. We must abandon the outmoded "weeding-out" philosophy with one of "bringing-in." We must emphasize the "value-added" aspect of education for all—the developing and nurturing of the human potential of all groups.

> *That there should one man die ignorant who had the capacity to learn, this I call a tragedy. To impart the gift of thinking to those who cannot think, and yet who could in that case think: this one would imagine, was the first function a government had to set about discharging.*
>
> **THOMAS CARLYLE**

Will leaders of higher-educational institutions provide creative ways and means of preparing students to participate in a more tolerant, more understanding, more progressive society? We need to prepare today's minority graduate students to assume faculty positions so they can serve as role models during this upcoming revolution. We must wisely deploy our human capital if we are to remain a global leader in education as well as in the production of goods and services.

Clifford R. Wharton, Jr. ("Education and Tomorrow's Work Force: A National Agenda," from *A Century of Service: Land-Grant Colleges and Universities, 1890–1990,* Chapter 10; Transaction Publishers, New Brunswick and London, 1992) shared insightful glimpses of the "promise" and the "peril" which may accompany this revolution in the U.S. labor market. The promise lies in potential expansion of employment opportunities for women, African Americans, and those in other groups of minorities. The peril lies in the fact that these individuals may not be properly educated and trained for the jobs at hand.

According to Wharton, several factors could compound the peril side of the equation. These include an aging population, lower high-school graduation rates, excessive teenage unemployment, lower college attendance and graduation rates, lower propensities to attend graduate school, low minority faculty representation, failure of U.S. corporations to promote blacks and Hispanics into executive policy-making roles, and failure of society to produce and bring ample numbers of role models and leaders into the system.

Today we must pay more attention to those who may be at the margin—those who, with a little development effort, can be transformed into superstars.

JAMES DUDERSTADT

Census data indicate that members of groups now minority comprise 26 percent of the U.S. population. By the year 2000, a third of college students and more than a third of the nation's workforce will be persons of color. Yet minorities comprise only about 12 percent of higher education's full-time instructional faculty (Table 3.1). Social justice and national self-interest compel higher education to aggressively confront the problem of underrepresentation

TABLE 3.1. **Ethnic group representation, as a percentage of the United States population, at various educational levels. (Note that minority underrepresentation tends to increase as educational level increases.)**

	Total U.S Citizens	White	African American	Hispanic	Asian	Native American
United States Population	255,082,000 100.0%	181,873,466 71.3%	30,864,922 12.1%	22,957,380 9.0%	7,397,378 2.9%	2,040,656 0.8%
High School Graduates	2,228,100 100.0%	1,622,660 72.8%	299,520 13.4%	197,560 8.9%	90,960 4.1%	17,400 0.8%
Undergraduate Enrollment	12,440,000 100.0%	9,508,000 76.4%	1,299,000 9.9%	804,000 6.5%	559,000 4.5%	106,000 0.9%
Bachelors Recipients	1,094,538 100.0%	904,061 82.6%	65,338 6.0%	36,612 3.3%	41,622 3.8%	4,513 0.4%
Masters Recipients	337,168 100.0%	255,286 75.7%	16,136 4.8%	8,382 2.5%	11,180 3.3%	1,136 0.3%
Doctoral Recipients	39,294 100.0%	25,328 64.5%	1,212 3.1%	732 1.9%	1,458 3.7%	102 0.3%
Faculty	520,551 100.0%	456,316 87.7%	24,611 4.7%	11,424 2.2%	26,545 5.1%	1,655 0.3%

Sources: Adapted from *Chronicle of Higher Education Almanac*, August 25, 1993, and *The Road to College* (Western Interstate Commission for Higher Education, Boulder, Colo., July 1991).

of minorities in the ranks of the faculty. Proper representation of minority groups on faculties is crucial and must receive the attention of higher education.

Minority faculty members serve as role models for minority students. They communicate the possibility of personal success. They serve as mentors. Seeking out students, providing them individual support, intervening to help resolve problems, contributing to their personal and professional growth. Minority faculty can best understand issues of particular concern to students belonging to minority groups and thus help to develop a knowledge base that will serve a diverse society.

What is just as important, faculty of underrepresented groups communicate the diversity of our society by their presence. They verify that professional talent flourishes without regard to color or culture. They make essential contributions to a whole society that can function successfully only if all work together. Fortunately, public programs are responding with increased attention—both to our nation's growing diversity and to the historical, contemporary, and future importance of multiculturalism.

3.4 Providing Access to Higher Education

No race that has anything to contribute to the markets of the world is long in any degree ostracized. It is important and right that all privileges of the law be ours, but it is vastly more important that we be prepared for the exercise of these privileges. The opportunity to earn a dollar in the factory just now is worth infinitely more than the opportunity to spend a dollar in the opera house.

BOOKER T. WASHINGTON

The United States cannot move forward with its founding ideals of freedom, equality, and social justice—nor succeed in a competitive world—without assuring equal opportunity for a college education to members of all sectors of the citizenry. Indeed, when a society is indifferent to its responsibility of providing equal access to educational opportunities, it is indifferent to its future.

To engender sustained public support, the makeup and programs of land-grant colleges and universities must reflect the diversity of our general population with regard to gender, race, and ethnicity. Our admissions policies must reflect a mission which embraces the challenge of meeting the educational needs of all parts of our society. And our curricular and noncurricular responses must reflect greater diversity as we broaden and widen our human services mission.

A larger proportion of our population—especially those from working class, poor, and minority backgrounds—must be encouraged to enroll in and complete college. The cost of a college education as a percentage of median family income has approximately tripled in one generation. This means more scholarships, work-study opportunities, and loans are needed. The obligations of federal and state governments to assure access for all to higher education is clear.

There is reason for serious concern about increasing admission standards at a time when higher education must embrace a rapidly growing underclass. As admission standards and entrance requirements are increased, is an important segment of society being excluded, the great American dream of equal opportunity for all denigrated? The land-grant college and university system was conceptualized and mandated to provide equal access to all. As we spend approximately four times as much on legalized gambling in the United States as in support of higher education, it would seem our society can well afford to assume a bit of risk on behalf of every young person who expresses and demonstrates a desire for a college education.

> *We must recruit more of the "marginal" students; at the end of four years, we'll be both glad that we paid attention to the ones we did, and we'll be sad we didn't pay attention to more of them ... we must pay more attention to the development of human resources made available to us; we must acknowledge their scarcity.*
>
> **JAMES DUDERSTADT**

According to a 1990 publication of the Massachusetts Institute of Technology entitled "Education That Works: An Action Plan for the Education of Minorities," each year's class of dropouts costs the United States an estimated $240 billion in terms of crime, prisons, welfare, health care, and other public services. For every dollar spent on education, it costs nine dollars to provide services to dropouts. Approximately 80 percent of all prison inmates are school dropouts; each costs the nation more than $28,000 annually. One of the fastest growing population groups in the United States is prisoners. Deplorably, the United States of America is a world leader in the percentage of its population that is incarcerated.

In 1990, more than 14 million children were being reared in the United States by women who were single parents with an annual income averaging only $10,982, whereas children living with two adults had a mean annual family income of $36,872. Demographers predict that 60 percent of today's children will live with a single parent before reaching the age of eighteen. In 1960, only 5 percent of all births in the United States were to unmarried mothers; today the figure is approaching 30 percent. And in 1990, 166 of every 100,000 juveniles were behind bars.

Analyzing the demographic realities that are developing, we quickly conclude that the United States cannot afford a situation where those in the numerical majority are destined to minority status—that is, to be trapped in conditions of poor education, housing, health care, and other important aspects of a reasonable lifestyle. Today there are more college-age African American males confined in America's jails and prisons than living in our college residence halls. One-in-four black males is either behind bars, on parole, or on probation. And a young black female has a probability of only one-in-21,000 of receiving a Ph.D. in engineering, mathematics, or the physical sciences, but a one-in-five chance of dropping out of high school before graduation, and a two-in-five probability of having a baby before her twentieth birthday.

These are serious societal problems closely related to the levels of encouragement received to continue an education and the financial means to do so. Land-grant colleges and universities were founded to respond to needs of the public. They forged a covenant with the people to provide equal access for all to higher education. Great are the opportunities and challenges these institutions face today as they strive to form collaborative partnerships with the public in resolving these problems.

The future is a race between education and catastrophe.
HERBERT G. WELLS

Currently, numerous cultural and economic constraints combine to deny access and educational opportunity to many who would benefit from a college education. We must build new partnerships involving secondary schools and higher education, business and industry, government, and local community leaders to provide incentives for students to pursue advanced education. To do so, we must develop new strategies to provide greater numbers of scholarships, fellowships, and other forms of student financial aid. Meaningful internships and summer enrichment programs should be made more accessible so students can build knowledge and professional experience in their chosen fields of endeavor.

Every child must be encouraged to get as much education as he has the ability to take. We want this not only for his sake—but for the nation's sake. Nothing matters more to the future of our country; not military preparedness—for armed might is worthless if we lack the brainpower to build a world of peace; not our productive economy—for we cannot sustain growth without trained manpower; not our democratic system of government—for freedom is fragile if citizens are ignorant.

LYNDON B. JOHNSON (1965)

According to a 1994 General Accounting Office report, only a small portion of available scholarship monies are targeted for underrepresented groups. Only 5 percent of the total value of all undergraduate scholarship dollars are minority-targeted, and only about 15 percent at the graduate level. These sobering statistics are not in keeping with the need to address multicultural diversity gaps in meaningful ways.

3.5 Mathematics, Science, Engineering, and Technology: Challenges and Opportunities

Concentrate on the golden road ahead, filled with opportunities, but even more importantly with ever-increasing obligations.

D. HOWARD DOANE

Multicultural diversity is not merely something to be tolerated. It is an asset to be promoted. Nowhere in higher education is the application of this philosophy needed more than in mathematics, science, engineering, and technology. Minorities are noticeably underrepresented among students pursuing careers in these disciplines. In 1992, minorities comprised more than 30 percent of school-age youth (aged five through seventeen). By the year 2010, the school-age population is expected to be more than 40 percent minorities. And after 2005, more blacks than non-Hispanic whites are projected to be added to the U.S. population each year. Further, after 1995, the Hispanic population is projected to add more people to the nation's population each year than any other group. In California, Hawaii, Louisiana, Mississippi, New Mexico, and Texas, whites currently represent less than 50 percent of the school-age population.

These demographic data—when coupled with concerns over our nation's economic competitiveness, the level of preparedness of our workforce, society's ability to cope with advanced technology, and the pipeline that feeds the nation's pool of scientists and engineers—clearly point to the importance of assuring the enrollment of an increasing proportion of underrepresented students in mathematics and science classes at secondary and college levels. Raising the achievement of all groups in these disciplines is an important prerequisite to our addressing the technological challenges of the twenty-first century. We must better communicate these career opportunities as well as the fact that technology is color-, gender-, nationality-, and religion-blind.

Between the years 1977 and 1991, the number of science and engineering master's degrees earned by African Americans in the United States dropped from 4197 to 3825 per year, and between 1980 and 1990, the number of African Americans earning Ph.D.s in science and engineering decreased from 276 to 264 annually. In 1992, only 11.8 percent of all doctorates awarded in the United States—3041 of 25,759—were to underrepresented students of all kinds.

These data do not provide much basis for optimism regarding our making sufficient progress in adding underrepresented faculty in the foreseeable future. And colleges and universities that do not achieve balance in their faculty ranks with regard to multicultural diversity, including gender considerations, will not be viewed as academic leaders among world-renowned institutions of higher education. Other reasons why colleges and universities should want to broaden their faculty memberships of underrepresented groups include (1) demographic realities—major changes are in store with regard to the proportion of minorities and women entering higher education during the next two decades; (2) moral and political aspects—society advances more quickly when economic opportunities are available to all segments of the population; and (3) benefits that accrue with broadened perspectives—recruiting more broadly assures better balanced and richer perspectives on various public issues.

Organized efforts directed at achieving greater faculty diversity interlace many partners: university faculties, graduate schools, and administrators; state offices and boards of higher education; state and regional higher-education alliances; state legislatures; the U.S. Congress; business and industry; and private foundations. The all-important goals of educating more minority doctoral students and thereby having the potential for more minority faculty members can be achieved only if these groups are committed and carefully coordinate their efforts. Ultimate success will be reflected by a diverse faculty to prepare our nation to address the broad range of problems and opportunities in the next century.

Having no secure source of financial support for graduate study leads to higher attrition rates and slower progress toward degrees. Minority students are more likely than others to rely on personal rather than federal or institutional resources to support graduate study. In 1992, personal sources (loans, earnings, and family contributions) accounted for 60.9 percent of the primary support for African American predoctoral students and 53.4 percent for Native Americans but only 47.4 percent for whites (Paula Ries and D. H. Thurwood; Summary Report, 1992: "Doctorate Recipients from U.S. Universities," National Academy Press, Washington, D.C., 1993). These data point once again to the importance of providing clearly identified public and private funding to support the pursuit of graduate studies by students in underrepresented groups. Priorities precede funding. If there is to be noteworthy progress in multicultural education and affirmative-action initiatives, faculties and administrations must make provisions for incentive funding of these programs. Otherwise, it will be assumed that the priority assigned such efforts is not high, which would result in slow, limited progress on these important fronts.

Measures of accountability, incentives, and rewards can spur faculties and administrators to envision the funding and academic progress of underrepresented graduate students as being important to their individual and collective contributions to teaching, research, scholarship, and outreach, as well as to the overall health, integrity, and richness of the university community.

3.6 Achieving Multicultural Diversity

The only real hope for the human race, I am convinced, is to find a way for the peoples of all colors, all races, and all religions to agree, not necessarily on politics or economic philosophies, but on how to get on with peaceful efforts at solving the most important human problems.

JOHN A. HANNAH

Diversity is not about numbers or quotas. And merely living within the law is not enough. For many years, racial discrimination was de facto legal in this country, but it was never right. And now it is not enough to simply know what is right. We must have the commitment and courage to do what is right. Human rights were not invented in the United States. Human rights invented the United States. Diversity is not an issue that will permit us to sit idly by, uninvolved, neutral, uninformed, unchallenged. Racial, ethnic, and cultural diversities in society are important issues that span the range of human emotions, from reverence to cynicism, from anger to hatred. Multiculturalism will be successful only if we prove able and willing to bring about broad-based acceptance of the values, perspectives, and political ideals many share in this regard. We must give high priority to identifying and cultivating abilities in the previously excluded and still disadvantaged. And we must inspire these citizens to aspire to use their talents and abilities to *make a difference* in our society's quality of life.

Especially important among the new strategies to be devised to serve the needs of an increasingly diverse student body are those aimed at supporting students who are at risk of academic failure. As we have seen, failure of these students can lead to failure of our nation. We must create a new educational order in which the success of students is our primary aim.

Reasons for the underrepresentation of minorities on every facet of higher education are deeply rooted in American society. At no stage in our education system do enough minority youth succeed, and many of those who do advance to higher levels lack sufficient academic grounding to excel. The task we face is as readily apparent as it is monumental. We need to improve elementary and secondary education, to dramatically increase the number of minority undergraduate and graduate students, and to increase the number of graduate and professional degree recipients planning academic careers.

Recent studies suggest that academe may no longer have as much appeal to minorities as a primary route to career success. For example, in 1977, 67.3 percent of African American and 71.3 percent of Hispanic doctoral degree recipients chose to work in academe, whereas fifteen years later the percentages had decreased to 54.5 and 59.4, respectively. Many of the minority doctoral degree recipients received attractive offers for positions in industry and government, where of course more minority doctoral graduates are needed as well.

Unfortunately, some outstanding minority graduates are being dissuaded from pursuing academic careers because of the perception that opportunities for satisfying academic careers are limited. And while there has been a significant amount of recent publicity with regard to a shortage of academic positions available to new degree recipients, projections indicate that a large number of current faculty members will be retiring in the years after 1996. These projected faculty openings are expected to offer a one-time opportunity to achieve the objective of a greatly improved minority representation among faculty ranks. But qualified candidates must be available for these projected appointments. Preparing a larger pool of minorities for college and university faculty positions will require a consistent, persistent, and carefully planned effort—and it must begin now.

3.7 Summary and Synthesis

No other nation has so successfully combined people of dif-

ferent races and nations within a single culture than in the
United States of America.

LADY MARGARET THATCHER

Our nation has progressed steadily over the years because it has been able to bring its most precious national resource—diverse, resourceful, talented people—to bear on the challenging opportunities at hand. The one dependable force that has consistently sustained and empowered all people has been the power of education (Chapter 1). Our schools and colleges have equipped individuals to take their places in the great work of transforming visions into realities, needs into deeds.

As land-grant institutions of higher education prepare for the twenty-first century, they have as an awesome responsibility the moving closer to fundamental goals that underline multiculturalism, pluralism, and cultural diversity. This is nothing less than a challenge to transform the academy into a place where differences in skin color no longer make any difference.

The issue of diversity is one of balance and fairness. We must work cooperatively to achieve a fair society in which differences are respected, prejudices overcome, and human potential fully realized. The importance of the struggle for equality and diversity in American education can hardly be overstated. It will be critical in determining the future quality of education in the United States and thus the future quality of this nation itself.

One of the greatest challenges in the coming century is for the United States to find satisfactory ways and means of wisely developing and using the varied potential of our highly diverse population. At-risk students represent an important part of the nation's future. They must be granted equal access and then be given the academic support services necessary to assure adequate progress and ultimate academic success. The economic and social state of black Americans compels us to make major shifts in how we educate and train these citizens in future generations. Declining participation of blacks in higher education and disproportionate underrepresentation of blacks in the physical, chemical, and biological sciences calls for a bold response from the land-grant community. In the food and agricultural sciences, African Americans represent fewer than 2 percent of the master's and doctoral degree candidates. These data are alarming in a society that is struggling to hold its competitive edge in global markets—a situation that has resulted in part because we failed to fully utilize the creativity and diversity of the nation's time-tested land-grant system.

While most academic leaders recognize that shortcomings in faculty diversity is an issue of considerable magnitude, commitments and efforts to yield more minority doctoral recipients are woefully inadequate. How do we move multicultural diversity from a peripheral concern and commitment to being a central and enduring one that permeates the value structure and decision-making of the entire institution? This goal and its stewardship must be the concern of all members of the academic family, beginning with the institution's chief executive officer. It must be broad-based both on- and off-campus. It must be addressed through compacts forged by all concerned—state and national governmental officials, business and industry leaders, and academics—all working in concert. Goals must be established and pledges for sustained commitments to satisfactory resolution of the matter must be made and kept.

One such compact involving the New England Board of Higher Education, the Southern Regional Education Board, and the Western Interstate Commission for Higher Education—with financial support from the PEW Charitable Trusts and the Ford Foundation—has embarked on such an effort. It identified five strategies to ameliorate the faculty diversity problem: (1) motivate states and universities to address the problem by increasing the base of financial support for minority doctoral study; (2) offer promising minority graduate students a support package of multi-year fellowships and research and teaching assistantships that promote success by integrating students more fully into the academic life of the department; (3) introduce incentives for academic departments to create supportive environments for minority students, especially through strong mentorship; (4) sponsor an annual institute providing opportunities to build support networks and promote teaching; and (5) develop a collaborative approach to student recruitment by drawing from undergraduate faculty and programs targeted to minority students.

Laws can be enacted to give equal opportunity. But in practice equal opportunity comes only from those who can care about people and put skin color aside. Regrettably but certainly, affirmative-action programs still are needed in our society. When such programs function to overcome the effects of years of discrimination and serve important societal goals, they are consistent with equal-protection principles.

Higher education's commitment to multicultural diversity is of surprisingly recent origin. The scale of American higher education is a product of the post–World War II era. It began with the "GI Bill"—an educational opportunity passed by Congress in June 1944 that brought approximately 30 percent of all veterans—more than 2.5 million people of varying age, ethnicity, and race—to study in American institutions of higher education. It reinforced the land-grant act of 1862 in guaranteeing access to higher education for qualified students, regardless of their financial means.

As is society more broadly, higher education is in the midst of difficult transition. Our commitment to diversity requires colleges and universities to substantially increase the number of people from underrepresented groups in our student bodies, on our faculties and staffs, and in our administrative offices. This challenge requires new thinking about the structure, purpose, and values of higher education.

Ultimately, it is our task to help others appreciate the splendor of the diversity of cultures within our nation and to emphasize the unifying aspects of individual human rights. These are ideals associated with our nation's heritage. Ideals that can empower people of all continents, races, and creeds to strive for more meaningful and satisfying lives.

In all things that are purely social, we—Black and White— can be as separate as the five fingers, yet as one as the hand in all things essential to mutual progress.

BOOKER T. WASHINGTON

Telecommunications and Distance Education Initiative

Concern for man himself and his fate must always form the chief interests of all technical endeavors. ... Never forget this in the midst of your diagrams and equations.

ALBERT EINSTEIN

4.1 Introduction

Policy makers must determine how to sustain, in an electronic age, the democratic and equal access to information that free public libraries have provided in the age of print.

JAMES H. BILLINGTON

When Frank Whittle first presented his ideas for the design of a jet engine, he was met with massive doubt and indifference from the scientific community. They were interested in new solutions to old problems, but the kind of new solutions they sought were better pistons, improved propellers, and the like. His ideas—albeit brilliant and refreshing—failed to mesh with the conservative approaches of investors of the time. It received a modicum of support, and then only because a few individuals, like Launcelot Law Whythe, decided to back the innovative, well-conceived vision. "There is a clue here of wide significance", said Whythe. "The most fertile new ideas are those that transcend established, specialized methods and treat new problems as a single task. ... Cooperative groups, from great industrial concerns to small research teams, inevitably tend to rely on what is already acceptable as common ground, and that means established, specialized techniques."

Just as surely as the jet engine revolutionized the airline industry in fundamental ways, telecommunications and distance education are destined to have monumental impacts on how the body of truth, information, and principles are transmitted in the teaching-learning process in the United States. Moreover, the whole of information technology will be the part that dramatically repositions the learning enterprise in our society.

Advances in communications already have wrought profound changes in the patterns of civilization. In all of history there have been only a few sweeping changes in communications—those of the magnitude of the wheel in transportation—and most of these have come during the past century. For thousands of years, information could travel only as fast as a person could run.

The Romans were the first to substitute the horse for the runner, a revolutionary advance that remained unchallenged for some 2000 years. Paul Revere dashed across the countryside on a borrowed horse to warn the colonists that the British were coming in 1775. Two days before his famous midnight ride to Lexington, he galloped to Concord to warn patriots there to move their military supplies. Prior to the American Civil War, then, news could travel only as fast as a horse could run.

Samuel B. Morse laid the foundation for today's communication explosion when he invented telegraphy, a timely development that was greatly depended upon by President Abraham Lincoln and the Union Army during the Civil War. Soon thereafter, Alexander Graham Bell invented the telephone, which by the turn of the century had begun to transform the business and social life of the nation.

In the 1920s, the radio began yet another communications breakthrough that greatly expanded capabilities for dissemination of information. It facilitated instant transmission of a human voice across the airways in all directions, over great distances.

As we prepare to enter the twenty-first century, communications technologies still are leaping forward—statewide, nationwide, worldwide. Global satellite communication is expected to be available by 1997. A person equipped with a mini-transceiver will be able to speak to people, send a facsimile, or even tie into computers throughout the world, twenty-four hours a day. In a globally competitive environment, this nation cannot afford to lag. To stop further development and application of communications technologies would by default benefit our competitors. Many believe that where the industrial revolution increased productivity by a factor of 10, the development of information technologies will enhance productivity by a factor of 100. For example, calculations that once took days to complete now require only slight fractions of a second.

Just as the system of rivers, railroads, and highways provides conduits through which people and products move across a state, nation, and world, telecommunications networks linking information bases with powerful computers already are conduits for the transfer of useful information. And, just as vehicular highways promote the growth and development of cities, electronic superhighways are promoting the growth and development of academic endeavors.

Technology will be the single greatest force for change in higher education in the foreseeable future. It will affect not only the day-to-day nature of academe, but also the relationships among students, faculty, and institutional leaders. For state policy makers, it may significantly shift our investments from today's vertical structures to tomorrow's horizontal ones that cut across institutions, sectors, and even states. Increased competition and capacities, especially telecommunications capacities, will be powerful forces shaping the foundations of coordination upon which state boards of higher education are ever more relying.

Anyone wondering what the twenty-first century holds for the United States can find the answer in America's classrooms—K-12, vo-tech, and higher education. The ambitions, attitudes, and visions of today's young people will be seen in education, business, government, and elsewhere in the early decades of the next century. Nothing better defines what we will become than the education of our children. But how can we assure that broadly based courses and high-quality instruction will be available to those enrolled in all schools—small and large, rural and urban, poorly- and well-financed?

The answer lies in telecommunications and distance education. The term *distance education* is used to describe teaching and learning over a distance. It involves the process of educating people at a distance. Widespread, pervasive, effective use of educational technologies will dramatically change how and what students learn.

Telecommunications enables educators to hurdle matters that heretofore have been barriers to the flow of information—including budgets, location, and school size. This opportunity can greatly reduce differences and distances. The ability to provide instruction via satellite enables remote geographic areas to share in the benefits of comprehensive, high-quality programs. Land-grant colleges and universities especially will transmit and coordinate telecommunications programs to off-campus locations as they fulfill traditional and nontraditional missions.

Telecommunications and learning technologies have enormous capacity and potential to restructure teaching and learning. Yet the gap between opportunity and actuality remains great. Adoption has been impeded by many within higher education who have viewed this technology as compromising quality education and a threat to job security. As a result, use of technology resources has been low, resistance to replacing existing delivery systems with electronic ones, high. This and other technologies should be employed to free faculty *for* students not *from* them.

The test of a first rate intelligence is the ability to hold two opposed ideas in the mind at the same time, and still retain the ability to function.

F. SCOTT FITZGERALD

Through expanded use of distance education technologies, institutions of higher education soon will be competing electronically in one another's backyards. More students will be completing courses and even full degree programs entirely over computer networks. Alert alumni directors will need to become more creative in programming to solicit dues-paying alumni memberships from these new graduates, as they will not develop the same degree of bonding with their alma mater that those who spend a number of years on campus do.

4.2   Why Distance Education?

Long range planning does not deal with future decisions, but rather with the future of present decisions.

PETER DRUCKER

Since the Renaissance, people have looked to science and technology to solve problems and create opportunities. Communications technologies promise to create new forms of as well as new suppliers of post-secondary education. The interdependence of higher education and the national economy is much the same as two people on a seesaw. If one jumps off, the other surely falls. Moreover, telecommunications advances offer universities cost-effective means of meeting the educational challenges of the twenty-first century, as a rapidly maturing and increasingly multicultural American society makes greater demands on higher education. In a time of burgeoning needs and diminishing resources, telecommunications technology can be a vital resource in keeping higher education accessible, affordable, and excellent.

In addition to the home, distance education enables students to complete courses at community sites or in the workplace, and to combine these approaches with on-campus options. Recent technologies, such as those listed below, give both students and faculty members opportunities for more communication and greater involvement with one another and other resources that enrich the learning experience.

electronic mail
optical fibers: Flexible transparent fibers, commonly made of extremely pure glass, designed and manufactured to guide rays of light. Optical fibers

have a greater information-carrying capacity than do copper wires. Light-emitting diodes send light through the fibers to a detector which converts the light back into electric signals. Fiber-optic lines have more bandwidth than any other type of line. They can carry full-motion video as well as compressed video.

voice mail

CD-ROM: This high-capacity optical computer storage medium is an electronic publication on a compact disk (CD) that can be accessed with a computer. It has read-only memory (ROM), meaning the disk cannot be changed.

DVD: The digital video disk resembles audio CDs (CD-ROMs), but can pack fifteen times as much information.

T-1 line: High-capacity telephone lines having sufficient bandwidth to transmit compressed video.

teleclassroom: A learning environment connected by interactive electronic media to any other place, potentiating live interaction of individuals at a distance.

computer conferencing

floppy disk: A magnetic computer storage medium.

audio bridges: Allow high-fidelity conference calls involving many parties, facilitating instructional situations in which many individuals at various locations need to be in voice communication (e.g., for a seminar).

audiographic devices: Facilitate, for example, an audiographic conference, which combines a telephone conference call—enabling all members of a class to be in voice communication—with some means of graphic support such as an electronic chalkboard, writing table, still video, or computer-generated visual material. All participants can converse while viewing the same text and graphics on their computer screens. In a chemistry class, for example, any student could display an equation, a graph, or a still video image, which then would be displayed on the computers of all other students; point to a component of the equation, and everyone would see the cursor on their screens; draw a new graph, which then would appear on each screen; and simultaneously describe aloud what they are doing and why.

Video cassette recorders (VCRs) allow students to access programs at will when and where they need to in order to review course materials at their convenience. Students can participate in a seminar via computer conferencing, then use a computer to access databases for research and to request that books from other libraries be delivered to a local site. Computer-conferencing systems—sometimes called text-based conferencing—enable people to type messages that appear instantaneously on receivers' computer screens, making them real-time communication. As comments accumulate, discussion takes the form of a transcript scrolling up the computer screen.

The interactive power of telecommunications is opening the way for various means of not merely conveying information, but of responding to questions that arise in the usual course of learning as well. The time-honored concept of classroom time could come to seem but a quaint anachronism when considered against the ability of the proposed information superhighway to guide students to dependable sources of information. Even a simple network of electronic mail makes possible a system of rapid and frequent interaction between students and those who encourage and evaluate their learning. The results can be improved student mentoring as well as an enriched form of Socratic inquiry.

What telemarketing did for catalog sales, what the Quality Value Channel (QVC) did for home shopping, what automatic teller machines (ATMs) did for banking, the information superhighway is about to do for higher education. The high-stakes battle among corporate giants for control of quickly emerging information and entertainment networks clearly demonstrates keen awareness in for-profit circles as to just how important it has become to control these enabling technologies and the novel markets they are spawning. Distance education offers access to vast, insatiable markets at home and abroad. It features interactive telecommunications networks, including video-based teaching and learning; instructional projects, including simulations; telecomputer usage for learning at home or work locales; and asynchronous long-range group teleconferencing supervised by qualified mentors. The public demand for this service will be met, if not by land-grant institutions then by other public or private entities.

Most states are faced with significant differences in educational capabilities and fiscal resources among school districts. Higher education also is faced with an increasingly restricted resource base as well as increased demand for teaching and other services. Distance education can greatly aid in resolving differences in the quality of educational offerings. Moreover, it can enhance delivery of education and training at virtually any location.

What will be the effects of distance education on teaching and course offerings via fiber optics and in a wireless world of ubiquitous hand-held computers, communication devices, and user-friendly software (prototypes of which already are being marketed in products such as Apple's Newton)? Will there be concerted efforts in distance-education endeavors among institutions of higher education to collaborate with businesses and other entities?

> *Great discoveries and improvements invariably involve the cooperation of many minds.*
>
> **ALEXANDER GRAHAM BELL**

According to a recent Congressional Office of Science and Technology study, U.S. businesses already have in use more than twice as many personal computers per worker as Germany, almost four times as many as the Japanese. An estimated 75 percent of this nation's homes will have computers by the year 2001, compared with about 30 percent in 1994. The United States leads in producing equipment and services of the new information age, which can be translated into important short- and long-term growth in our exports. American producers of cellular equipment, satellite systems, sophisticated switching and transmission equipment, and mobile personal computers have pioneered global production of these new technologies. For example, our international sales of modern telephone equipment increased by 210 percent between 1989 and 1994. And U.S. companies now hold approximately 90 percent of the world market in video-conferencing equipment and sell approximately 70 percent of their microwave radio systems products in the global marketplace. Additionally, the United States enjoys about 70 percent of the world market in satellite communications equipment and 50 percent in ground systems to connect with satellites.

4.3   The Role of Distance Education in Continuing Education

The possession of facts is knowledge; the use of them is wisdom; the choice of them, education. Knowledge is not power but riches, and like them, has its value in spending.

THOMAS JEFFERSON

Recent U.S. Department of Labor statistics indicate that the average worker today will change jobs approximately eight times, and half of the changes will be involuntary. Comprehensive, well-integrated, life-long learning opportunities must be created for a work environment in which three of four new jobs will require more than a high school education. Many individuals with only high school diplomas may well face the prospects of declining incomes.

An obsolete machine can be melted down and recast into a modern one. But an obsolete person—whose professional skills are no longer needed in a rapidly changing workplace—cannot be. An obsolete person must be retooled to serve a useful role in society. With the avalanche of new technologies, there soon will be great need and opportunity to retool major segments of the workforce.

Will our education system be prepared to provide the continuing education needed by the fastest growing group of students—those in the thirty-five-years-and-older category? Already in 1990, such students represented 19 percent of higher education's enrollment, and they are expected to account for 23 percent or more by 2002. The proportion of students in the twenty-five- to thirty-four-year-old range, which increased during the 1980s, is expected to decline from about 25 percent to approximately 20 percent by the year 2002. Only approximately half of students enrolled in institutions of higher education during the 1990s are expected to be less than twenty-five years of age—the so-called traditional students.

In recent years, the demographic picture of undergraduate life has significantly changed. It is no longer the norm for a student to graduate from high school, proceed directly to college, study four years, and around age twenty-two enter the workforce with college degree in hand. Many students are delaying their entrance into college, and are as likely to study part- as full-time. Also, they are likely to have work and family responsibilities outside the classroom. All of these and other factors have led to an increase in the number of students interested in distance education.

The overriding reason students enroll in distance education courses is convenience, important because (1) many students are time-bound—those who work on shifts, travel a great deal, or whose heavy responsibilities at home or work do not permit regular classroom attendance; and (2) many students are place-bound—some simply live too far from a campus to pursue educational goals in the traditional manner. Others may be homebound due to family responsibilities, illness, or disability or may be confined to hospitals, rehabilitation facilities, or prisons.

Educational systems need formal guidance and frequent attention. The formal-guidance phase of higher education enables students to expand their knowledge base, enrich their lives, increase their understanding of themselves and others, and search for new truths. The frequent-attention phase comes in many forms. An important one is continuing education, which is in the process of being reconceptualized in land-grant colleges and universities. This process is part of a general pattern of change that includes greater emphasis on technology transfer, including forging stronger relationships, cooperation, and interaction with business and industry (Chapter 5). These are excellent opportunities for land-grant institutions to regain public support that has been waning of late as they provide timely information, new knowledge, and continuing education for various sectors of our free-enterprise system. Continually honing and expanding the minds of these constituents is vital to mental renewal as well as to improved relationships with alumni, professions, and businesses. Using tools associated with distance education to provide this form of public service will be top priority in the attitude and commitment of land-grant institutions that achieve higher levels of public support in the twenty-first century. Rural America will rightly expect full access to the on-ramps of this nation's Information Highway, and land-grant institutions must fulfill this need if they expect to receive continued public support.

4.4 Who Will Provide Distance Education?

A university is not outside, but the general social fabric of a given era. ... It is not something apart, something historic, something that yields as little as possible to forces and influences that are more or less new. It is on the contrary ... an expression of the age, as well as an influence operating upon both present and future.

ABRAHAM FLEXNER

Historically, the economic growth and related national security of the United States has been inextricably linked to the development of human resources and applications of advances in science-based technology to all sectors of the nation's business and industry. The accelerating rate of technological change in the workplace makes it more essential than ever before that employees be prepared to adapt to changing job requirements. The more advanced the technology, the more dependent the system is on highly prepared people.

In an increasingly internationalized economy, the most important competitive advantage the United States possesses is the quality of its human resources. The people part of the equation is no place to be in second or third place. This holds true for metropolitan economics just as for the national economy. The capacity of a metropolitan economy to perform well depends substantially on improving the quality, resilience, and productivity of its current and future labor force. The greatest number of new workers entering the force in the next two decades will be immigrants and members of underrepresented groups. United States citizens are increasingly ill-prepared to enter a workforce that must be more highly educated and skilled and more capable of adapting to changing technologies and markets than ever before.

A coordinated distance education program can provide an important service in assuring a properly educated workforce as well as serving as a dependable means of building collaborative relationships with business and industry. But will universities respond to this public-service opportunity? Or will the prevailing academic culture impede this relationship—frequently perceived "non-scholarly"—and thereby encourage entrepreneurs in the private sector to embrace the opportunity?

The unseen environment in which higher education functions might be called the institutional culture. The unwritten ways of doing things. The culture also includes the common values, expectations, standards of excellence, assumptions, traditions, general atmosphere, and behavioral patterns of the people involved. The people and the culture are related in complex ways. For example, each student brings a unique set of interests and traits to the institution; interacting with fellow students, exerting influence upon each other. Through such interaction, a student subculture evolves, and it becomes an influential source of change for all inducted into it. Similarly, individual faculty and staff members bring their unique interests and traits to an institution. Collectively, they create a subculture that influences those with whom they associate. The various subcultures combined becomes the campus culture.

Academic culture—the invisible tapestry that represents a shared way of thinking and collective way of behaving—could be a serious impediment to the opportunities and needs of distance education that are at hand. The success of technology and information transfer activities in a university community depends in large part on the degree to which they are consistent with the goals of the institution's prevailing academic culture.

In this setting, then, it is the prospect of delivering high-quality, lower-cost educational programming conjoined with the rising demand for advanced education that creates the business opportunity for potential competitors of a tradition-locked system of higher education. Access to a computerized, high-performance information infrastructure is essential for research and development teams.

Advocates of information technology are amazed at the exploding popularity of the international network—Internet[1]—as well as the great potential of such developments as interactive video for distance education, multimedia software for classroom presentations, and wireless communications that permit people to link computers without the use of telephone lines.

Numerous software suppliers and cable conglomerates are interested in all this. These firms have substantial capital and human expertise they want to invest. An obvious early target of suppliers of interactive distance education will be adult students, who constitute the fastest growing group of those in

[1]Internet was created some twenty-fve years ago as a nuclear-attack-proof U.S. military communications network. In December 1994, this worldwide network connected more than 42,000 computer networks, thereby interconnecting more than 500,000 computers ranging from the smallest to the most powerful in the eighty-four participating countries. This Information Superhighway is now being traveled by an estimated 40 million people, with a million more being added each month. And it is truly turning the world into a global village.

search of baccalaureate degrees, as well as the increasing ranks of those who seek educational opportunities for retooling. The cost of continuing their education is highly important. The lure of campus life is not strong. Their choice of institution has more to do with accessibility than institutional loyalty. This large group of students is likely to embrace well-conceived programs that offer degrees at less expense and greater convenience even if they are offered by non-traditional suppliers.

Historically, accreditation has provided adequate protection against those who would encroach on higher education's traditional monopoly over postsecondary credentials. But it is unlikely to hold against today's powerful contenders. Developers of the new learning programs conducted by interactive electronic means will demonstrate that their students perform as well or better than do those who obtain their education through more traditional avenues.

The power of the public's search for a more accessible and lower-cost set of educational products has not yet been translated into a sense of urgency within most institutions. Many out-of-touch faculty members and persons holding positions of administrative leadership are either largely unaware of or refuse to take notice of these already emerging developments (Chapter 2). They are therefore unprepared for this new competition. In economic terms, one goal of higher education must be to have the most possible students taught by the fewest possible faculty members without compromising educational excellence. Most faculty members simply still have not grasped the fact that technology is going to greatly alter the market for educational services. Moreover, while most universities possess the intellectual capital to compete in the emerging market for information services, too often they lack the vision, motivation, and leadership to adapt accordingly (Chapter 11). The specter of new, well-financed competition—armed with ways and means of producing alternative learning programs—looms large on higher education's horizon. A major challenge for faculty and administrators alike will be to assure increased access to high-quality programs at lower cost without losing the sense of community that has long characterized the culture of higher education.

4.5   Serving Students Enrolled in Distance Education

> *Since new developments are the products of a creative mind, we must therefore stimulate and encourage that type of mind in every way possible.*
>
> **GEORGE WASHINGTON CARVER**

A major challenge to faculty members is to accept and use new technologies that make learning fun and more exciting. Distance education programs should reflect on educational philosophy, goals, and purposes that clearly complement institutional missions. Moreover, it is crucial that faculty and staff working with alternative degree programs share a commitment to serve adult learners and come to possess the attitudes, knowledge, and skills needed to teach, counsel, and assist such students.

Many believe a major technology-driven restructuring of academe is at most no more than ten years away. This will include a realigning of the ways faculty teach and are rewarded, the ways they create a desirable learning environment, the manner in which they reach out to students to take advantage of new technological capabilities. Expanded telecommunications will bring about more accessibility, accountability, connectivity, networking, and openness of people and ideas. As a result, it will be an important instrument for social transformation.

As institutions of higher education move into distance education, administrative and support services will have to be changed. For example, because of work and family obligations and other constraints, distance learners frequently find it difficult to come to campus for course registration or to use resource materials at an on-campus library. Colleges must revisit issues of students' accessibility to support services and creatively bring these into conformance with needs. Because of the economics and logistics of distance education, university librarians should be involved in planning the initiatives.

A compelling need exists to share resources, not only among institutions, but among states and regions as well. Telecommunications makes this possible. Rather than moving students to other institutions and states, educators can easily move information and programs to students wherever they may be. Distance education enables universities to offer coursework anywhere, anytime, on any topic. It does not respect boundaries of any kind.

Finally, since many students enrolled in distance education degree programs may rarely if ever come to campus, colleges and universities will be challenged to find creative ways of encouraging these students to feel a part of the institution. Possibilities include use of a uniform identification card and equal access to cultural events, graduation, sports, and the computer bulletin board for all students. This also will be important in working with them in the future as alumni and hopefully supporters of the institution.

4.6 Summary

Once a new technology rolls over you, if you are not part of the steamroller, you are part of the road.

STEWART BRAND

Technology's growing capacity to facilitate instruction at remote sites is causing colleges and universities to revisit basic policy issues. What kinds of education should they provide? Of what quality and quantity? For how many students? At what costs?

Live two-way video connections can bring virtual classroom experiences into students' homes, workplaces, and other settings. So far, distance education remains largely outside the mainstream of campus life, concentrating mostly on part-time students—those who cannot conveniently travel to a campus and those interested in non-credit or adult-education courses and curricula in selected graduate programs, such as engineering or business administration.

But distance-education specialists and academic policy makers see the opportunity to do much more. They expect technology to help colleges provide a wide range of programs, including undergraduate and graduate degree courses, to an increasingly larger portion of the population—and for less money than would be required to build new campus facilities or hire new faculty members.

Already, some 45 percent of all college enrollees are part-time students, a group for whom anytime, anywhere education holds much appeal. Approximately 25,000 students were enrolled in distance education courses in 1994. The number is expected to triple by 1997, and to rise much higher by the turn of the century.

The world of the twenty-first century will be deeply interdependent economically, closely linked technologically, and progressively and at unprecedented speeds more homogenized through the global mass movement of information, ideas, people, and capital. Via the technology of distance education, universities will participate in a network of resources, offering students global and multicultural perspectives.

In a world in which information is capital and capital synonymous with information, wealth becomes virtually unlimited, universally accessible, and highly decentralized. Unlike the industrial revolution, which imposed economies of scale, the information revolution imposes economies of microscale. A single five-cent plastic disk can store millions of dollars worth of programs and access codes that put the world economy within the reach of any individual.

Technologies that undergird distance education are continuously evolving. Much we readily accept and even take for granted today was considered revolutionary ten years ago. And many things we can only dream of today will be commonplace in another decade; scientific knowledge is doubling every thirteen years.

Higher education faces the challenges of expanding the reach, quality, and effectiveness of instruction within the context of shrinking resources as well as organizing itself to serve students regardless of where they reside. In addition to serving the needs of traditional college-age students, colleges and universities have the challenging opportunity to help retrain workers for a changing workplace. The term *college-age* itself has taken on new meaning as an increasingly large proportion of students fall into the broad category of adult learners, who bring new demands on the nature, timing, and delivery of higher education.

In response to these new challenges, a growing number of institutions are turning to the use of telecommunications technologies—especially distance education—as a means of providing educational services to more students and addressing a broader range of instructional goals. Developing and implementing successful distance education programs is a complex task that requires consideration of numerous policy issues including faculty development, incentives, and rewards; intellectual property rights; promotion and tenure considerations; student residency requirements; faculty workloads; program development and evaluation; and standards related to academic quality.

Unfortunately, many colleges and universities are only remotely aware of and therefore poorly prepared for the new competition that is certain to come as a result of this telecommunications and distance education revolution. The impact of the public's search for a lower-cost, more accessible set of educational opportunities simply has not yet been translated into a sense of urgency within most institutions of higher education.

While most colleges and universities possess the intellectual capital to compete in the emerging market for information services, they lack the governance leadership and institutional courage to adapt. Moreover, many members of their faculties are out-of-touch with the realities associated with current public needs and expectations. Taxpayers also are questioning the level of support for public institutions of higher education. The bottom line: major changes are coming to this aspect of the higher education system. Institutions will be faced either with self-imposed adaptation or with having it thrust upon them by outside forces. Knowing this, many business entrepreneurs are carefully evaluating the economics of the nation's higher-education needs and opportunities.

Monumental changes in communications have come about in recent years. More are certain to follow. Distribution and application of information has been the foundation of the land-grant system since its inception. Information that does not reach the user group is of limited public value (Chapter 5).

In a society driven by information, technology, and fierce competition, an individual's best survival strategy is to attain the best possible education. We must utilize telecommunication networks to enhance the development and application of science and technology. But it is important to keep the use of these new technologies in appropriate perspective. We must not fail to remember that technology is a tool. Education is the goal. Alas, those who believe that sending a videotaped lecture over a satellite or a digitized lecture over fiber-optic cable can completely replace faculty-student interactions do not understand what happens in a classroom.

Technology Transfer Initiative

The physicist, who, having completed a research no matter how attenuated, on reaching the street cannot explain his findings and its usefulness to the first man he meets, should return to his laboratory; his research is not complete.

LORD KELVIN

5.1 Introduction

Changes in technology tend to precede changes in social and cultural ways of life.

WILLIAM OGBURN

As I was growing up in rural America, it did not perturb me that the family radio required two or three minutes to warm-up. Nor was I especially bothered that I had to talk with an operator to place a telephone call. And I was perfectly satisfied with the family's first black and white television (with no accompanying VCR), a manual typewriter, or even my small slide rule. Now I have come to depend on the remote controller to change channels on a color television that accesses thirty times the number of channels our first model received—and it was plagued with "snow" and limited reception.

Things never dreamed of yesteryear we cannot imagine doing without today. Inventions frequently seem more the mother of necessity than vice versa. While this observation is not profound, it is nevertheless well to occasionally step back and recognize the role of the transfer and application of science and technology in our modern society. We can best advance society by advancing science and technology. Sustained economic growth is the key to providing Americans with rising real incomes and thus the material resources to fulfill their needs and wants. The fearsome scenarios conjured up by those who believe technology is the cause of most social problems notwithstanding, it is a powerful agent of social and cultural change.

The twentieth century has been a period of continuous high tide for science and technology. An era during which great strides have been made in improving upon the goodness of Nature. Before joining the ranks of those who advocate a back-to-Nature movement, it is well to appreciate how, through the application of research and technology, people have enjoyed significant improvements in hundreds of the things Nature gave us. For example:

Nature put mildew on roses; plant breeders and human ingenuity took it off.

Nature put parasites on and in pigs; veterinary researchers developed means of controlling them.

Nature gave people polio; Jonas E. Salk and Albert B. Sabin developed vaccines to protect them against that dreaded disease.

Nature gave us corn blight; agronomists solved that serious economic calamity for corn growers and consumers.

Nature struck humans with smallpox; medical researchers developed a means of eliminating that destructive disease on a global basis.

Nature gave us mosquitoes and they gave us malaria; entomologists developed ways of controlling the mosquitoes.

Nature gave us nematode pests of soybeans; scientists developed nematode-resistant strains of soybeans.

Nature limited corn yields; agricultural researchers developed hybrid corns that yielded enormous increases in production and lowered the cost of corn to consumers.

Nature gave us drought, plant diseases, and other inhibitors of optimal food crop growth and quality, resulting in starvation of people and animals in many countries; researchers developed drought- and disease-resistant varieties of crops that better feed the world's people.

Nature gave people the ability to greatly overpopulate the world; humans developed ways and means of controlling population expansion without interfering with the natural pleasures associated with procreation.

Nature gave rabies to dogs and other animals that can transmit that life-threatening disease to humans; science and technology gave us vaccines to combat the disease.

Nature gave us screwworm flies and the resultant toll their presence takes on the health of livestock and the economics of animal production; USDA scientists developed and successfully transferred the technology that has eradicated these enemies of animal health.

Nature put ugly worms in the apple and other fruits and vegetable crops; scientists gave us the technology to keep them out.

We could cite hundreds upon thousands of similar examples of improvements in our lifestyle enabled by new technology. The automobile for the horse and buggy, pasteurized milk for raw, electric lights for kerosene lanterns, personal computers for typewriters, refrigerators for iceboxes. But suffice it to say that the transfer of science and technology makes it possible to do things never done before (e.g., fly in an airplane); do things mechanically that had been done manually (e.g., to sew a skirt); and do more efficiently something previously done laboriously (e.g., filling milk cartons).

In his book *The Rise and Fall of the Great Powers,* Paul Kennedy points out that over the past 500 years, winners have risen in power because of first, education and research; second, technology transfer and application; third, the economic development that follows.

A strong technology base is critical to this nation's economic performance. In the long run, living standards, personal income, and industrial output would be much less than they are today were it not for the technological advances that have occurred during recent decades. Total returns for technology transfer activities—such as public goodwill and partnering between university and industrial scientists—cannot be accurately measured.

In the global economy in which our free-enterprise system functions, knowledge reigns supreme. Those nations that excel in creating new knowledge and transforming it into new technologies will prosper in the next century. If the United States is to remain a leader in the development and commercialization of new technologies, we must take steps to increase the output of new knowledge through investments of research and development.

Scientists are driven by curiosity and the personal satisfaction associated with intellectual exploration. Modern technology is based on fundamental discoveries made by scientists who conduct basic research which in turn produces basic knowledge of the structure and function of physical, chemical, biological, economic, and social systems (Chapter 7). Developmental research yields products and services with potential practical application and commercial utility. Technology transfer is the process by which the products of scientific investigation are implemented for the public good. Stages include technology creation, technology extraction and development, technology distribution and application, and technology productization and consumption.

5.2 Researching Ideas, Developing Knowledge, Applying Technologies

One new idea leads to another, that to a third, and so on through a course of time until some one, with whom none of

*these was original, combines all together, and produces what is
justly called a new invention.*

THOMAS JEFFERSON

When Frenchman Julius Herisson developed a device to measure blood
pressure in humans in 1835, physicians sneered. "This is one of the most
ridiculous baubles ever foisted on the profession," they said. No one sneers at
medical technology today. We are intently interested in alleviating dreadful
diseases and lengthening human lives. The fundamental component of Herisson's sphygmomanometer was an idea. Sound ideas create technologies that
lead to action.

Discovery and scientists are full partners in the spawning of technologies
that improve the lives of people. Conversion of ideas into processes and products requires command of an ever-expanding science and engineering knowledge base. The avalanche of technological advances notwithstanding, the fact
remains: it was people who conceived the ideas for these modern applications
of science, and only people can make them workable.

Technology per se is not a precise democratic principle. It potentially ac-
cords a few people the power to dramatically affect the balance of Nature and
thereby the lives of other people. We all need to appreciate the responsibility
of using the power of knowledge, the power of science. Technological advancement is important, but it alone is insufficient for economic development
and social progress. In general, the more advanced the technology, the more
dependent the system is on highly trained, highly responsible individuals to
make things happen for the betterment of all.

Winning the race for global technological leadership will ultimately
amount to winning the struggle to advance the human condition to the highest possible level in the years ahead. And it is important that we not view our
commitment to scientific research and technology transfer as merely contributing to the economic development of our states and nation. It is as well a
workable means of upgrading the lives and overall lot of the society we serve.
We need to appreciate more the value and importance of the information age
as a tool for advancing our economic and social objectives. During the industrial age, we invested natural resources and added value to obtain new
processes, products, and services. Now we must use readily accessible information, give high priority to creating new information, and then add value to
obtain even newer processes, products, and services.

*A Nobel Prize is waiting for the person who figures out the
economics of information.*

JAY OGILVY

It is practically impossible to predict where new technologies are most likely to emerge. History is replete with examples of scientific discoveries that have led to practical applications in areas far removed from the original objectives of the research. Fundamental research on electromagnetism contributed directly to the development of modern communications. Investigations in solid-state physics led in 1956 to the invention of the transistor, a scientific feat recognized by the awarding of a Nobel Prize. The recombinant DNA technology that facilitated the biotechnology industry evolved from studies of unusual enzymes in bacteria. Mathematics, often regarded as abstract, is at the core of applications as diverse as aircraft design, computing, and prediction of weather and climatic change. Much of the motivation to conduct fundamental research is not necessarily to develop new applications per se but rather the desire to discover new truths and thereby better understand natural phenomena. Nevertheless, the inherent motivation to explore, discover, and expand the knowledge base in the end brings society scientific advances and technological applications that simply cannot come about in any other way.

Born around the midpoint of the twentieth century, biotechnology consists in large part of two processes, genetic engineering and fermentation. In the early 1950s, scientists deciphered the genetic code by which deoxyribonucleic acid (DNA) controls cellular mechanisms in all living organisms. Through replication of DNA molecules, inherited traits are transmitted from one generation to the next. By the early 1970s, researchers could alter the genetic code by a process called recombination—cutting out a piece of DNA and splicing it with another piece. This gives the resultant synthetic microorganism specific qualities it did not originally possess. Hence, the term **"genetic engineering"**—a process through which the recombinant DNA (rDNA) molecules can be inserted in a host organism (bacterium, fungus, protozoon, plant, or mammal) to yield a mutant, which can then precisely reproduce itself. In recent years, manufacturers have used fermentation to produce food proteins, insulin, interferon, and hemoglobin, among others. Genetic engineering holds enormous potential benefits not only for agricultural and pharmaceutical concerns, but for chemical and energy firms and others as well. Fragrances, paints, plastics, resins, and solvents can be produced using genetic engineering technology.

Social aspects of utilizing biotechnological knowledge are far-reaching. In medicine and public health, for example, biological advances either now can or in the future might provide screening for genetic diseases of prospective parents or offspring; new vaccines and new cells to fight diseases; and new microbes to digest sewage, detoxify wastes, and convert the residue into substances suitable for consumption by animals.

Attempts to regulate biotechnology, pesticides, and herbicides are manifestations of a generalized public concern about the quality of American life. This concern led to the creation of numerous state and national regulatory agencies in the 1960s and 1970s. The Environmental Protection Agency (EPA) established in 1970 and Occupational Safety and Health Administration (OSHA) in 1973 are among the most powerful at the federal level.

5.3   Land-Grant Universities and Technology Transfer

Our nation is at an educational crossroads. Education must prove that it is equal to the challenges of technology and the information age. The success of our economy, and, indeed, the survival of our democracy have become more dependent than ever before on each individual's ability to master increasingly complex knowledge and skills.

GREGORY R. ARIG

Just as the white- and rose-flowered fishhook cactus does not flourish in the frigid arctic, nor Scottish Highland cattle on the Sierra desert, new entrepreneurships are unlikely to take root and existing businesses unlikely to expand if environmental conditions are unfavorable to the expansion of research efforts designed to fuel economic development. One important factor that favors business growth is a clear commitment to research/development/technology transfer and a strong spirit of partnership between academe and the private sector. Our nation's long-term economic health is coupled to that of its colleges and universities. We look to land-grant and other research universities for both discovery of new knowledge and development of new technology, as well as for those individuals educated and trained so as to be prepared to effectively use these results. These are generally well-understood prerequisites for economic development.

There are notable differences among major research universities with respect to faculty attitudes toward involvement in technology transfer. The degree of impact technology transfer activities have on a university will be measured largely by the extent to which such activities are incorporated into the regular work of the faculty. This, of course, depends on faculty attitudes.

University cultures—more policy-based and traditional than those of most other kinds of organizations—tend to insist that sanctioned activities be related to institutional goals and missions. In research universities, this commonly is accomplished by persuading faculty members that an activity, such as technology transfer, is either in their best interests or coincident with the long-term goals of the university. The long-term success of university-sponsored economic development activities is related to the level of faculty commitment to that opportunity for public service, a commitment that would be especially well-received by a public weary of the independence and disregard for such service faculty members are generally perceived to demonstrate (Chapter 2).

Europe, particularly Germany, led the way during the mid-nineteenth century in embracing the notion that universities are appropriate places to foster development of new ideas in technology. This proposition was intrinsic to the creation of land-grant colleges in the United States. It was readily apparent that there would be high economic payoff to the systemization and expansion of knowledge in agriculture, engineering, and other applied sciences.

The Massachusetts Institute of Technology (MIT), founded in 1861 and becoming a land-grant institution in 1863, was one of the first institutions of higher education to adopt the basic tenets of close cooperation with industry, a partnership that has flourished to this day. In 1918, in response to a challenge matching gift of $10.5 million from George Eastman to construct the first building at its newly acquired Cambridge site, MIT established its technology plan, a forerunner of subsequent liaison/affiliates programs, which served as its first formal link with industry. As part of the plan and in return for donations, MIT agreed to help companies identify and recruit engineering graduates by maintaining a file of resumes; to give companies access to the Institute's libraries and files; and to arrange for faculty to provide advice on planning research programs and solving industrial problems. More than 180 companies pledged over $1.2 million as a result of this effort.

The 1945 Vannevar Bush report, "Science—the Endless Frontier," presented to President Harry S Truman conveyed a simple but important message: progress in overcoming disease, defending our nation against post-war aggression, and developing new products and more jobs depends on new knowledge that can be obtained only through basic research. The report highlighted two overriding principles: (1) "that American colleges and universities should assume responsibility for providing the nation with new knowledge and requisite talents," and (2) "that the federal government should be responsible for providing funds to enable institutions of higher education to meet their commitments to basic research and training human capital."

In his 1949 inaugural address, President Truman said, "Greater production is the key to prosperity and peace. And the key to greater production is a wider and more vigorous application of modern scientific and technical knowledge." Then, on the occasion of establishing the National Science Foundation in 1950, President Truman said, "No nation can maintain a position of leadership in the world today unless it develops to the full its scientific and technological resources. No government adequately meets its responsibilities unless it generously and intelligently supports and encourages the work of science in university, industry, and its own laboratories."

Now, nearly a half-century later, we are enjoying the fruits of President Truman's vision. Major scientific progress has been made in medicine, new materials, agriculture, environmental science and technology, and computer and information technology as a result of those earlier initiatives and investments.

We can expect science and technology to play an even more important role in the twenty-first century. With the Cold War ending and a global economy fast becoming a reality, national and international goals are being shaped by new forces of economic interdependence and competition. The new knowledge being generated by scientists, mathematicians, and engineers must be utilized to the greatest extent possible if we are to foster sustainable development in all nations and contribute to the solution of global problems.

5.4 Expanding Institutional Outreach: Industrial Extension

It is not learning but the spirit of service that will give a university a place in the public annals of the nation.

WOODROW WILSON

Land-grant colleges and universities have been engaged in knowledge transfer since their inception. This has come through education of students; various publications, conferences, and workshops; consulting; and other means. Technology transfer is a form of knowledge transfer, but it goes further. It assists with the commercialization of research findings, which commonly requires significant effort at all stages of the process. More specifically, technology transfer involves the actual application of the research results to the design, development, production, and commercialization of new or improved processes, products, and services.

Historically, there usually has been a considerable lag between discovery and the time inventions and technological developments have entered the marketplace. Fluorescent lighting was invented in 1852 but was not produced commercially until 1934. The ballpoint pen was invented in 1882 but was not marketed for over fifty years. Television took twenty-nine years from the time of its invention to its commercial production. But now global competition and ready access to new information translates into much greater emphasis on reducing the lag from discovery to commercial adoption. Currently, this period averages about seven years.

We might do well to take a lesson from the Japanese as to the systematic transfer and exploitation of foreign technologies. Great Britain has received some ten times as many Nobel Prizes in the sciences as Japan since World War II. But note the relative differences in their expanded businesses. The fruits of scientific research are highly portable, and the economic pay-off for new technologies generated by scientific research lies downstream. So it is crucial that we not neglect development and application.

The United States led the world in the development of electronics. We did the basic research—and some development and application of electronic research technology—but concurrently shared our basic research findings with competitors abroad. They were well-organized and prepared to exploit these basic findings. Soon they came back with new electronic applications that have made them tough competitors. This example of borrowing and exploiting technology is not new. Indeed, Americans obtained basic metallurgical technology, the steam engine, and machine tools from the British. In fact, much of the fundamental technology that underpinned the Industrial Revolution in the Western Hemisphere came from Great Britain. We improved it, but our rapid development of an industrial economy was based on transferred technology.

The average annual rate of growth of manufacturing productivity for the 30-year period 1960–1990 was 5.17 percent in Japan but only 1.21 percent in the United States. Whether measured in terms of economics, ethics, or politics, this does not augur well for our long-term global competitiveness.

Increased emphasis on university technology transfer activities reflects an important aspect of the public's view of land-grant colleges and universities serving society in today's globally competitive environment. For several years there have been frequent discussions and even initiatives in several states concerning the merits of extending the agricultural Cooperative Extension model to a new "Industrial Extension Service" directed at providing technical assistance to small businesses. While this concept for public service presents many challenging opportunities, there are several notable differences between traditional agricultural extension and what is being proposed in other fields:

• Agricultural extension has been heavily subsidized by federal and state funds, but large subsidies are unlikely for industrial extension activities.

• The target audience for traditional agricultural extension—farmers and ranchers—has been easy to identify, whereas potential users of the proposed Industrial Extension Service will be more difficult to pinpoint.

• Agricultural extension usually confines its activities to a well-defined discipline that exists in units within universities (mostly in colleges of agriculture, forestry, home economics, and veterinary medicine), whereas a comprehensive Industrial Extension Service would have to include many more disciplines and departments—from biology and chemistry to mathematics and mechanical engineering, among others—and frequently arrange for these disciplines—along with the computer center, library, business college, and other academic and service components—to cooperate in solving industrial problems.

• The service dispensed by agricultural extension commonly has been delivered directly to the user group (especially farmers and ranchers) in usable form by a staff worker who possessed broad knowledge and could address a wide array of problems, whereas the advice delivered to industrial users frequently would require considerable adjustment and implementation before it could be useful, and moreover the problems encountered would span such a wide range of disciplines that a single extension worker could not be expected to be knowledgeable and thus able to be helpful across the board.

• Agricultural interests were much better organized and therefore probably carried more collective political clout than most potential users of the Industrial Extension Service being proposed.

The above concerns notwithstanding, many business and government leaders agree that U.S. manufacturers can regain their global competitive edge only with the help of a greatly expanded national network of industrial extension programs funded mostly by the federal government. These programs, they believe, should be modeled after agricultural extension programs and other services of land-grant colleges, and should reach out and work directly with manufacturers. Land-grant institutions are ideally positioned to participate in such an ambitious industrial extension network. They should aggressively pursue this opportunity.

In the late 1980s, the federal government became involved in the industrial extension network concept through the efforts of the Department of Commerce National Institute of Standards and Technology and the Department of Defense. An expanded national Industrial Extension Service network, sponsored jointly by federal, state, and local efforts, is needed to (1) build on successful programs already initiated; (2) make available to manufacturers a wide range of services, including access to technology, training and engineering, and management advice and expertise; (3) promote greater cooperation among national and local governments; small, medium, and large business firms; applied research and engineering institutions, training centers, and management organizations; (4) respond quickly and flexibly to the needs of local firms; (5) emphasize cooperation and outreach; (6) use federal funds to leverage those from state and local governments and private sources; and (7) minimize duplication of services.

Iowa State University (ISU) has been a national leader in extension programming throughout the twentieth century. In 1963, ISU, with financial support from the Iowa legislature, created the Iowa State University Center for Industrial Research (CIRAS). Now an important part of ISU Extension, CIRAS uses its budget of approximately $1.8 million yearly from state and federal sources and some twenty-four full-time staff members to provide management and technical assistance to Iowa-based firms, 90 percent of which have fewer than fifty employees.

It is especially important to demonstrate support of small businesses because they have certain advantages in commercial environments characterized by fast-moving technologies and rapidly changing consumer needs. A keen receptivity to new product ideas found outside their operations often typifies this efficiency. Small businesses supplement internal product development with new product ideas drawn from dealings with customers, suppliers, government laboratories, universities, and others to ensure useful innovations. Approximately half of all U.S. high-tech companies operating in 1993 were formed after 1979. To assure their continued growth and development, many of these new companies would benefit greatly from the services of an industrial extension network.

An important advantage land-grant universities have in working with industrial manufacturers is the vast array of resources available, including people, physical facilities, library, computer facilities, business and engineering colleges, and many other useful assets. For example, a small Iowa manufacturer held a contract to make a product for one of America's railroads, but the railroad would purchase the product only if it passed stringent abrasion and bonding tests. The small firm could not perform the tests and feared it might lose the contract. It called ISU's CIRAS, which in turn called on the professional expertise of engineering faculty members who reviewed the railroad's specifications and quickly made arrangements to perform tests on the product at ISU's Mechanical Engineering Laboratories. The product ultimately was found to actually exceed the specifications. Armed with these results, the manufacturer was able to market the product with confidence. Similar anecdotes could be shared by many other land-grant institutions.

According to a May 1994 report from the National Association of State Universities and Land-Grant Colleges (NASULGC) entitled "Universities and Industry Working Together," the nation's small- and medium-sized manufacturers comprise 99 percent of the nation's manufacturers and employ more than 60 percent of all manufacturing workers. They produce more than half of all components used by large industrial firms and are the source of most new jobs in the manufacturing sector. Yet their productivity is only about two-thirds that of U.S. firms with 500 or more workers. Many of these smaller manufacturers have lost their competitive edge because they lack the expertise and capital needed to adopt improved and rapidly changing technologies. Japan has approximately four times as many small firms using advanced machining centers and handling robots as does the United States. And half again more small Japanese firms than small American firms use computer-controlled machine tools.

Again, government and business leaders concur that these manufacturers can regain competitive edge with the help of industrial extension programs that reach out and work directly in speeding the flow of technology and information, often using field agents to service a local or regional area in much the same way extension agents do for agricultural programs.

5.5 University-held Patents, Business Incubators, and Technology Transfer

One key component of a uniquely American strategy for innovations is beginning to emerge. It is the enormous burst of industry-university cooperation in research and development leading to new products and technology.

THOMAS MOSS

While land-grant colleges and universities are dedicated to educating students, pursuing new knowledge, and providing public outreach, they have an opportunity to pursue commercial activity as a means of directly and indirectly generating greatly needed public support and budgetary revenue. By examining their institutional assets—physical, financial, and intellectual—and using the fundamental strategy of being more entrepreneurial, they can expect to directly enhance institutional revenue through patents, licensing of intellectual property, and entering into joint ventures with corporate America. For the most part, academe heretofore has stewarded a nearly antiseptic relationship between the scientific discoveries of institutional research and the industrial sector, where the primary aim is to develop scientific findings into new transferable technologies.

Such a new order for research universities has been encouraged and accelerated through discussions in recent years of attempts to attract and develop more "high-tech" industries, such as manufacturers of microcomputers, fiber optics, lasers, video equipment, robotics, machine-vision systems, and genetic engineering firms. Two examples are cited frequently: (1) Route 128—the freeway running through the suburbs ten miles west of Boston and (2) Silicon Valley—the popular name for the center of this nation's semiconductor industry—located in Santa Clara County south of San Francisco and until 1940 a quiet, productive agricultural area.

The person usually credited as being the primary architect of Silicon Valley was Frederick Terman, a visionary Stanford University electrical engineering professor and administrator. He encouraged his graduates to establish infant electronic companies near the Palo Alto campus. He set up for them and others the innovative Stanford Research Institute in 1946 and the nation's first industrial park, Stanford Industrial Park, in 1956. Terman pioneered new university-business-government partnerships that have since become models for others.

By 1970, Silicon Valley had become the world's densest concentration of high-tech enterprises, and Santa Clara had become one of the wealthiest counties in the United States. General Electric and Kaiser had set up branch manufacturing plants in the area, and they and others, including IBM and ITT, also had established research centers at Stanford Industrial Park, which leased space only to high-tech firms that would benefit Stanford University both intellectually and financially.

The numerous universities that have attempted to emulate Stanford have had varying levels of success. Most have not done well economically. Fundamental factors affecting the success of such pursuits include having "heavy hitters" on research teams, important scientific discoveries, and breakthroughs in the application of new technologies. Such technological progress drives productivity, which in turn serves as the engine of economic growth.

The indirect means of enhancing institutional revenues—from joint technology development through partnering with business and industry—comes from the increased tax revenues collected from those employed in the new jobs created as well as from renewed public support of education and research on the parts of those looking to institutions of higher education to demonstrate through readily apparent ways and means their interest in assisting with the on-going challenges of economic growth.

Wise people realize that investments in science and technology are essential to building a prosperous and sustainable economy, creating high quality jobs, improving education and health care, and maintaining a dependable level of national security. To neglect these is to neglect national economic survival. One does not buy a violin today and play in Carnegie Hall tomorrow. Similarly, investments must be made in research today if one of our goals is the surfacing of new technologies that can be commercialized tomorrow. New research discoveries and their transfer to business and industry is a debt due from present and future generations.

Patent policies at most universities have been liberalized in recent years to enhance the sharing of royalties between the university and the researcher-inventor. This has resulted in more patents being obtained by U.S. colleges and universities (1,491 patents were received by institutions of higher education in 1992, a fourfold increase since 1980). Still needed is a better mechanism to evaluate the commercial potential of ideas, assistance in determining patentability and in obtaining patents, as well as assistance in prototype development and in providing advice related to patent marketability.

The Patent and Trademarks Amendment Act (PL 965-17) signed by President Jimmy Carter in 1980 allowed nonprofit organizations (including universities) and small businesses to retain title to inventions made in the course of government-funded research. It is commonly referred to as **uniform federal patent legislation** because it clarified federal policy and abolished many regulations that had previously governed the ownership of inventions produced by universities using federal funds. It set forth the intent of Congress to use the patent system to transfer government-financed inventions to the public sector. This encouraged technology transfer by fostering enhanced interaction between universities and commercial businesses through giving inventors and owners of proprietary rights a protected monopoly on inventions and thereby encouraging economic growth and competition.

Principal objectives of university patent policies should include provisions to:

• Readily facilitate the transfer of university-developed technology to business and industry, and encourage the broadest utilization of the findings of scientific research to provide maximal public benefit;

• Encourage creative research, innovative scholarship, and a spirit of inquiry that assures the generation of new knowledge;

• Provide a procedure for determining the economic importance of discoveries, so commercially valuable inventions may be brought to the point of public utilization;

• Establish principles that determine the rights and obligations of the university, inventors, and research sponsors, respectively, with regard to university inventions, and to define equitable disposition of interest in inventions among the university family, the inventors, and research sponsors;

• Provide incentives to inventors in the form of personal development, professional recognition, extended research support, and direct financial compensation;

• Protect the intellectual property of worthwhile inventions until appropriate patent protection is attained; and

• Facilitate invention and patent management agreements with external entities.

Of course, patents are but one form of commercializable intellectual property. Copyrights are another, and with the extension of copyright law to computer software they have become especially important in technology transfer.

In 1970, the Stanford University Board of Trustees adopted a resolution permitting employees (faculty, staff, and students) to retain all rights to inventions made by them. This liberal intellectual property policy was an important step in establishing a culture that encouraged invention disclosure and technology transfer. Stanford also established an Office of Technology Licensing which attempts to sell particular technologies before they are patented by contacting companies that are involved in the particular technology being considered. In 1993, Stanford received $31.2 million from patent royalties. The University of California received $45.4 million.

During FY1989 and FY1990, the thirty-five universities studied by authors of the "1993 Science and Engineering Indicators" granted 197 exclusive licenses and 339 non-exclusive licenses. They earned $29.3 million from exclusive licenses and $52.7 million from non-exclusive licenses. Typical licenses granting exclusive rights to commercialize the discoveries of federally funded research were made to small businesses. Most such licenses were awarded to pharmaceutical, biotechnology, or other medical companies.

As centers of technology transfer in their regions, universities are recognized as having the resources needed to provide a steady stream of technological know-how and human capital that can fuel innovation and entrepreneurship. In FY1993, inventions developed at 117 of the nation's leading research universities produced some $242 million in royalties and a total of 1307 new patents, often directly benefiting local and regional companies. For example, faculty at the University of Pennsylvania made some 90 invention disclosures per year during the past three years, resulting in many collaborative research and license agreements with Pennsylvania businesses.

One important aspect of technology transfer in land-grant universities is the strengthening of ties with current constituencies and the expanding of interaction with new ones. Another is responding to the call of local and statewide requests for universities to aid in economic development through participation in research parks and business incubators designed to nurture start-up business ventures through their early stages. They frequently provide fledgling businesses with building space at below-market rental rates as well as other services, including technical and business advice. University-sponsored incubator firms commonly have access to university libraries, computers, and other facilities and equipment. As with most technical assistance programs, business incubators are primarily a service offered to the community. The fact that university-sponsored business incubators have increased during the past decade indicates the underlying trend among research universities toward increased direct involvement in economic development.

Several major research universities take equity in companies based on university research in lieu of royalty income on patents because:

• Patent licensing is often an unsatisfactory means of capturing the value of the university's intellectual property. Patents often lose value by being "invented around," improved upon, infringed upon, or rendered obsolete. Accepting stock in licensed companies is a way to share in the profits from an invention. A recent study found that 404 companies in Massachusetts were founded by MIT graduates. They employed some 160,000 people and had gross annual revenues of approximately $127 billion—about one-fifth of the state's gross income. Another study found that 156 of the 216 high-technology companies in the Boston area were created at MIT facilities, which is one reason the institution has embarked on an aggressive program of equity ownership in start-up companies. At MIT, industry sponsors more than $60 million of research annually. Scientists at that world-renowned institution receive more patents than do all federal research laboratories combined, and MIT routinely licenses more than half of these patents to business and industry.

• Ownership in start-up companies can be an effective way of associating a university with the economic development efforts of a region and of demonstrating involvement in technology transfer.

• The university can serve as both an effective advisor and negotiator for the faculty and a buffer between the faculty and the company when operations begin. Moreover, this can aid in the recruitment and retention of faculty.

Selected recent noteworthy developments related to patent policy include:

March 31, 1981: First patent issued on a genetically engineered microorganism. In 1972, A. M. Chakrabarty applied for a patent on a bacterium he had developed that would clean up oil spills. The U.S. Supreme Court (in a 5 to 4 ruling) upheld his application in 1980, and he was issued a patent in March 1981.

June 8, 1981: Congressional hearings on the commercialization of biomedical research. This two-day hearing was spurred by a research partnership between the Hoechst Corporation of Germany and Massachusetts General Hospital (Harvard University), which raised the question of a foreign corporation benefiting financially from federally-sponsored research.

October 12, 1984: PL 98-620 became effective. This law, spurred in part by developments in biotechnology, included plant varieties in the term "subject invention."

April 10, 1987: Executive Order: Facilitation of Access to Science and Technology. Signed by President Ronald Reagan, it articulates federal commitment to economic development through technology transfer. It refers to universities as being part of several "partnership" programs, including the research center programs of the federal government.

April 1988: First patent issued on an animal. Harvard University received a patent on a genetically altered mammal (a mouse) that can be used to detect cancer-causing substances. Harvard had applied for the patent in June 1984.

When in October 1980 it was proposed that Harvard University consider taking an equity position in a new company that was to be formed to exploit a professor's discoveries in biochemistry which it was believed would enable scientists to produce drugs and other products by manipulating the genetic makeup of bacteria, a great deal of publicity and public debate followed, after which then-Harvard President Derek Bok issued the following statement:

> The preservation of academic values is a matter of paramount importance to the university, and owning shares in a company would create a number of potential conflicts with these values. ... I have concluded that Harvard should not take such a step, even on a limited experimental basis, unless we are assured that we can proceed without the risk of compromising the quality of our educational research.

Approximately eight years later (September 1988), Harvard announced that a fund had been established that would invest in companies formed to bring Harvard faculty members' research to the marketplace.

5.6 University-Industry Partnering in Technology Transfer and Economic Development

> *Pinpoint your purpose and you will head toward achievement.*
>
> **WILLIAM A. WARD**

Technological developments fuel economic growth by increasing productivity, generating more jobs, and creating new processes and products for consumers to want and purchase. The desire for economic growth reflects a belief that growth leads to expanding economic opportunity, which frees people from elemental wants and offers them increased capability to pursue individual fulfillment in individual ways. It is not merely the technology itself that makes the world a better place in which to live; it is the economic growth the technology engenders.

United States industry, challenged by the exceedingly competitive demands of an increasingly integrated global economy, is going through a difficult period of restructuring and downsizing in which research and development activities compete with other (often short-term) company priorities. In this environment, there is almost a gold-rush enthusiasm for converting new research findings into marketable processes and products.

To better effect technology transfer, an organized effort to introduce industrial representatives to university scientists and their research findings is crucial. Expanded collaboration, communication, and cooperation among university researchers, scientists and engineers, and business and industry is essential to develop and market new technologies. The argument that we cannot afford to broaden our emphases and priorities to include expanded collaborative partnering with industry and government in research programs and activities (and the subsequent technology transfer that underpins business growth and economic development) would parallel the foolishness of concluding that wheat growers cannot afford to use seed and fertilizer.

The burden of expectations on universities to become more heavily involved in economic development is increasing. This comes at a time when the institutions' traditional functions of teaching, research, and outreach have never been more crucial. The term **"economic development"** as it relates to institutions of higher education refers to institutional activities designed to promote economic development. Providing technical assistance to business and industry; helping train or retrain employees; sharing computer, library, and other resources; as well as providing direct involvement with research parks and business incubators, are examples of ways in which universities can engage in economic development.

Following is an example of university-industry partnering in technology transfer. Flight Safety International is a New York City-based international company that trains pilots for advanced commercial and military aircraft. It has thirty-eight learning centers in the United States. Most of the flight simulators used by Flight Safety are designed and built by its Simulation Systems Division in Broken Arrow, Oklahoma. With a modest company grant, faculty and students in the School of Electrical and Computer Engineering at Oklahoma State University developed two new simulator subsystems for Flight Safety. The first enables the flight simulator to create maneuver movements that reflect realistic g-forces. The second accurately reproduces the critical sensory cues reflecting movement and the feel of the controls the pilot would experience. This movement and feel of the controls (termed "control loading") functions exactly as it does on the actual aircraft.

Such research partnering is another example of how industry needs can be addressed through new technologies developed by and transferred from the university directly to industry. The new digital control loading and motion systems became new product lines that enabled Flight Safety to receive a five-year, $40 million contract to build flight simulators for the McDonnell Douglas C-17 transport aircraft, which resulted in creating approximately 100 new jobs.

According to the National Science Foundation, the United States invested an estimated $161 billion in research and development activities in 1993. These important expenditures in the discovery of new knowledge and the application of knowledge to development of new and improved processes, products, and services was equivalent to 2.6 percent of the total U.S. gross domestic product. The absolute magnitude of the effort and the manifold tasks to which it is directed are indicative of the critical role research and development play in addressing such concerns as national defense, industrial competitiveness, public health, food, environmental quality, and social well-being.

5.7 Public Concerns and Technology Assessment

We must match the advances of mind and machines with an advance of heart and wisdom.

THOMAS J. WATSON, JR.

Land-grant universities have established themselves as respected enterprises working in the best interests of the general public in terms of health, wealth, and welfare. This means partnering with businesses, helping to modernize manufacturers, and helping to advance cutting-edge technologies.

Technology assessment is the systematic study of possible impacts of a particular technology. It is especially concerned with effects that are unintended, indirect, or delayed. Such assessments have covered such technological issues as automobile safety, consumer products safety, occupational health and safety, and nuclear power safety.

Seeking individual input encourages people to participate publicly in deliberations about technologies, which provides participants with a sense of belonging, of being part of a group decision-making process. The establishment of networks of individuals—being part of the group—becomes the end result of these deliberations, not the means to adjudicate technologies. No matter what the outcome of any given assessment, no matter what the ultimate decision, those who voiced an opinion on any side of the issue can revel in knowing that theirs was a job well done; they proved themselves responsible and eased their consciences by contributing their views and inputs.

Disparity of opportunity may be magnified by technology-driven market forces. For example, the United States has made improvements in infant mortality in recent years, resulting in large part from technological innovations that allowed for more effective treatment of underdeveloped lungs. The dark side is that, as overall infant mortality rate has declined, the disparity between black and white infant mortality rates has increased, because benefits of new technologies for treating underdeveloped lungs are limited to those better able to pay for medical care.

5.8   Technology Transfer and Global Competition

The skill, dexterity, and knowledge of a nation's people is the most powerful engine of economic growth.

ADAM SMITH

From Singapore to the Emerald Isle, national governments are becoming increasingly aware of the role science and technology will play in future economic growth and development. Leadership in science and the transfer of technology has become one of the defining characteristics of a great nation. The United States has risen to a position of global prominence largely through its strengths in science and technology. This enterprise continues to be essential. It is central to our future, vital to our economic growth, invaluable to our personal health and well-being.

Against a backdrop of new political realities—the end of the Cold War, collapse of the former Soviet Union, and the resultant concomitant changes in defense requirements—the demand for national investments in research and development and in educating and training our workforce is particularly significant. Increased globalization of national economies underscores the need to analyze and understand current trends in both cooperation and competition in science and technology. Many nations have increased their scientific and technological capabilities, resulting in growing competition from abroad in the processes, products, and services of technology, which has resulted in numerous U.S. manufacturing firms having difficulty keeping pace. The twin challenges of vigorous foreign competition and rapid technological change are terrific.

Globalization of capital, labor, and product markets has intensified during the past two decades. This in turn has changed the dynamics of poverty in the United States. The export of jobs, especially in manufacturing, has reduced employment opportunities in certain geographic areas. As capital—faced with foreign competition and more profitable alternatives elsewhere—has been disinvested in steel towns in the Rust Belt and textile mills in the South, new poverty has been created in specific spots.

The U.S. trade deficit results mostly from products such as oil and automobiles. We are the most efficient producers of many services, such as computer software, finance, entertainment, and higher education. The service sector now accounts for approximately 60 percent of the U.S. economy. The

McKinsey Company recently found that we have a trade surplus in services with other countries of more than $65 billion per year. This has come about because we have been successful in transferring technology.

What we need most now, in order to be more competitive in the global marketplace in the years to follow, is to have more new technology to transfer. We need a steady stream of new technology, and it is research that provides the discoveries that spawn the new technology. Hopefully, defense conversion—the process by which people, skills, technology, equipment, and facilities now in defense are shifted to alternative economic applications—will free up additional monies to support desperately needed expanded research efforts.

5.9 Summary

The significant problems we face cannot be solved at the same level of thinking we were at when we created them.

ALBERT EINSTEIN

The 1993 report, "Technology for America's Economic Growth—A New Direction to Build Economic Strength" identified three especially important technology goals: "(1) long-term economic growth that creates jobs and protects the environment, (2) a government that is more productive and more responsive to the needs of its citizens, and (3) world leadership in basic science, mathematics, and engineering." The United States cannot have a strong economy without having a steady flow of new technology, and we cannot have that without having an abundance of science underway. Fortunately, increases in federal support of science have averaged over 7 percent annually during the past decade. This bodes well for science and technology, providing the technology is adequately transferred to and applied by industry.

Discussion in this chapter noted the importance of having a more organized dynamic between technology development and technology deployment. In short, we need better mechanisms to transfer technology from research results into commercial processes, products, and services. Land-grant universities were originally founded and charged to serve people, government, and industry through education, research, and outreach. They are uniquely positioned to help revitalize the economy of the United States through a proposed national Industrial Extension Service network. The role land-grant institutions played in the economic growth, productivity, and efficiency of American agriculture is well known worldwide.

No other system can match their heritage of working shoulder-to-shoulder with industry to promote economic growth through continuing education programs, applied research centers, and intellectual resources across a broad range of academic disciplines. Land-grant university business and engineering departments always have had close ties with industry. University medical centers and life sciences schools have contributed immensely to the major changes in medicine, pharmaceutical applications, and biotechnology that have led to healthier people. Monumental advances in computer technology reflect synergistic interaction among industrial scientists and engineers and university researchers.

No other single organization can offer the special combination of resources, knowledge, outreach, experiences, and access already possessed by the productive and much-respected land-grant institutions. In effect, the land-grant system is the result of a social contract negotiated with the people of this nation. The proposed national Industrial Extension Service network would provide new opportunities for partnering and re-negotiating the social contract with regard to technology transfer (Chapter 14).

If we are to use science and technology to meet state and national objectives, we must have a strong, robust, ever-expanding knowledge base—one appropriate for economic growth, long-term job creation, protection of the environment, and improved social well-being. This will require a conscious commitment to strong, consistent, long-term support for research and education as part of a balanced portfolio of investments. The process of assuring research in fundamental sciences and engineering expands the knowledge base and contributes directly to strategic national goals through pioneering discoveries and the continued development of a cadre of educated people—individuals who are the primary source of new opportunities and new solutions.

For virtually all of the major problems the world faces—population-increase pressures, expanded educational opportunities for all, the environment, health care, urban development, substance abuse, transportation and its infrastructure, and even the need for stable democratic governments among fledgling nations—steady, reliable progress depends increasingly on science and the transfer of technology to business and industry.

Since the faculty comprises the heart of any university, it is important to engage faculty members in discussing and planning for extensive involvement in technology transfer. One way of achieving greater faculty support for technology transfer is to liberalize institutional patent policies. The primary goal of university patent policies should be to strike a balance between the interests and needs of inventors, institutions, research sponsors, invention developers, and the general public. Policies should clearly encourage commercialization of research and protect the intellectual property produced in the university, while at the same time protecting the inventor and the institution from conflict of interest and any appearance of misconduct.

Teaching Initiative

In the end, inspired teaching keeps the flame of scholarship alive. Almost all successful academics give credit to creative teachers—those mentors who defined their work so completely that it became, for them, a lifetime challenge. Without the teaching function, the continuity of knowledge will be broken and the store of human knowledge dangerously diminished.

ERNEST L. BOYER

6.1 Introduction

One thing is certain: if we get everything else right but fail to provide for the education and nurturing of our children, we will lose our place as a great nation.

DAVID L. BOREN
Personal correspondence, June 6, 1994

Thomas Jefferson believed that "a nation cannot be both ignorant and free." Confronted by ignorance and its companions—illiteracy, intolerance, injustice, and poverty—the people of the United States have invested wisely in education. Faith in education has sustained free inquiry, free expression, free enterprise, and all the other values that lie at the heart of American life, including fairness, opportunity, and the dignity of each and every citizen.

Self-government, Jefferson noted, can succeed only through the participation of an educated electorate. And the more complex the nation's problems become, the greater the need for education. Moreover, in a democratic free-enterprise society, it is important to call on the leadership of all groups, thus necessitating the education of all groups (Chapter 3). It is imperative that the United States make a quality education a high priority for all of its people. Indeed, students should be provided with as much education as they are capable of achieving and willing to seek. An educated populace is a productive populace, returning a portion of what it earns to society in the form of taxes, which in turn support additional education, research, and many other public services.

Education is not a luxury. We cannot be strong economically or in any other way unless we are strong educationally. And before our gross national product can enter an accelerated and protracted growth phase, we need an accelerated and protracted growth of our gross national mind. This can come only through greater emphasis on education at all levels.

Education is everybody's business! The quality of education of our citizenry, especially our youth, will determine whether the United States can enlarge its business and industrial base, create meaningful jobs, be competitive in the global marketplace, and thereby prosper. In the end, it will determine whether the overall quality of life in this country will improve and whether we can decrease the number living on welfare and in prisons.

Education is the gateway to a better life. The right to a high-quality education is fundamental, for education is freedom's foundation. This struggle is at the heart of our ongoing quest *for liberty and justice for all.*

The United States can compete either with low-wage laborers whose productivity is limited by educational underdevelopment or with well-educated and well-trained workers, eager to learn more, flexible and innovative. Moreover, the nation's needs cannot be met by an elite few. It is neither just nor economically sound to leave any of our nation's youth unprepared to assume their responsibilities as members of the national workforce and as participating citizens.

Public institutions of higher education serve many purposes. They develop human potential; advance knowledge through research and other scholarly activity; and fulfill many of society's needs through outreach programs. They help attract business and industry. They make continuing education available broadly and provide affordable, unbiased expertise to business and government.

Clearly, because it is inextricably linked with the progress of the nation, education should be a national function. It has been estimated that, during the period since World War II, half or more of our nation's growth can be explained by the better education of our people and by improved technology, also an important product of universities (Chapter 5).

Needed for the twenty-first century are ideas that would make institutions of higher education less labor-intensive; simplify the curriculum; transform academic departments into efficient teaching, research, and outreach collectives. Such institutions would be more responsive, more capable of shifting various resources to meet pressing public needs, and better prepared to address inevitable changes in technology and strong competition from alternative providers of post-secondary education (Chapter 4). These responses must emerge from a sense of internal discontent that—combined with external inducements—will yield an effective recasting of institutional function.

The public is conveying a clear message: **Put greater emphasis on undergraduate education and teaching, including the assurance that all teachers can communicate effectively.** Undergraduate education constitutes the strongest constituent influence on elected officials as well as the strongest advocate base among alumni and other supporters of higher education. To help restore our "most favored institution" status in the hearts and minds of the public, we must make it clear that undergraduate education will be a high priority for enhancement as we prepare for the twenty-first century (Chapter 2). The importance of graduate and professional education, research and other scholarly activity, and technology transfer as functions of American higher education notwithstanding, the stature, reputation, and level of public support of any land-grant institution will rise or fall in the next twenty years on the basis of the quality of the learning environment it creates for undergraduate students.

Public support of higher education is strongly connected with the national mood. It advances when there is convergence between national aspirations and institutional capabilities. Such a situation occurred during the three decades that followed the Civil War, when the sweeping new land-grant movement contributed so much to advances that occurred in agriculture and industry. Another such period came in the 1950s and 1960s, when higher education contributed immensely to the post-Sputnik science and civil rights movements. The vitality of higher education depends on opportunities to respond to the nation's needs as expressed through the political process.

6.2   The Synergistic Effects of Teaching and Research

Academic research has a twofold purpose, educate students and produce results. I believe that the former is far more important than the latter. Yet, the recognition and reward system in the university places greater weight on the latter than the former. In academic research, more emphasis must be given to what is in the best interest of the student, what is in the best interest of the nation, and what is in the best interest of the university.

JOHN WHITE

Today we engage the benefits that accrue from four major overlapping functions in research universities: (1) the scholarship of teaching, (2) the scholarship of discovery, (3) the scholarship of integration, and (4) the scholarship of application. Land-grant colleges and universities are well known worldwide for their tripartite mission: **teaching** at both undergraduate and graduate levels; **research, scholarship, and other creative activity**; and **public service, extension education, and outreach**. To ask which of the three is the most important is to miss their obvious interrelatedness. Indeed, they are equally important. However, if one mission needs more attention at one time or another, it is appropriate to commit extra attention to that front for a while.

The current public perception is that teaching is the mission needing special attention right now. All teaching and service activities flow from the professoriate's scholarly efforts, and scholars also learn as they teach. The French essayist Joseph Joubert wrote, "To teach is to learn twice over. Teaching is an integral part of the scholar's life."

Saying that research is important nearly to the point of being dominant is not saying that teaching is unimportant. Faculty members actively contributing to our knowledge base in their respective disciplines have a high probability of being vibrant teachers. Students prefer to drink from a running brook rather than a stagnant pool. Whether new knowledge is acquired through learning and synthesis or through original research, one's scholarship is essential to maintaining one's disciplinary zest.

Nationwide, less than half of higher education's faculty members are actively engaged in scholarly research. But there need not be a dichotomy between teaching and research. They go hand-in-hand. In a Virginia Polytechnic Institute and State University study it was found that faculty members with top credentials as teachers on average garnered about 35 percent more external grant funds than the rest. Similarly, in a University of Arkansas study it was found that those engineering faculty members having the highest student ratings of teaching effectiveness also had the greatest research funding and productivity. And in a survey of faculty at Virginia Commonwealth University it was found that 79 percent believed that research to create new knowledge improves teaching performance.

Scholarly activity is the yeast of excellence in any university. Students appreciate that they are more likely to be introduced to the latest information in their chosen disciplines when the teacher also is a scholar actively engaged in the academic discipline.

Teaching and research are part of the same process—learning. Teaching solidifies what has been learned and identifies that yet to be learned. But it is not enough to be only a great teacher just as it is not enough to be only a great researcher. Faculty members should demonstrate excellence in both. It is an abrogation of responsibility for a young faculty member to emphasize research more than teaching in the early career years.

The intellectual rigor required by scholarly research carries over into the classroom. In the long run, discipline, the excitement of discovery, and continued renewal via original research, scholarship, or other creative intellectual activity is needed to keep teachers professionally enriched. Without it, teachers will not grow in the wisdom and disciplinary breadth needed to maintain over time a high level of instructional effectiveness.

The naturalist J. Arthur Thompson noted that humans can live without air for minutes, without water for days, without food for weeks, and without ideas for years. But it should be added that universities have no such luxury. Without a steady stream of new sound ideas, institutions of higher education soon become out-of-touch and out-of-focus with the needs of students and the rest of the public they serve.

The national and international reputations of comprehensive research universities grow in proportion to the expansion of their programs of research and graduate education. All colleges and universities serve as repositories of knowledge, and all pass it on to students. But only a small number—probably fewer than 200 of the approximately 3,400 colleges and universities in the United States—have the discovery of new knowledge as a truly major component of institutional focus and mission.

The public frequently fails to appreciate the research university's role as a center for advanced study. Professors are often criticized for spending too little time in the classroom. There is a tendency by some to forget that universities are institutions of *higher learning*, not merely *higher teaching*, and that scholarly activity is the most appropriate mechanism for learning the most advanced knowledge and techniques. Teaching is not simply conveying information to students. It also is inspiring students by demonstrating the passion that led the teacher into a lifelong study of the subject matter. This passion is obvious only in those actively engaged in their discipline, in those who delight in sharing a glimpse of their excitement with their students. A highly significant undergraduate research experience can provide the student an exhilarating "whitewater" feeling of working at the cutting edge of the disciplinary knowledge base.

6.3 Teacher Attitudes

No greater gift can a person bestow than giving of his or her life to help others grow.

L. W. HYER

With high esteem, I fondly remember the young woman who taught me to read in the first grade more than half a century ago. She was a caring, enthusiastic, kindly person. It was immediately obvious that she enjoyed her work and that she loved and respected each and every one of us. The classroom was decorated with the magical world of words. We had books, we had story charts, and we had the motivation of wanting to become a member of her "reading club." But most importantly we had Ms. Duffield, a committed teacher who knew how to make us feel important as she showed us the joy and excitement associated with learning. By the end of the school year, we could read well because Ms. Duffield guided us methodically through the fundamentals of the reading process and encouraged us never to fear the possibility of making a mistake but always to launch out aggressively in attempting to achieve the next level of learning.

When she sent me on to the next grade, I was a devoted reader, a passionate lover of books. Throughout the next eleven years, I was fortunate to be in the presence of numerous master teachers who made learning fun and meaningful and who demanded much from us as they engendered self-confidence and self-respect. Indeed, Ms. Duffield's enthusiasm for learning was contagious, and her sincere respect for students made all of us want to do everything possible to meet her expectations. After what seemed like a very short period with her—a school year in which she guided, nurtured, and inspired me, a time during which she left marks that have not faded with time—I knew what I wanted to be when I grew up—a teacher!

Fortunate are those who have the opportunity to be a student of teachers who convey the pleasures associated with a proper attitude. While teachers ordinarily can not expect much in terms of monetary reward, they can and do—as Ms. Duffield did—enrich the lives of others. So teachers' main rewards come rather in the form of the personal satisfaction that comes from serving others, from making a positive difference in the lives of others. The most meaningful power and lasting satisfaction in life derive from being respected at one's craft, from having the enthusiasm to do it well, from being motivated to find creative ways of sharing it with others, from seeking excellence for its own sake. A high level of personal pleasure derives from realizing that one is in control of what he or she is doing as well as knowing that what is being accomplished is being accepted and appreciated for its intrinsic worth. Former Michigan State University author and master teacher G. Malcolm Trout put it this way:

> He has achieved success who has lived well, laughed often and loved much; who has gained the respect of intelligent men and the love of little children; who has filled his niche and accomplished his task, whether by an improved poppy, a perfect poem, or a rescued soul; who has never lacked appreciation of earth's beauty, or failed to express it; who always looked for the best in others and gave

the best he had; whose life was an inspiration and whose memory a benediction.

Sharing kind deeds and thoughts—things which cannot be purchased—with others is more valuable than giving material gifts. Norman Vincent Peale said:

> The man who lives for himself is a failure. Even if he gains much wealth, position or power he is still a failure. The man who lives for others has achieved true success. A rich man who consecrates his wealth and his position to the good of humanity is a success. A poor man who gives of his service and his sympathy to others has achieved true success even though material prosperity or outward honors never come to him.

Displaying a warm "I-want-to-help-you" attitude in the classroom as well as other places is the first prerequisite for effective teaching and learning; it captures the goodwill of others. The importance of goodwill was put in perspective by J. D. Snow when he said:

> The most precious thing that anyone can have is the good will of others. It is sometimes as fragile as an orchid and as beautiful. It is more precious than a gold nugget and as hard to find. It is as powerful as a great machine and as hard to build. It is as wonderful as youth and as hard to keep. It is an intangible something, this good will of others, yet more to be desired than gold. It is the measure of a person's success and it determines their usefulness in life.

Research and practical experience show that the most important aspect of providing students with a high-quality education is having high-quality teachers. Neither books nor buildings, laboratories nor classroom designs are as important as the teachers. Neither degrees held nor academic knowledge acquired assure effective teaching. Instead, combination in the teacher of attitude, enthusiasm, competence, experience, technique, and a spirit of "learning partnership" lead most assuredly to teaching excellence.

Teaching is more than the transmission of knowledge and skills. It is the evocation of promise and performance in life by someone who cares about students. Teaching involves an intimate encounter between teacher and student. It requires a vast range of knowledge, ability, judgment, skill, and understanding, and is best accomplished by a thoughtful, caring person. When teachers recognize that they are learning partners with their students in life's challenging and complex journey, when students are treated with the dignity and respect they deserve, teachers are on the road to becoming respected and even revered as individuals and even as master teachers.

Attitude is the way one thinks. Teacher attitude is a personal trait that students readily sense. They can hear it in the voice, see it in the teacher's postures and movements, feel it when they are in the presence of their teachers. A teacherly attitude expresses itself in everything one does. Positive attitude invites positive results.

Most students are skillful interpreters of silent language. They quickly and unerringly detect the attitudes and feelings of teachers. They learn best when they feel good about themselves and others, when they trust the environment and people in their lives, when they feel safe, secure, and needed. Learning is powerful and fun when information is integrated into experiences and larger personal contexts. As individuals, students and caring teachers long for community, for places of common vision, shared purpose, cooperative effort, and personal fulfillment within collective commitment.

Teaching, if it is to be done effectively, must be built on commitment to a vision. Learning, if it is to be enjoyable and meaningful, depends on imagination, risk-taking, intention, and invention. Stripped of these elements, teaching is mechanical and sterile, and learning takes on the form of mice trying to figure out a maze.

It is impossible to lay out a generic set of criteria that will assure excellence in the teaching-learning process. But there are certain important basics that begin with teachers having the right attitude about the opportunity to teach; the right set of professional competencies in their discipline; and an abundant supply of enthusiasm. There is no reason for students to be expected to be more enthusiastic about the subject matter than their teachers. Add to these fundamental teacher characteristics that of being an interested, caring, and compassionate person, and the stage is set for the individual to become a beloved, highly respected teacher. If and when that title is achieved, the teacher will share the personal feelings about teaching expressed by one of Yale University's most respected and beloved master teachers, W. L. Phelps:

> I do not know that I could make entirely clear to an outsider the pleasure I have in teaching. I had rather earn my living by teaching than in any other way. In my mind, teaching is not merely a life-work, a profession, an occupation, a struggle: It is a passion. I love to teach. I love to teach as a painter loves to paint, as a musician loves to play, as a singer loves to sing, as a strong man rejoices to run a race. Teaching is an art—an art so great and so difficult to master that a man or a woman can spend a long life at it, without realizing much more than his or her limitations and mistakes, and his or her distance from the ideal.

6.4   Education and Teaching Philosophy

Education is the foundation of democracy. There is no more powerful force in the world than a well-developed mind. It is not your aptitude, but rather your attitude, that will determine your altitude with a little intestinal fortitude. When external forces say you cannot, you must have the internal resources to say that I can. If you can conceive it and believe it, you can achieve it.

GAIL E. THOMAS

Education is a continuum that extends throughout one's life. It is as beautiful and gradual as a sunrise, as admired and inspirational as a sunset. The continuous process of education represents the accumulation of life's experiences. The fundamental purposes of an education are simple but profound. Achieving an education is to better prepare for the future in order that one may live a meaningful and productive life, one that enables an individual to contribute to the lives of others.

Education means different things to different people, but to all it is much more than the accumulation of knowledge. To be well-educated one must be competent in one's own language; have an understanding of the biological world of which we are a part; have an understanding of fellow human beings' behavior and motivations. Moreover, being educated should enable a person to better understand one's self and then to develop a personal philosophy that makes life meaningful, satisfying, and rewarding.

A well-rounded education should attempt to expose students to diverse and conflicting perspectives on themselves and their society, to challenge previously untested assumptions. It should create conditions which stimulate students' intellectual, moral, and emotional growth so they may better establish their skills in a mature, humane framework of values. A comprehensive education deliberately encourages students to reformulate their goals, the manner in which they think, and their view of their role in society. A liberal education enables one to develop the essential tools for thinking, making value judgments, and communicating.

Each student enters college with a specific background, with unique desires, expectations, abilities, intentions, and needs. Separated from family, the student welcomes the caring hand and listening ear of the teacher. A survey of National Merit Scholars revealed that the teacher trait they cherished most was personal interest. Students like teachers who like students. When the teacher's philosophy is one of personal trust, sincerity, fairness, and interest, it usually has a great motivational effect on students.

Teachers should reach out to students—get *in touch* with them. Most students welcome a thoughtful, caring teacher in their lives. A friend who will nurture and challenge, coach and guide, understand and care. Happily, most people are attracted to teaching because they sincerely love young people, enjoy being with them, like watching them open up and grow and become more able, more competent, more powerful, and more self-confident.

Most students who enter college experience a few bumpy spots in the road. Caring teachers can serve as "shock absorbers." It is important for teachers and students to develop a seamless web within which they are connected in a special bond of knowledge exploration, transfer, and growth. The harder teachers work at doing a good job of teaching, the harder their students will work at learning.

Many students are not self-starters. They need help in learning how to best benefit from educational opportunities. A large percentage need the caring but firm attention of faculty members who demand the development of critical thinking skills. Students benefit from those faculty who "raise the bar" of expectation with regard to what they are capable of achieving in their studies.

6.5 Curricular Considerations

There is not magic, but neither is there any mystery, about the best way to draw individuals of intellect and character into our public life. The answer is through our educational institutions, which are the training ground of our leaders.

J. WILLIAM FULBRIGHT

Rembrandt did not limit himself to a palette of one color. He created masterpieces by employing a rainbow of hues. As with the diverse choices available to Rembrandt, students should not limit their educational experiences but should instead seek a wide range of curricular opportunities.

The curriculum comprises much more than an assemblage of pieces of information, subject matter, and disciplines. It is an ongoing engagement with the problem of determining what knowledge and experiences are most worthwhile and thus most needed. A college education commonly comes to students packaged in courses that are to be experienced systematically. And students, pressed for time and caught in a hectic routine, work their way through the forest of courses much like industrious beavers chomping their way through riverbank saplings.

In a seeming race to modernize the curriculum, colleges and universities frequently lose sight of the need to teach critical thinking, writing skills, values and ethics, or even basic facts about the world. We need to be more mindful of the importance of properly developing the minds of young people, of stimulating them to find the truly great resources of the mind, and of having the ability to gain wisdom by and for themselves whereby they can make sound decisions that favorably impact society the rest of their lives.

Institutions of higher education have a social responsibility to inculcate basic moral values into the curriculum as well as to help students to better understand the social and intellectual significance of these matters. Such fundamental values as honesty, promise-keeping, free expression, and nonviolence are values upon which learning and discovery depend.

Since most students will spend their productive careers dealing and working with people in a business-oriented world, all students should have exposure to social sciences and business. These would include studies of individual and group behavior (principles of psychology and sociology); operation of political systems (principles of government and politics); operation of economic systems (principles of economics); and operation of business (applied business principles). Knowledge of other languages also is important in our global economy. One can purchase in any language, but it is far better to sell in the language of the customer. The study of foreign languages also can serve as a bridge to understanding other cultures (and thus better understand one's own).

Food, clothing, and shelter were recognized prehistorically as the basic needs of human beings. Yet many students graduate from college with little knowledge of the processes, problems, and people involved in providing these essentials. They know little about human nutrition, which is highly important to their own mental and physical well-being. Many graduate with little knowledge of economics, yet will be expected to provide industrial, political, cultural, and social leadership.

Much of the world's unrest stems from want of food. Problems and challenges of agriculture involved in production, prices, people, poverty, policy, and potentials are not studied by most students, but they are of considerable importance to every consumer. Therefore, just as surely as it is desirable for all students to appreciate art, music, and the like, it would be well if every college student were required to enroll in an overview course in agriculture and renewable natural resources. Students need more knowledge of food:population ratios in various geographic regions if they are to be prepared to constructively deal with the many challenges. With world population approximating 5 billion—and increasing steadily—a curriculum is incomplete without reference to demographic trends and changes. Furthermore, a situation in which food crops are grown abundantly in certain regions, while people in others are starving necessitates a study of distribution systems and balance of payments as well as a consideration of economic, political, and social concerns.

Students benefit greatly from travel and study abroad, hence more emphasis should be given to these opportunities as well as to providing students more opportunity to benefit from internships and cooperative-learning experiences. These are powerful educational tools, as they expand the student's knowledge base, provide a more global view of human interrelationships, and afford a significant means of developing and honing teamwork and leadership skills.

Cooperative education (co-op) is a structured educational strategy that combines classroom learning with productive work experience in a field related to the student's planned academic or career goals. Co-op is an educational partnership among students, institutions, and employers. Each has specified responsibilities that include:

• Formal recognition of the co-op experience on student records and by the institution as an educational strategy;
• Productive work experiences related to planned career and academic goals in an appropriate learning environment;
• Pre-employment preparation as well as ongoing advising for students;
• Agreement among institution, employer, and student with regard to: job description and expected learning opportunities; minimum work periods; college enrollment during off-campus employment; evaluations of quality and relevance by student, institution, and employer; and remuneration.

The more than 200,000 college and university students who participate in cooperative education programs annually and the thousands of co-op employers throughout the United States who are both mentors to and beneficiaries of this extraordinary talent pool are indicative of the emphasis that will be given in the years ahead to experience-based learning.

A common concern expressed by employers of our graduates is their lack of proficiency in communications, both written and spoken. Clearly, more curricular emphasis is needed in teaching the basics of speaking and writing well.

6.6 College Admission Policy

We want to be a gate opener, not a gate keeper.

JOHN GIDO

Over the years, land-grant institutions have had a policy of giving students the right to try in college. This is in keeping with the original intents and purposes of the Morrill Land-Grant Act of 1862 to provide a "liberal and practical education for mass society" (Chapter 1). It also impedes the schism of the U.S. citizenry into two groups, the educated and the uneducated. This policy has served these institutions and their publics well.

Many students enrolled in land-grant colleges had graduated from small (often rural) high schools where academic offerings were marginal. Most of these students entered college with a strong work ethic and determination to succeed, then proceeded to study hard and graduate in good academic standing, many with honors. Appreciative of their having been given the right to try, they have been for the most part strong, loyal supporters of their alma mater. Fortunately, most of these students were reared in families which believed in the value of education. An important aspect of a student's success is their family members being supportive of education. Parents and others must instill an abiding respect for education and create an environment in the home that is conducive to learning.

More recently there have been those who want to apply much more stringent selection criteria in admitting new students into land-grant institutions. This has led to considerable ill will among alumni as well as taxpayers and legislators. The following excerpt from a recent letter written by a graduate of a major land-grant university to the editor of his alumni magazine is typical:

> When our son applied to the College of ... with his ACT of 28 and top 1/5 of his class, he was rejected. ... I will argue that the University of ... has lost two generations. It has lost the talent of young people who were brought up thinking that the University of ... was a very special place. And it has lost the dollars of the older generation who are able to support special programs, special needs and all those little "extras" that the state no longer supplies. ... Our family has found today's University of ... a very uninviting place.

In the spirit of the true land-grant tradition and free-enterprise system intended to afford equal opportunity to all, I favor a philosophy of being more accommodating on admission, then tougher in terms of performance expectations and graduation standards.

Strong encouragement should be given to all individuals to achieve the level of education commensurate with their abilities and ambitions. This is based on the premise that learning is essential to both personal fulfillment and cultural advancement. The extension of education in this manner does not mean that everyone would be expected to graduate from college at age twenty-one or twenty-two, but rather that each person would be given the opportunity to develop educationally during his or her lifetime. To this end, the educational system would adjust and diversify its programs to accommodate persons of varying backgrounds, interests, talents, and ages. Such a plan of educational opportunity would provide a broad array of programs, available at convenient times and places.

Land-grant universities should not set as their goal merely the education of a group of intellectually elite. Rather they should strive to educate members of a broad range of constituencies and to make the benefits of learning accessible by all who wish to take advantage of them. Ultimately, the public will not support a system of higher education that addresses only the educational needs of the privileged while leaving the have-nots to fend for themselves. Moreover, mere access is not enough. Students must be helped if we expect them to succeed academically. Some students are late-bloomers, and they too should be encouraged to continue their education and thereby become more productive citizens.

Providing equality of public support to youth from all sectors of the populace relates to the political question of whether or not society is ready and willing to make the investment required to liberate the intelligence of a large number of young people from the career-stunting environments in which it is confined. The land-grant community—in keeping with the public mandate that accompanied the provisions of the land-grant acts of 1862 and 1890—should take the lead in addressing the educational needs of both well-prepared and inadequately-prepared students.

6.7 Upgrading Student Services

Education is to be aware of the uniqueness of each individual and to treat that uniqueness with loving concern. To provide each student with the opportunities appropriate to his or her abilities and interests. To encourage each to develop an "I will, I can" attitude. To help students go a step above and beyond what they, themselves, or others, might expect of them.

ROGER ROWE

Student services should be examined from top to bottom with the objective of improving the manner in which we relate to and serve our students. For example, many land-grant institutions need a comprehensive new-student information system. Provisions should be made for students to apply for admission using computer disks rather than paper applications; to register for classes by touch-tone telephone; and to have their transcripts transmitted electronically when transferring among institutions as well as in responding to prospective employers. Support services for students should be literally user-friendly.

The stewardship of students is highly important to the future of land-grant institutions. If these institutions help close the gap by accepting their share of students poorly prepared academically to compete with mainstream and above students, provisions must be made for the appropriate academic support services to increase the probability of collegiate success. Upgrading

K-12 education would eventually result in the universities being able to discontinue most remedial education.

6.8   Assessment/Outcomes-based Education

The strength and power of a country depends, most of all,
on the level and quality of education among its men and women.
JOHN RUSKIN

Assessment is first and foremost an effort to improve quality. In essence, assessment is a means of determining the educational value-added aspects of instructional programs. It is the testing of each student to measure the education gained. It also is an attempt to gain greater public trust in higher education through increased accountability.

The question often arises, How frequently should academic progress be assessed? There is no clear-cut answer, but vegetable growers agree that it is not a good practice to pull up the carrot too often to see how it is growing. At a minimum, students would be tested as they enter and again as they exit an institution of higher education.

Another question frequently asked is, How long should a student remain in college before being granted a diploma? Academicians have long debated whether the length of time spent in college is a relevant prerequisite to a college degree. Consider this: Imagine taking your clothes to a laundry and being asked, "How long do you want them to be washed?" Many would view this question as absurd. "Long enough to get them clean" might be a typical response. Similarly, colleges should define what is needed to acquire the essential education and training for a particular field, and then make certain that students achieve those given levels as the basis for conferring the degree. Some students will master the skills needed more quickly than others. But the objective is for all students who receive the degree to possess the necessary education. This philosophy fits with the current emphasis on outcomes-based education.

6.9   Summary

Teaching is an art, and the teacher an artist, differing from
the painter or sculptor in the very essential fact that he deals
with living material. His task is to guide the development of na-

ture's culminating achievement, the human intellect and personality.

VICTOR A. RICE

Education, like any pursuit of excellence, is a dynamic, lifelong, incremental process that calls on individuals and institutions to embrace the merits of teaching excellence during the collegiate experience as well as through continuing education programs that extend and continue intellectual development.

This nation's ability to produce educated students—those having global perspectives on human knowledge and interpersonal relationships—depends in large part on moving toward more interdisciplinary programs and more interdisciplinary appointments in land-grant colleges and universities. As the United States assumes an ever-greater role in the international community and marketplace, the need for greater numbers of persons having a comprehensive understanding of foreign cultures, languages, and social institutions becomes increasingly apparent.

Land-grant universities are confronted by challenges that reflect public expectations of changing patterns of federal and state financial support. The public is demanding that research universities focus more on the undergraduate experience and serve groups heretofore not well-represented in higher education, including nontraditional students and students from ethnic groups that are rapidly increasing demographically. They are being asked to play an increasing role in continuing education and outreach, to link research activities more directly to national and international needs, and to participate more directly in solving society's problems.

Concurrently, intense consumerism has made the public resistant to tuition increases and has brought new accountability and regulation pressures to bear on both universities and members of their faculties and staffs (Chapter 14). Alternative learning enterprises, such as corporate training programs, are competing with research universities for students and financial resources. There has been limited growth in state, federal, corporate, foundation, and private support of universities at the same time expenditures for things such as financial aid, library, maintenance, and employee benefits have had to significantly increase.

The basic goal of an undergraduate education is to lay a foundation for lifelong intellectual and professional development, crucial to one's achieving a successful and personally rewarding career and life.

Teaching is a professional activity that flowers over time. Teaching excellence requires a thoughtful, caring teacher who is committed to the lives of students. Good teaching is not something that can be readily scripted, planned, or prescribed. It is in large part a matter of love—love of students, love of subject matter, love of life. Teaching is an act of hope for a better future. The material rewards of teaching are modest. The rewards tend instead to be internal, of the moment. There comes a particularly powerful satisfaction from caring in a time of carelessness and from thinking for oneself in a time of thoughtlessness. The ultimate reward of teaching is knowing that your life **made a positive difference** in the lives of others. What could be a more noble career than being part of the educational experiences of the nation's most precious asset, our young citizens? It is impossible to determine the net worth of individuals who measure their wealth in terms of friendships established and nurtured with students.

Teaching is more than communicating truths. It also is preparing the mind to see truths by virtue of its own capacity. Few students rise higher than the teachers who inspire them. For students to develop critical thinking abilities, they need the benefit of having been taught by faculty who are themselves critical thinkers. Master teachers are quick to discover strengths in students and then identify creative ways to leverage these against weaknesses in their students. Since students typically conceal more than they reveal, teachers must get to know their students before they can relate with them well.

Next to parents, teachers are students' strongest links with the world. The dreams and hopes of students are greatly influenced by their teachers—the teacher who touched your life, who cared about you as a person, who understood you, whose passion for his or her discipline was infectious and energizing. Indeed, teachers comprise a large presence and make major impacts on the lives of students. Consequently, universities would be wise to include in their mission statements the expressed goal of infusing the love of learning into the lives of students.

While achieving the level and balance of excellence desired in teaching, research, and extension may seem to involve pulling in different directions, it is important to pursue excellence on all three land-grant mission fronts concurrently and with equal fervor. Excellence is a matter of purpose, commitment, and resources, not of size. Achieving excellence in academe fulfills the faculty, staff, students, alumni, and friends who comprise the university family. But excellence is a fleeting state. Never permanent, it must be pursued continually and fervently. Excellence is best realized in an environment where **ordinary** individuals are inspired to strive for and accomplish **extraordinary** deeds.

> *One machine can do the work of 50 ordinary men. No machine can do the work of one extraordinary man.*
> **ELBERT HUBBARD**

> *Next to excellence is the appreciation of it.*
> **W. M. THACKERAY**

Research Initiative

Research is to see what everyone has seen, and to think what no one has thought.

ALBERT SZENT-GYORGYI

7.1 Introduction

What we know is a drop. What we don't know is an ocean.

ISAAC NEWTON

Scholarship, research, and related activities generate knowledge of intrinsic value. It is through research that new truths are discovered. The quest for new knowledge is ennobling, and the public has an abiding interest in science. As curious humans, we are driven to search for new facts, principles, and laws and new models that might be manifest in our curricula as well as applied in business and industry and in our inexorable endeavors to improve our quality of life. Science enables us to explore the earth, venture into outer space, study exotic cultures, create new life forms, develop new medicines, probe the human psyche, and do many other exciting things. Scientific achievements arouse wonder, stimulate imagination, calm curiosity, provide adventure, confer pride. Science has about it simultaneously the mystery of poetry, the beauty of art, as well as the exhilaration of spectator sports. During the twentieth century, the expansion of knowledge has been enormous, but that which remains unknown must be absolutely awesome.

Science never remains static. New truths are learned and old ideas are modified or discarded as our body of knowledge continues to grow. Now we find that science and technology are ahead of schedule in that possibilities people once thought might be realized in the twenty-first century already have been adopted. More people are engaged in research today than ever before. The continuity, excellence, productivity, and utility of the scientific enterprise are all critically important to the well-being of the people of the United States.

Academic research can be traced back to Egypt, more than 2500 years ago. At Alexandria, teaching was limited to what was necessary to train researchers for the next generation. The focus was on understanding so each generation could inherit a more advanced civilization. Johns Hopkins University, established in 1876, was the first American institution designated a research university, where undergraduate, graduate, and professional education and research all came together. The second was the University of Chicago, founded in 1891. Land-grant institutions became recognized as research universities during the twentieth century.

Research discoveries and applications directly and indirectly affect human beings everywhere everyday. There are thousands of examples. One is the classical research that gave us penicillin. Sir Alexander Fleming of Great Britain ushered in the life-extending era of wonder drugs in 1928 when he observed that certain bacteria did not survive when in the vicinity of a green mold. But it should be noted that, many years prior to Fleming's monumental discovery, there were those in Great Britain who collected copper coins and copper kettles, smeared them with lard, and placed them in a damp place where mold growth flourished. This mold was then scraped off and packaged for sale. People came, for example, to the great-grandmother of Eva Wood of Bungay, Suffolk, to purchase her "remedy" for whatever ailed them. While the users did not know how the mold helped them, the important thing to them was knowing that it did.

Fleming and his co-worker, Sir Howard Walter Florey, with whom he shared the 1945 Nobel Prize in Physiology and Medicine, already had devoted more than a decade to isolating penicillin in relatively pure form by 1941, an opportune time for it to be field-tested in World War II. Working as a research bacteriologist at the University of London, Fleming also discovered lysozyme, a substance found in human tears and nasal secretions that, even when diluted, literally dissolves the cell walls of certain germs. Typical of many research discoveries and the resultant new technologies, penicillin was initially very expensive, costing $60 per dose. But through cooperative research between scientists working in the academic and industrial sectors, the cost of production was eventually reduced to about a dime per dose.

From a human health standpoint, the mold that yielded penicillin is much appreciated. But mold is highly undesirable to the bakers of bread. We hear that "necessity parents inventions," but some discoveries are not readily applied. More than five centuries ago, a Swiss scientist observed that bread treated with a thin film of the vinegar made from peaches inhibited mold growth. He did not know why, and this discovery was apparently not pursued until sliced bread was becoming commonplace in the United States. The baking industry was experiencing difficulties because the sliced configuration greatly increased the amount of surface area for molds to grow on, and the slicing knives scattered these molds throughout the loaf. Then researchers at

DuPont turned to the Swiss literature and set out to learn what was special about peach vinegar. They learned it is high in propionic acid rather than the acetic acid found in most vinegars. Further research provided the information needed to use propionic acid as a food preservative. Today, propionates are commonly incorporated into packaging materials to inhibit the growth of molds on foods inside the package.

So we see that a significant amount of scientific discovery is evolutionary. New research is based on past findings. One new discovery often serves as the basis for a subsequent knowledge breakthrough. Moreover, application of a given research finding often calls for additional discoveries and inventions. Electricity was a discovery that needed several primary inventions to bring it to the city and countryside—power generators, distribution means, and development of incandescent lamps and electric motors.

Breakthroughs in scientific research are less frequent than home runs in baseball, touchdowns in football, slam dunks in basketball. But they are just as exciting and inarguably more useful to society. German bacteriologist and chemist Paul Ehrlich founded chemotherapy when he showed that injections of certain dyes will cure certain tropical diseases. He became best known for discovering salvarsan (arsphenamine), a remedy for syphilis. Salvarsan is also called "606" because it was the 606th compound tested by Ehrlich, who shared the Nobel Prize for Physiology and Medicine in 1908. Rugged individualism and unfettered competition among scientists have led the United States to world leadership in the total number of Nobel Prizes awarded, scientific papers published, and patents received.

Experimentation is the fundamental tool of science. Ideas, curiosity, and alert observations are critical to scientific progress, and sometimes they arise where least expected. Only recently, for instance, the nine-banded armadillo was found to be capable of producing antibodies against the microbes that cause leprosy. For people in Asia and elsewhere, this was a significant finding. Thanks to this previously insignificant animal, the potential exists to wipe out another terrible disease. And consider, too, the fact that about half of all medicines used today are components of plants. Natural plant gene pools must be preserved for the future well-being of humans. The cure or preventative for cancer just might be part of one of Nature's wild plants, waiting to be discovered.

Research and public service always have been at the core of land-grant institutions' activities. First they serve as essential adjuncts to education. Teaching in an environment devoid of inquiry and creativity and without significant contact with the general public would be irresponsible (Chapter 6). Excellence in research enhances the value of what is being taught. Hence, we should not be overly critical of the "publish-or-perish" adage, although a concept of "grow-or-perish" would be better still. This approach has been a significant strength of faculty members of land-grant colleges and universities through the years.

> *It has been my observation that the most distinguished scientists present the results of their research in the simplest possible form. They do not undertake to obscure the results of their work by excessive use of technical language or obscure sentences which may have a double meaning or at least leave the reader in doubt as to the real meaning. Writers should not suffocate the reader by excessive use of technical language.*
>
> F. B. MUMFORD

7.2   Research Philosophy

> *There is no longer margin for doubt that whatever the mind of man visualizes, the genius of modern science can turn into fact.*
>
> DAVID SARNOFF

We are responsible for continuing the enterprises of research and scholarship that contribute to the preservation of our human heritage. Research universities are charged with pursuing truth, with discovering new knowledge. They are expected to serve the public by providing critical analysis unaffected by outside influences.

The strength of the United States has traditionally rested on our people and our vast knowledge base. The genesis of new knowledge is the raison d'être of research universities. The academic research community should view research challenges as its opportunity to be an integral part of resolving problems that confront the nation.

Scholarship is the ultimate use of the human mind. It advances the frontiers of knowledge. Responsible academic administrators minimize expenditures for nonacademic activities in order to direct the most monies possible to scholarly endeavors. Responsible scientists commit much thought and effort to enriching and expanding their scholarship. Artisans aim for excellence and originality in their work as well.

Knowledge can be advanced only by fresh thinking. For ideas to arise and thrive, they must be encouraged and nurtured by the free play of unencumbered imagination. Even incomplete knowledge is a vital adjunct of wisdom so long as it is free to be probed. This may explain, in part, why Montaigne recorded that he learned more from poor examples than from good ones. One he cited was of a lawyer on horseback who he claimed taught him more about how to seat a horse than any accomplished cavalier. Ideas are alive, driven by hopes, but susceptible also to decay. An education that provides information without imagination, that treats ideas as inert and serves them up for passive consumption, is unsound.

The research that leads to new discovery comes from curious, perceptive, and discriminating minds. Austrian monk and botanist Gregor Johann Mendel discovered the principles of heredity by observing characteristics of individual plants. His classic experiments in growing garden peas supported the conclusion that there is a definite pattern in the way contrasting characteristics are inherited. He discovered that one of each pair of certain characteristics is dominant while the other is recessive, that it is possible to grow a line of plants that show only recessive characters, as well as one of those that show only dominant characters. When Mendel reported his experiments and discoveries—in a paper published by the Austrian Society for the Study of Natural Sciences in 1866—he founded the scientific study of genetics and heredity. But, as more than three decades passed before the importance of his work was appreciated, his work was not acknowledged during his lifetime.

My scientific work brought me a great deal of satisfaction, and I am convinced that it will not be long before the whole world acknowledges it. My time will come.
GREGOR JOHANN MENDEL (1822–1884)

Throughout history scientists often have questioned the appropriateness and advisability of reporting their research findings. When Anton van Leeuwenhoek, a Dutch lens maker, discovered human spermatozoa through a microscopic lens in 1677, he described what he saw as "man swimming in his own pool." In reporting findings from his investigations of semen to the Honorable Viscount Brouncker, president of the Royal Society, he wrote, "If your Lordship should consider that these observations may disgust or scandalize the learned, I earnestly beg your Lordship to regard them as private and publish or destroy them, as your Lordship thinks fit."

7.3   Research Categories and Terms

Surely scholarship means engaging in original research, but the work of the scholar also means stepping back from one's investigation, looking at the connections, building bridges. Build-

ing bridges between theory and practice and communicating one's knowledge effectively to students.

ERNEST L. BOYER

The twenty-first century will impose greater responsibilities on those who have a stake in the discovery and use of knowledge. A more rapid pace of discovery that responds to a sense of urgency in a competitive global economy, the increasing importance of multidisciplinary research, and the confluence of research interests and opportunities across institutional lines call for academe, industry, and government to forge new partnerships and approaches. The fact that more than 35 percent of all articles authored by industry researchers in 1991 were co-authored with academic scientists is indicative of the magnitude of this trend.

"Research" is the term commonly used in the generic sense to refer to scientific inquiry of all kinds as well as other forms of scholarship and artistic contributions. **Basic research** involves systematic study in which the primary aim is fuller knowledge of the subject rather than a specific practical or commercial application. Basic research comprises a voyage of discovery. Sometimes it reaches its objective, but even then it often reveals unanticipated facts and principles that lead in turn to more voyages. In industry, basic research is commonly thought of as that which advances scientific knowledge but does not necessarily have immediate commercial objectives (although it may be in fields of commercial interest). Most basic research provides fundamental knowledge that, either alone or in concert with other discoveries, eventually leads to innovation, technology development and application, and economic growth.

Applied research is systematic scientific study in which the primary aim is gaining knowledge necessary for determining the means by which a recognized specific need or commercial objective may be met. In industry, applied research commonly is oriented toward discovery of new scientific knowledge that has specific commercial objectives with respect to products, processes, or services. Because of its goal orientation, applied research generally tends to restrict creativity and serendipitous discovery.

Development is the systematic direction of knowledge gained from research toward production of useful materials, devices, processes, systems, or methods. For example, the world economy is now undergoing an epochal transformation from The Machine Age to The Information Age. The new source of wealth is less materials and more information. Carburetors, for example, enabled automobiles to travel twelve miles on a gallon of gasoline, whereas computerized fuel injectors enable them to travel twenty-two or more miles per gallon, effectively increasing the supply of gasoline by more than 80 percent.

Distinction should be made between a **research project** and a **research program**. A research project is of limited scope and duration, and commonly focuses on the resolution of a particular research problem. A research program is an ongoing effort to coordinate research projects that address larger, more comprehensive research issues.

An **individual investigator** is a single scientist or small research group receiving funding for an independent research project. A **research team** is a group of investigators, often at more than one institution or firm, pursuing common research objectives and considered by the funding source to comprise a team.

A **research center** is a more or less formally organized group of scientists, frequently multidisciplinary, using shared resources to pursue coordinated research focused on one or a few research themes. Research centers are frequently used to bring university scientists having common interests and complementary skills together as a means of attracting funding from business and industry, governmental agencies, and private foundations by calling attention to the combined strength of professional colleagues who are conducting related research. They are especially useful in describing interdisciplinary groups.

Research consortia are programs of university research funded by a number of corporate sponsors, and often by federal and state governments, as well. Corporations participating in such consortia commonly provide annual funding for ongoing investigation in a specific field of research and are to some degree involved in setting the research agenda. Universities typically maintain close contact with the sponsors and make periodic reports on research progress.

Multidisciplinary and **interdisciplinary research** are research approaches in which a problem is identified that requires the attention of more than one scientific discipline for the discovery of knowledge and development of solutions. The **multidisciplinary** approach involves a joint planning and coordinating activity that identifies research agendas for the respective disciplines involved. Scientists from each of the disciplines pursue their portion of the research independently. The **interdisciplinary** approach goes a step further by forming a working team of persons from different disciplines whose deliberate collaborative synergy is directed toward the understanding, development, assessment, or technological improvement of a concept, phenomenon, or problem. An interdisciplinary team follows a common research plan so an integrated model of the problem's elements is generated. This approach facilitates giving due attention to the complex interrelationships that often exist among the various elements of a technological solution.

Since Nature does not present her secrets along compartmentalized disciplinary lines, the interdisciplinary/multidisciplinary collaborative-research-team approach is emerging as the best accepted workplace for achieving the research objectives in the twenty-first century. Many fundamental problems faced by society require interdisciplinary research approaches rather than reliance on traditional disciplinary paradigms. There is a recognized need for closer cooperation among private- and public-sector scientists, among U.S. scientists and those of other nations, and among researchers in the natural sciences and the social sciences. As these trends continue, boundaries between basic research and applied research will be increasingly more difficult to demarcate.

The internal structures of colleges and universities always have been characterized by a high degree of segmentation. In the best interest of the whole, these disciplinary (often departmental) fences need to come down in favor of more nearly seamless research endeavors. The need for interdepartmental research approaches has increased to the extent that a new type of organization may be needed. But reorganization presents both opportunities and dangers.

7.4 Research Linkages Among Academe, Business and Industry, and Economic Development

Some people regard private enterprise as a predatory tiger to be shot. Others look on it as a cow they can milk. Not enough people see it as a healthy horse pulling a sturdy wagon.

SIR WINSTON CHURCHILL

In Thomas Jefferson's day, the common people worked twelve hours a day, six days a week, for a total of seventy-two hours a week. Workers were criticized when they asked for a sixty-hour work week. Today, most workers have a forty-hour work week, and this is likely to drop to 36 as a general rule in the foreseeable future.

The prospect of having a work week only one-half that of Jefferson's day—thereby freeing up time for the enjoyment of life, family, travel, Nature, reading, and related recreational pleasures—has been made possible primarily through research and technology. Hundreds of advances have put the United States at the world's vanguard in terms of applying science and technology for the improvement of the quality of life. But to remain competitive in today's global economy, the United States must become even more efficient and productive. This calls for renewed commitment by leaders of academe, business, and government and partnering more fully now than ever before to increasing scientific findings and applying technological developments (Chapter 5).

The foremost function of land-grant colleges and universities—as for any college or university—is education. This is not likely to change. But modern research universities must change in that they must become more active partners with business and industry and with government in addressing the challenges of international competition, especially as it relates to economic development. Properly utilized, the principal product of research universities—knowledge—could well have the same invigorating effect on economic development in the United States during the next few decades that the railroads had during the second half of the nineteenth century, the automobile during the first half of the twentieth.

Economic development is a process that increases the capacity of individuals and organizations to produce goods and services and thereby create wealth. Economic development is becoming synonymous with entrepreneurial development. Universities can contribute to such initiatives through joint research and development, education and training, and entrepreneurial assistance services.

> *Now universities have become absolutely essential to the economy and to the very survival of nations. Forces from outside the university, which formerly had only a marginal effect upon the evolution of the university, are now likely to exert a powerful influence on this evolution. Universities therefore have to strike a balance between an adaptation which is too inflexible. To achieve this balance universities need to initiate and control their adaptation to society, not to allow it to be imposed on them from outside.*
>
> **SIR ERIC ASHBY**

Research is the engine of economic growth and development, the single most important source of economic expansion. As the speed with which change occurs increases, the need for new knowledge increases. Such is the case today. A great challenge facing us is the translation of research discoveries into widespread commercial use. Since the academic sector performs nearly two-thirds of the nation's basic research, meeting the challenges of global competition calls for stronger university-industry collaboration. This provides a great incentive for higher education in the United States to change current public perceptions of what it is and what it can do (Chapter 2).

Collectively, we must secure new advantages in the global marketplace as well as maintain the advantages we already enjoy if we are to sustain a healthy economy in the long run. Public and private recommitment to research is essential to achieving these goals. A strong case can be made for a significantly increased federal responsibility for national economic development and thus for ensuring equal opportunity in higher education. A key to successful competition in the global marketplace during the twenty-first century will be the increased importance of a well-educated and well-trained, flexible, and adaptable workforce. Again, more than ever before, federal responsibility for ensuring adequate national investment in the education and training of human capital is absolutely critical.

Given the nature of our national economy today, and especially the mobility of capital and labor and increasing interdependence of economies around the world, the federal government has the greatest of incentives to ensure optimal investment in human capital, physical capital, and science. The same argument holds for technology development and adoption. The benefits of research and technology do not accord with the boundaries of any particular state. If access to higher education is restricted to those in the most advantageous positions to benefit from it, both institutions of higher education and society will be diminished. The talents of all citizens need to be developed if we are to deal effectively with the problems of society. Moreover, social justice requires that we share access to new knowledge and its rewards as fully as individual talents and motivation permit.

According to a study conducted by Employment Research Associates, a $1 billion federal investment creates 31,000 jobs in military procurement, 43,000 in housing, 47,000 in health, and 48,000 in education. As the United States phases back its expenditures for national defense, it can create more jobs by investing the recouped monies in education than in many other forms of employment.

During the past two decades, there has been a significant increase in industry's interactions with university scientists. By supporting academe, industry gains access to both cutting-edge research and a downstream employment pool. For entrepreneurial university researchers, industry collaboration offers an additional source of funding and intellectual stimulation and often access to state-of-the-art facilities. Special educational opportunities have benefited from a variety of federal and state programs explicitly designed to encourage such collaboration. Nationwide, industrial support for academic research and development increased by more than 300 percent (constant dollars) between 1978 and 1993. Knowing that we live and operate in a global economy, that the economy is in large part knowledge-driven, and that in the future American businesses will look to universities for well-prepared employees as well as new knowledge, the research universities that choose to strongly partner with industry have sound reason to expect strong support from the business sector in the years ahead.

University-industry liaison programs are important means by which research universities establish productive relations with industry. Typically, in return for an annual fee of $10,000 to $50,000, corporate members are provided facilitated access to the university and its research efforts. **Facilitated access** commonly includes the opportunity to send corporate representatives to an annual conference summarizing research being conducted at the university; access to special university facilities, equipment, and data bases; receipt of periodic newsletters and research publications; opportunities to attend meetings, workshops, and lectures on topics of special interest; and special arrangements that encourage exchange of information related to research issues.

Most focused liaison programs provide for close association between research faculty and technical representatives from industry. Specific benefits typically include scientist exchanges, opportunities to forge agreements for licensing results of sponsored research, and access to students for in-house projects, summer employment, and recruitment. Such programs are commonly viewed by all parties as true collaborations.

Monies received from membership fees often are spent at the discretion of the sponsoring academic unit to support additional research. Results of recent studies indicate that liaison programs constitute the most effective mechanism for technology transfer from university to industry. Continuing education ranks second, patent offices third.

Research parks are real estate developments dedicated to serving research-oriented corporate entities. They frequently have a contractual or operational relationship with a university which partners with industrial firms to assist the growth of new ventures or promote economic development.

A major factor in improving university-industry relationships was the federal policy of certain funding agencies, such as the National Science Foundation (NSF), which leveraged federal funds by requiring industrial matching monies for certain research projects. The NSF Centers of Excellence program is an important example of this trend. Another significant change in federal policy was revision of patent law, especially passage of the Patent and Trademarks Amendments Act in 1980 (PL 96-517), which gave universities the right to patent and license discoveries made under federal contracts. Patent protection also was extended to new categories of discoveries and inventions, including bacteria produced in research laboratories using biotechnology and later genetically altered plants and animals.

7.5   Research and Graduate Education

Teach me well so I may have a more complete set of the ba-

sic tools to become an effective researcher—and may I then re-
search well so others may use my findings to become more effec-
tive teachers.

R. J. MALL

Graduate education can be expected to be of high quality only when it is part of a genuine research process. The blending of undergraduate education, graduate education, and research that occurs in comprehensive research universities creates an exceptional opportunity for learning.

Universities are known largely for the excellence of their graduates. This in turn is immensely affected by the excellence of the instruction. And the excellence of instruction in turn is related closely to the excellence of the research from which the teachers derive their information.

Down through the ages, wise people have been willing to invest in the education of those who will follow them. The public has a logical stake in developing the mental capacities needed to secure the future. We must attract not merely competence but brilliance across the spectrum of science—and this among underrepresented groups, men and women, those with conventional and nonconventional views alike, those who seek their own frontiers, those who practice independent thinking. Alas, the cost of identifying, educating, and training the scientific Mozarts in the public interest is not free of cost. But the cost of the alternative—a state of ignorance, scientific stagnation, and non-competitiveness—would be incalculably higher.

The United States needs proportionately more young scholars entering research than is now the case. Insufficient numbers of new minds are choosing to probe the wonders of Nature. During the past decade, there has been a significant decrease in the number of scientists under thirty-five years of age applying for new monies from the National Institutes of Health (NIH). Is the public interest being well-served while our biomedical research community steadily grays? At every stage of the human talent pipeline—from high school to postdoctoral research—we are experiencing significant decreases. It is important to reverse this erosion of the foundations of our nation's human capital.

Postdoctoral students are commonly those who recently completed the Ph.D. degree, and are conducting research full-time under the tutelage of a professor for one to three years prior to accepting a more permanent position in academe, industry, or government. Postdoctoral students contribute significantly to institutions of higher education as well as to the general society. They advance the research mission, assist in recruiting and training graduate students, are the academicians of the future, and help secure the United States' place as the world's scientific research center.

Emphasis given postdoctoral education has significantly increased during the past two decades, and there is reason to expect this trend to continue. For one thing, there is an increasingly market-driven need for research specialization. Also, postdoctoral experience serves as a holding pattern for new doctoral recipients in a competitive job market.

7.6 Marketing the Discoveries of Research and Technology

Our ability to get better at the innovative process—to drive new products from idea to market faster and with fewer mistakes—is the key to winning the product war.

ROBERT G. COOPER

As more faculty engage in research sponsored by private entities, the issue of ownership of ideas becomes increasingly important to both academe and industry. In an environment of intense global competition, the economic stakes with respect to intellectual property have grown higher. We must think new thoughts and dream new dreams; we must change and improve. Research and development are needed to encourage new concepts in our effort to retain competitive advantage. The rapid pace of research in molecular biology puts a premium on staying at the forefront of this fascinating field. The genetic code can now be read, understood, and used. It is an intellectual feat of unique and staggering proportions.

Proprietary research and industrial outreach activities are motivated largely by pecuniary incentives. Public benefits may result, but they usually are subordinate to private firms' primary interests. Additionally, there is the risk of failing to discover a commercially exploitable technology. Proprietary research requires a return on investment. Anticipated market potential sometimes indicates a lower-than-acceptable rate of return, and so the work is not started.

Both the public and competing firms are prone to complain that funneling promising technology to a university-owned company is self-serving and inappropriate, especially when the research that spawned the technology was funded by the public. Yet universities cannot ignore the potential financial returns that might be realized through ownership of research-based start-up companies. Other considerations supporting such ownership include widespread public acceptance and support of technology transfer as an important goal of the university, as well as recognition that the university can play an effective part in bringing embryonic technology to commercial fruition.

Some universities have entered into ownership of research-based companies through buffer organizations established specifically for this purpose. In 1981, the University of Rochester established a wholly owned, tax-exempt venture-capital organization called University Ventures, Inc., with $67 million of endowment funds. It is a subsidiary of the university, and its board of directors is comprised mostly of university officials. In 1989, The Johns Hopkins University formed a for-profit enterprise—Triad Investors Corporation—to commercialize university research. Triad is owned by the Dome Corporation, which in turn is owned jointly by The Johns Hopkins University and The Johns Hopkins Health System. Triad seeks outside investors willing to make major investments (initially $2 million each). With this funding, Triad evaluates the results of Johns Hopkins research, obtains rights to patents on promising inventions, and then helps develop business plans and provides first-stage financing for new ventures.

In contrast to Triad, which was established to make a profit from university research, the Pittsburgh Foundation for Applied Science and Technology was founded to support state economic development programs and encourage expansion of high-technology industry in Pennsylvania. A substantial proportion of its funding comes from the Commonwealth of Pennsylvania.

Equity ownership in companies has paid handsome dividends for universities in many cases. As a professor of economics at the University of Pennsylvania and Nobel Prize winner, Lawrence Klein established the Wharton Economic Forecasting Association (WEFA). In return for use of the Wharton name and a $250,000 line of credit, the university received equity in the venture. The university ultimately received about $150,000 annually in dividends from WEFA, and in 1981 sold 80 percent of its stake for a reported $7 million.

The late 1970s are remembered by many as the time of the biotechnology gold rush. Participating in this rush to fame and fortune was Walter Gilbert, a Nobel Prize-winning biologist at Harvard University. His research in gene cloning—particularly on what came to be known as the **lambda repressor**, which was potentially significant in the fight against cancer—propelled Gilbert to the front of this exciting new field. He was instrumental in founding Biogen, one of the first companies formed to exploit the commercial potential of DNA research. Eventually, the degree of his involvement with the company caused him to resign his American Cancer Society Chair at Harvard to become Biogen's Chief Operating Officer (COO). (Interestingly, after serving several years as the COO of Biogen, Gilbert resigned and rejoined Harvard as a tenured professor.)

In January 1980, following a press conference conducted by Gilbert, Charles Weissman of the University of Zurich (Switzerland), and other scientists with Biogen at which a breakthrough in gene cloning was announced, the company's stock climbed rapidly, adding approximately $50 million to its paper value—and substantially to Gilbert's personal net worth. The announcement had to do with the cloning by Weissman of a human leukocyte interferon that had the potential to be especially important in the treatment of cancer.

Ten months later, when Genentech (another biotechnology company, founded by Herbert Boyer of the University of California at San Francisco) went public, its stock increased from an opening price of $35 per share to $89 in just twenty minutes, despite the fact that at the time Genentech did not have a single product to sell.

In the public eye, these and related events reflected and reinforced the direct connection between university research and commercial possibilities.

7.7   Federal Policy and Support of Contract Research

Good research projects produce fibers. Good research programs spin those fibers into threads. Good institutions, through well-organized and well-managed research and development programs, weave those threads into the technological, economic, social, and political fabric of the nation.

DONALD A. HOLT

Federal policy makers learned already during World War II that the federal government could not conduct solely in government laboratories all the scientific research it needed on a variety of topics. From the standpoint of human resources, physical facilities, and equipment needed, it was necessary and actually more efficient to contract with universities and private research laboratories.

Opportunities are increasing for research requiring large-scale organizational settings for its performance. But as funds-strapped state and federal agencies struggle with the need to do more with less, there is the need also for greater research coordination within and among public and private universities. With the public's call for more attention to undergraduate education, additional coordination is needed between the teaching and research programs. A report recently issued by the Federal Coordinating Council for Science, Engineering, and Technology stated, "Federal Agencies should examine the impact of federal research support on university undergraduate and graduate education and identify strategies to ensure against unintentional degradation of the educational mission and excellence of the research-intensive universities."

There are approximately 200 research and doctorate-granting institutions in the United States. Of the research and development accomplished in universities, approximately 85 percent occurs in the top 100 institutions. Approximately two-thirds of the universities' research funding comes from the federal government (the federal share of academic research support was approximately 60 and 73 percent, respectively, for public and private research universities in 1988). Heretofore, industrial support of university research has been modest. With the advent of greater emphasis on university-industry partnering in technology transfer, however, this source of support is expected to increase significantly in the years ahead.

7.8 Research Productivity and Publications

Even the most significant research findings are of little or no use until they are published.

ROBERT T. MARSHALL

Researchers are evaluated in large part not on the basis of their attitudes, intentions, or philosophies, but on that of their accomplishments as reflected by their scholarly publications. In 1991, there were 177,805 scientists and engineers holding doctorates earned at U.S. institutions working in science and engineering in our nation's colleges and universities. That same year, U.S. authors published more than 142,000 articles in the natural sciences and engineering in more than 3500 major technical journals worldwide. More than 70 percent of these publications came from academe, and the total number of U.S. articles accounted for 35 percent of the world total. In 1991, the United States produced 23 percent of the world's literature in chemistry, 30 percent in physics, and about 40 percent in other major fields of science. More than 60 percent of U.S. publications in 1991 were in the life sciences, particularly in clinical medicine and biomedical research, which together accounted for more than half of all U.S. publications. There is wide variation in the amount of faculty participation in the authorship of scholarly publications. Approximately two-thirds of all college and university faculty members in the United States have never written or edited a book, and about one-third have never authored a single refereed journal article.

Scientific leaders and research models are defined mostly at research universities. They are strongly influenced by disciplinary and departmental structures. Many believe the intellectual influence of higher education emanates from a few major research universities. But, although a select group of highly reputable institutions are major contributors to the intellectual-capital base of the nation, there are productive researchers, scholars, artists, philosophers, students of public policy, and social critics on the faculties of virtually every institution of higher learning.

7.9 Summary

The greatest joy of those who are steeped in work and who have succeeded in finding new truths and in understanding the relations of things to each other, lies in work itself.
CARL VON VOIT (1831–1908)

Education is an investment in human capital. It must again rank at the top of state and national agendas. The future prosperity of the United States depends on the quality and quantity of teaching and learning, which in turn depend on the discovery of new truths. Investments in research and technology transfer aimed at strengthening the United States of America's competitive edge in the global marketplace must be increased. We must convert research discoveries into products, processes, and services that can be commercialized, and thereby create jobs and expand the tax base required to provide needed governmental services, including education and research. After all, they are among the most cost-effective activities in which a government can be engaged.

Research is the mechanism for learning, for advancing the knowledge base, for developing new technology. The public needs a clear vision of the true values in science as one means of advancing human civilization. This can be accomplished. There is in virtually every human being the desire to know, and this is strongest about phenomena which influence our daily lives. How are we to satisfy this hunger for knowledge? Spawners of new scientific knowledge need to communicate their findings via the media, and the public should better develop its powers of observation and abilities to analyze and understand what it reads and sees.

The knowledge industry is permeating business and government. The production, distribution, and consumption of knowledge in all forms is estimated to account for between one-third and one-half of our gross national product, and knowledge production is growing at more than twice the rate of the rest of the U.S. economy. Never before in history has knowledge been so central to the conduct of a society. Just as railroads greatly impacted our nation's economic development during the second half of the nineteenth century and the automobile during the first half of the twentieth, the knowledge industry will be remembered as the focal point of economic development during the second half of the twentieth century. Key contributors in the knowledge industry will continue to drive the economy well into the twenty-first century. Land-grant and other institutions of higher education should strive to continue being at the center of this knowledge-generation and -dissemination process.

If land-grant colleges and universities are to effectively contribute to the advancement of learning and scientific inquiry and be more responsive to the ever-changing needs of society in the twenty-first century, it is important that faculty members and administrators evolve formal mechanisms which make self-examination, self-renewal, change, and innovation integral components of the creative academic life. Education is a continuous process of discovery, and land-grant institutions should maintain their substantial capacity for sustained adaptability.

The clear trend in research is toward more cooperative ventures. Scientists and engineers, often from several disciplines, join in preparing research proposals. Research specialization, expensive instruments, and the need for extensive computer facilities encourage such cooperation.

It is important to recognize that technical advances depend on basic research in science, mathematics, and engineering. Scientific advances are the wellspring of the technical innovations, the benefits of which are reflected by economic growth, improved health care, and many other areas. While the creation of new scientific knowledge does not guarantee the utility, diffusion, and implementation of that knowledge, the greater challenge—and the real payoff—is the conversion of promise into practice. It is not always possible to link specific scientific discoveries made in university laboratories with particular new products or processes. There are many stages and many people involved in the complex process of research and development, and each step is indispensable.

Society receives a hefty dividend from its investment in research. Why, then, is public support of academic research on the wane? Certainly one objective in securing wider recognition of and broader public support for scientific discovery is to increase public recognition of the essential value of science in a democracy. The first step in this process is to establish greater public trust, which in turn is associated with a reputation for devoting resources to resolving problems the public believes are important. Projects perceived as inconsequential or irrelevant arouse little or no public support.

Many of the social problems generally recognized as important may receive only modest academic research attention because they are not viewed as having considerable or immediate impact on the economy. But research in the social sciences may have many important uses, even though it may be difficult to assign a dollar value to it. In many cases it is essential to our understanding of ourselves and our society. Social-science research frequently fosters perspective and openness to change. It provides the data needed to monitor the performance of society and has numerous applications to practical decision making in both public and private affairs.

Extension/Outreach/Public Service Initiative

I have always believed that there need be no competition be-
tween the most scholarly academic program in the University
and those designed to help people earn a living or develop their
talents—so long as both serve the public interest.

JOHN A. HANNAH

8.1 Introduction

To be human, one must serve others.

ERNEST L. BOYER

From their inception, land-grant colleges and universities have evolved on the primary philosophical premise of service to the public. Farsighted statesmen recognized well over a century ago that the power of education must not be the privilege of a select few. Instead, our nation's destiny depends on bringing the benefits of education in its broadest sense to the entire citizenry.

Publicly supported universities have an obligation to do so. This is especially true among land-grant colleges and universities, institutions in which the extension, outreach, public service mission make them unique. Of course, all comprehensive universities provide instruction and conduct research, the other components of the tripartite mission of land-grant institutions.

This extension effort develops educational programming on important issues, addresses both their public and private dimensions, brings pertinent information to bear on problems and opportunities, and attempts to help everyone understand the nature of public debate in a pluralistic society. The overarching emphasis is on the application of learning to humanity's needs.

People appreciate the personal commitment to public service of intellectual leaders, the special kind of commitment that was demonstrated by the

135

brilliant author, physician, philosopher, medical missionary, and humanitarian Dr. Albert Schweitzer—recipient of the 1952 Nobel Peace Prize—in building his hospital at Lambarene, French Equatorial Africa (now Gabon).

> *In the middle of September, we got the first rains, and the cry is to bring all building timber under cover. As we have in the hospital hardly a man capable of work, I begin hauling beams and planks about myself. Suddenly I catch sight of a man in a white suit sitting by a patient whom he has come to visit. "Hello, friend," I called out. "Won't you lend a hand?" "I'm an intellectual and don't drag wood about," comes the answer. "You're lucky," I replied. "I too wanted to become an intellectual, but I didn't succeed."*
>
> **ALBERT SCHWEITZER**

Through teaching, research, and public-service programs, land-grant colleges and universities have contributed immensely to the overall growth, productivity, and efficiency of the U.S. economy. This greatly benefits all of society. Educated people contribute new ideas and ideals for the improvement of technology and organization applicable to business and industry, government, and nonprofit entities. Most ideas are not patentable, and they are quickly imitated, facilitating wide diffusion of their benefits.

8.2 Agricultural Extension

> *Each year, as every farmer knows, there is a rebirth on the farm. The first furrows plowed, the first pigs farrowed, the first wheat sprung. In this renewal lies a rich replenishment of the spirit. It is known only to the men and women who have dedicated themselves to the land.*
>
> **DONALD A. HOLT**

When the boll weevil from Mexico threatened to wipe out cotton crops in Texas during the 1890s, the U.S. Department of Agriculture sought the services of seventy-five-year-old Seaman A. Knapp—a former professor of agriculture and president of Iowa Agricultural College (now Iowa State University) who had broad experience as a farmer as well—to seek new ways to grow cotton. With federal, state, and private monies, Knapp employed field agents and set up farmer-operated demonstration farms. He noted, "What a man hears he may doubt, … what he sees he may possibly doubt, … but what he does himself, he cannot doubt."

The first county extension agent in the United States was W. C. Stallings, appointed to serve Smith County, Texas, in 1906. The number of county agent positions increased rapidly across the country during the next few years, giving sound credence to the value of extension service to farmers. Also in 1906, Knapp visited Tuskegee Institute, where he conferred with George Washington Carver about initiating a cooperative extension program for black farmers in the South. T. M. Campbell was hired at Tuskegee as the first extension agent employed in a cooperative extension program in the United States. Campbell also was the first black extension agent in the nation.

President Theodore Roosevelt expressed his concern and interest in 1908 when he appointed the Commission on Country Life chaired by Liberty Hyde Bailey, Dean of the College of Agriculture at Cornell University. The Commission's report strongly recommended adding "the third coordinating branch" to the established branches of teaching and research in land-grant colleges. This third branch, the commission stated, should comprise extension work "without which, no college of agriculture can adequately serve its State. It is to the extension department of these colleges, if properly conducted, that we must now look for the most effective rousing of the people of the land."

The successes that resulted from Knapp's leadership, coupled with the recommendation of the Commission on Country Life and experiences gained through early successful extension programs in DeKalb County, Illinois, and elsewhere, served as the basis for passage of the Smith-Lever Act—legislation introduced by Congressman Asbury F. Lever of South Carolina and Senator Hoke Smith of Georgia—by the U.S. Congress on July 1, 1914 (Chapter 1). This innovative means of extending agricultural knowledge and practices to those engaged in farming and ranching has played a central role in the highly productive food and fiber system of our nation.

In September 1993, this author was invited to participate in dedicating the new National Soybean Research Laboratory at the University of Illinois. Driving across central Illinois en route, another abundant crop of corn and soybeans lay as far in every direction as the eye could see. Following the ceremonies, the opportunity arose to discuss the 1993 harvest with a prominent livestock and grain farmer from west central Illinois. Yes, corn was yielding 160–175 bushels, soybeans 50–60 bushels per acre, he said. When asked what inputs the Illinois Cooperative Extension Service had made to the high yields, the farmer said,

> Many. Please let me cite a few. First, Extension people were directly involved in soil testing, terracing, and applying soil conservation practices on my farm. And I followed the recommendations of the area agronomy specialist as to application

of soil and plant nutrients, row width, and plant density per acre. The commercial hybrid seed company obtained its germ plasm from University of Illinois corn breeders. The grain drying, handling, and storage facilities reflected recommendations of agricultural engineering faculty members. The beef cattle and swine operations are just as dependent on the recommendations of university animal science Extension personnel. The feed formulations were made by animal nutritionists, the breeding program was based on recommendations of animal geneticists at the University of Illinois, the artificial insemination program reflected the latest advice of the reproductive physiologists there, and the ventilation and waste-handling systems were designed by the agricultural engineers. And the herd health program was outlined by the university's Extension veterinarian.

The farmer went on and on, noting further that the twenty-four-hour-a-day weather and market information, the farm records-keeping system, and the Extension short courses on applications of computers in managing the farm enterprise had been invaluable. And he mentioned the effectiveness of Extension's monitoring of herbicides and insecticides, the importance of his being able to readily obtain reliable, unbiased recommendations on the application of agricultural chemicals. He was especially appreciative of the concern Extension workers have demonstrated regarding environmental quality and other public concerns.

While all of the above, and more, College of Agriculture inputs were important to his farming enterprise, the farmer stressed even more the people aspects. The value to his family of Extension's 4-H and youth development programs; the undergraduate education of agribusiness leaders, Extension personnel, and others; and the array of Extension publications, newsletters, radio, and other communications initiatives designed to keep farmers well-informed on research findings, developments, and applications. Finally, he was most appreciative of the caring and service-oriented attitudes that characterize members of the land-grant family.

These reflections of an Illinois farmer about the critical role the Cooperative Extension Service has played in the success of his operation are much the same as those of farmers and ranchers throughout the United States. Technology provided by research and extension programs of land-grant colleges and universities has been invaluable in making America's agricultural enterprise the world's most productive and most efficient—truly the envy and the hope of a hungry world.

The sciences of agriculture are unlike most academic disciplines in that much of their classroom and laboratory is external to the institutional campus. The off-campus classroom and laboratory is tended largely through the land-grant university's Cooperative Extension Service, which serves the educational and demonstration needs of farmers, food processors, and those who provide goods and services to the agricultural and food industries.

In a matter of a few decades, agriculture has changed from being a labor-intensive enterprise to being capital-intensive. And now in the Information Age it is in the process of becoming knowledge-intensive. An important means of keeping farming enterprises economically viable is to assure their use of the best scientific information available. But these informational gold nuggets must be picked up and cashed in, and this is the responsibility of academic research and extension programs as well as farmer-stakeholders.

Throughout the twentieth century, land-grant colleges and universities have followed the philosophy espoused already in 1904 by Kenyon L. Butterfield, who said:

> Each land-grant institution should develop as rapidly as possible a definite tripartite organization that will reveal the college in its three-fold function—as an organ of research, as an educator of students, and as a distributor of information to those who cannot come to college. These are really coordinate functions and should be so recognized. The colleges should unify them into one comprehensive scheme. The principle of such unity is perfectly clear: We have in research, the quest for truth; in the education of students, the incarnation of truth; and in extension work, the democratization of truth.

The Cooperative Extension Service of land-grant colleges and universities has played a key role in the United States' worldwide reputation for agricultural efficiency. According to Sister Thomas Moore Bertels:

> Some ten years ago, a Dutch Bishop from Malaysia came to the United States to discover what it was that made American farmers and ranchers so successful in providing food in such abundance, of such high quality, and for so moderate a price. He wanted to bring back the secret to his people so that they could feed and support themselves. Someone suggested he visit farm organizations and "donated" my services. We spent two days visiting Co-ops, a Grange meeting, and so forth. At the end of the visit, I asked him if he had discovered the secret of America's ability to feed the world. He said, "Yes, I did, export your Extension."

8.3 Economic Returns on Public Investments in Extension

Let us develop the resources of our land, call forth its power, build up its institutions, promote all its great interests, and see whether we also in our day and generation may perform something worthy to be remembered.

DANIEL WEBSTER

Taxpayers deserve to know that their money is being prudently expended in society's best interests. Findings of studies conducted to determine economic returns from investments in agricultural research and extension consistently indicate an average annual rate of return in the 30 to 60 percent range. Specific cases—for example, hybrid corn—range to over 300 percent.

The rates of return on public investments made in research and in extension are similar. These investments complement each other, and reducing the research investment would hinder the extension investment. Both are required to capture the benefits of either.

Approximately half of the agricultural productivity gains enjoyed in this country—the world leader in efficient production of food and fiber—result from two factors: public investment in agricultural research and the educational level of farmers and ranchers.

8.4   Continuing Education

Instruction ends in the classroom, but education ends only with life.

F. W. ROBERTSON

Students who stop learning upon graduation from college will be uneducated soon thereafter. Continuing education is driven by the quickly outdated nature of industrial and professional knowledge. An aging population, single parenthood, and more women and others re-entering the workforce as well as the expansion of leisure activities will swell the ranks of continuing education enrollees. The success of Elderhostels—short-term, university-based educational programs designed for older citizens—demonstrates how institutions can adapt to changing needs. To effectively reach nontraditional students, colleges and universities need to restructure their modes of instructional delivery and related services (Chapter 4).

Successful institutions of higher education—often content to sort through admission applications in the past—will be reaching out to students who need education the most, including underrepresented ethnic and demographic groups. Among the fastest growing programs in higher education today are Institutes for Learning in Retirement (ILRs). Commonly organized on a membership basis and appealing mostly to people aged fifty and higher, they specialize in continuing education but also in members themselves providing some services, such as mentoring younger and international students as well as assisting in community projects.

8.5 The Importance of Recognizing and Rewarding Public Service

Quality public service is never an accident; it is always the result of high intention, sincere effort, intelligent direction and skillful execution; it represents the wise choice of many alternatives, the cumulative experience of many masters of craftsmanship. Excellence in public service also marks the search for an ideal after necessity has been satisfied and mere usefulness achieved.

WILLA A. FOSTER

Whether among the tea pickers of Kenya or the staff of land-grant universities and other institutions of higher education, people respond favorably to rewards. Kenyan tea industry workers are paid a basic salary plus a bonus. Similar incentives should be offered those engaged in outreach programs.

Members of university staffs engaged in public service activities often perceive that their peers and leaders do not value their work as highly as research and teaching. It is unfortunate if these perceptions are valid, because public service is closely associated with public support of land-grant universities, and this in turn directly affects all functions of the institution.

The university rewards system must be fairly based on merit. Unfortunately, administrators at some land-grant institutions place low priority on the missions of applied research and educational outreach. Some even find the "agricultural and mechanical arts" identity demeaning.

In the past, land-grant colleges and universities, among publicly supported institutions of higher education, have received above-average public support. This has resulted largely from the high-quality public service that has been rendered on a shared agenda. To plan and implement initiatives that will ensure a solid financial footing for land-grant colleges and universities as we prepare for even greater public service in the next century, it is crucial that all parties—those representing the public and the university alike—concur on the agenda.

The story is told of a Mexican bandit who robbed a bank in southern Texas and with the loot quickly escaped back across the border, being fully aware that a Texas Ranger was in peppery pursuit. The Ranger caught the bandit in a village just south of the border. But there was a problem. The Ranger could speak only English, the bandit only Spanish. So in time-honored fashion, the Ranger sought out the village elder, who could speak both languages, and deputized him to translate. The question went out: "Ask him what his name is." The answer came back: "He says Jose."

"Ask him if he robbed a bank in South Texas this morning."

"Yes, he robbed a bank today."

"Ask him where he hid the money."

"He refuses to answer."

With this development, the Ranger pulled his service weapon, put it to the bandit's head, and ordered the translator: "Try again."

At this point, the bandit—in very soft Spanish—said, "I hid it in the village well." But the translation came back: "He said he isn't afraid to die."

The poignant point is: It is essential that all parties involved share a common agenda, have common motives and values. Cooperative Extension programs have demonstrated that contributions of land-grant colleges and universities to society are based on a spirit of true collaboration.

8.6   Public Perceptions and Support of Outreach

The highest motive is the public good.

VIRGIL

The most important resource of any university is its faculty members—their professional abilities, their commitment to excellence. The most important off-campus resource of a public university is the public goodwill and trust that their investments in education and research are justifiable and relevant (Chapter 2).

Few institutions of higher learning will emerge unscathed from confronting the external environment, which is increasingly more hostile to colleges and universities. One dangerous possibility is that they have become less relevant to societal expectations because they have yet to accept the new demands that have been placed on them. If we fail in our effort to claim a higher level of credibility, it will unfavorably impact the very public we seek to serve. Achieving and maintaining credibility requires that institutional leaders understand constituents' values and hopes.

Land-grant colleges and universities should use public service opportunities to affirm the land-grant mission. They must focus on the needs of their clienteles, not merely on institutional agendas. As the expectations of society become increasingly diversified, each institution of higher education will search for its niche. Land-grant colleges and universities have the opportunity to expand their public mandate by responding to initiatives so as to secure their respective niches. A major challenge, however, is going to be satisfactorily resolving matters of increasing public expectations of service and decreasing public commitment to paying for that service. Reordering of institutional priorities must be accomplished and supported by institutional governing boards.

8.7   Challenges and Opportunities in Meeting Public Service Needs

Civilization is progress only if life improves because of it.
With all the progress of science, we cannot replace a species
once extinct. Men should never overlook the fact that the con-
struction of an airplane is simple when compared with the evolu-
tionary achievement of a bird. The challenge is clear; the final
answer will be given not by our amassment of knowledge, or by
the discoveries of our science, or by the speed of our aircraft, but
rather by the effect our civilized activities as a whole have upon
the quality of our planet's life—the life of plants and animals, as
well as that of men.

CHARLES A. LINDBERGH

It was apparently Heraclitus who first said, "There is nothing permanent except change." The primary role of land-grant colleges and universities always has been service to meet people's changing needs. The land-grant system was created in 1862 to answer the need for a more responsive educational system. This need is as valid today as it was then. Knowledge is as central to the betterment of society now as it was then. As a producer, wholesaler, and retailer of knowledge, land-grant universities must increase their commitment to public service.

In the practically minded United States, the concept of a university as a center for teaching, research, and public service was ushered in with the land-grant system. Now, well over a century later, the struggle with budgetary constraints comprises a serious challenge to land-grant institutions' ability to deliver on their promise. To retain their uniqueness in seeking public support, land-grant institutions must not let research and teaching interests crowd out proper consideration of the university's role as problem-solver, as unbiased expert for society at large.

Now the public is asking land-grant colleges and universities to help resolve nontraditional concerns, including:

Our children. Thousands of babies born each year have been damaged by their mothers' substance abuses. Many live in substandard housing, and only about a third of those eligible for Head Start are being served (Chapter 3).

Our public schools. Too many students are dropping out of school. Merely adding more requirements for high school graduation or admission to college will not solve the problem. We cannot ignore our schools' ills that are eroding the educational foundation of our nation. Ernest L. Boyer said it well: "The higher education family must become involved in K-12, if it is to enjoy the true eloquence of education."

Our cities. The national fabric's most serious strain lies in urban America. Violence, unemployment, poverty, poor housing, and pollution are neighbors with some of our most distinguished colleges and universities.

We need a twenty-first century land-grant vision to sustain us. We need common interests that transcend our differences. We must better communicate our common goals, build mutual trust among all involved, and then work together to achieve excellence in public service (Chapter 14). Cooperative Extension's involvement in specific local problems has earned the public's trust, respect, and support over the years. The Expanded Food and Nutrition Education Program (EFNEP) and Master Gardener Program that serve low-income urban families are examples of successful, well-received public service initiatives. Now it is time to revisit the successful ways and means of implementing the techniques that have worked before and employ them again.

8.8   Summary

Our troubled planet can no longer afford the luxury of pursuits confined to an ivory tower. Scholarship has to prove its worth, not on its own terms, but by service to the nation and the world.

OSCAR HANDLIN

Historically, the university has grown in concentric circles. It began with the philosophers in Greece and the first great library at Alexandria. It spread to the ancient professions, then to science. Thanks to our world-renowned land-grant college and university system, it has permeated agriculture and industry around the globe. Whereas education originally served the elite of society, it now serves all groups and classes, regardless of social, cultural, or economic background.

One of the greatest programs ever devised by the land-grant system was the Cooperative Extension Service. It was implemented at a time when the majority of the nation's people lived on farms and thus political support for it was broad and large. Today agriculture is still a major component of our economy, but with farmers decreasing in number its political clout has shrunk. The notion of combining the need for information-transfer technology with the needs of nonagricultural businesses could bring new importance to the land-grant university. If this were accomplished, land-grant institutions could expect taxpayers and legislators to be more supportive of their programs and services as we enter the twenty-first century.

While land-grant colleges and universities have a responsibility to reach out to the people and businesses around them, they also have a responsibility to look inward and to cultivate an attitude of sound citizenship among their own constituents—students, faculty, and staff. An effective way of communicating commitment to service is by incorporating more service-related topics—such as environmental, social, and global needs—into the curriculum.

The soothsayers of doom are pessimistic with regard to the future of outreach by academic institutions. But most leaders are in step with the attitude of Arthur D. Little, a pioneer in research on consulting. Little had substantial confidence in the human spirit. He refused to accept the notion of limits, and became restless when people said a project was impossible. *You cannot make a silk purse out of a sow's ear,* they would say. That phrase grated on Little so much that in 1921 he purchased ten pounds of gelatin from a Chicago meatpacker, complete with an affidavit stating that the gelatin had been made entirely from sows' ears. He took that gelatin to his laboratory where he spun it into thread barely distinguishable from silk. And from that thread, he fashioned an elegant purse. Thereafter, he displayed this purse over a plaque that read: *You **can** make a silk purse out of a sow's ear—and here it is!*

Of course, not everything is possible. But the "silk" purse story reminds us that there are untapped resources in this country and that those who act positively can and do achieve positive results. If those associated with land-grant outreach programs will determine the needs of the public and then respond with the necessary commitment to fulfilling them, increased public support surely will follow.

An idealist believes the short run does not count. A cynic believes the long run does not matter. A realist believes that what is done or left undone in the short run determines the long run.
SIDNEY J. HARRIS

International Initiative

*I have said over and over again in my work at the World Food Council that only **people** are important—this is as true in the poorest countries of the world as it is in the United States. Anything that a public or private university can do to provide opportunities for people at the bottom of society's ladder to help them climb a bit farther up is appropriate for the university to do.*

JOHN A. HANNAH

9.1 Introduction

I hold the unconquerable belief that science and peace will triumph over ignorance and war; that nations will come together not to destroy, but rather to construct; and that the future belongs to those who accomplish the most for humanity.

ADLAI E. STEVENSON

Nearly two and a half millennia ago, Socrates admonished his friends to think of themselves not as Athenians or Greeks but instead as citizens of the world. That counsel is as sound today as it was then, as we attempt to position the university to deal with the universe.

Our world is an increasingly interdependent place. In a world torn with revolution and terrorism, hunger and poverty, understanding among nations is essential to maintaining peace, providing adequate food, promoting economic growth, and improving health. Former U.S. Senator J. William Fulbright put it this way:

> Other countries are populated not by doctrines that we fear, but rather by individual people—people with the same capacity for pleasure and pain, for cruelty and kindness, as the people we were brought up with in our own country.

147

If ever there is to be a world at peace—safe for our children and our children's children—the United States must participate in facilitating it. While traveling in more than fifty countries, this author has observed that people everywhere wish to be treated with respect as human beings. It is incumbent upon prosperous developed nations such as ours to take the lead in creating a world in which people—of all religions, races, political views—can live healthy, safe, productive, meaningful lives.

One of the greatest challenges is assuring adequate production and distribution of food to the poorest people of the poorest countries. No human need is greater than the need to eat. Starving people are ungovernable. People do not peacefully accept chronic hunger. Lucius Annaeus Seneca, in a warning to the Roman Senate some 2000 years ago, said, "A hungry people listens not to reason nor are its demands turned aside by prayers."

Since starving, poor people are prominent in today's developing nations, finding ways to further lower the cost of food production offers the most realistic way to improve their quality of life. Some believe that because we enjoy an abundance of food in the United States, investing additional public money in the research and education that undergirds agricultural production is not in the public interest (Chapter 10). We should not, however, stand in the way of attempts to feed more people.

> *He who has too much bread has many problems; he who has no bread has only one problem.*
> **FIFTH CENTURY BYZANTINE PROVERB**

Globalization—the growing linkages of economic and political policies, trends, even modes of behavior and consumer habits—is transforming the modern world. There is increasing interest in problems associated with building more effective social, economic, and political systems in formerly totalitarian states and still socialistic developing nations. Political science, economics, and sociology have contributed much to our understanding of the character of democratic societies and free-market economies. A key challenge is to involve those engaged in these social sciences in international scholarship.

9.2   The World Population-Poverty-Food Equation

> *No individual has exclusive rights to the fruits of the earth;*
> *... all citizens have equal rights to the products of the earth upon*
> *paying a just indemnity to those who cultivate it.*
> **FRENCH ASSEMBLY** (1793)

Twenty years ago, those participating in the 1974 World Food Conference in Rome declared the following:

> All governments should accept the removal of the scourge of hunger and
> malnutrition, which at present afflicts many millions of human beings, as the ob-
> jective of the international community as a whole, and accept the goal that **within
> a decade** (author's emphasis) no child will go to bed hungry, that no family will
> fear for its next day's bread, and that no human being's future capacities will be
> stunted by malnutrition.

Unfortunately, these goals have not yet been realized. Now, **two decades
later,** an estimated 1 billion of the world's people live in poverty—without
enough jobs, without basic necessities, without much hope. Most reside in
rural areas of Asia and Africa. Each year, an estimated 3 million children die
from malnutrition.

In 1994, an estimated 5.6 billion people inhabited this earth. The current
rate of increase is approximately 1 billion per decade (more than 90 percent
of this increase comes in the developing nations). In some twenty countries,
average annual per capita income is below $300. Approximately 80 percent of
the world's people have annual per capita incomes of less than $750, one-fifth
the world average. The World Bank estimates that by the year 2030, there will
be approximately 3 billion more people to feed in the world than there are today. Approximately 2 billion of them will be living in developing countries—
nations where the average person lives on less than $2 a day.

Most of the additional population will live in cities and seacoast and
river-basin areas where the environment already is under stress. By the end of
the twentieth century, twenty-three cities in the world will each have more
than 10 million inhabitants, but only five of these—London, Los Angeles,
New York, Osaka, and Tokyo—are in the so-called developed nations. Without major breakthroughs in the genetic engineering of food crops, developing
nations also will need to build an environmentally unfriendly, fossil fuel-in-
tensive infrastructure. A major challenge to science and technology is to develop means of improving the standard of living in the developing parts of the
world without burdening the less-developed countries with the consequences
of environmental pollution.

Land-grant colleges and universities in the twenty-first century will be
able to participate by maintaining adequate public support while devoting
significant human resources to world development. We must remember that
only 200 years ago poverty was the status of most human beings in virtually
every country of the world, including the United States. Today, we find in
marked contrast to each other two sets of nations—the rich and the poor—
with a widening gap between. Technological revolution has had two profoundly different effects. In the rich countries it has progressively improved
human standards of living. But among the peoples of the poor nations its ef-

fect has been to expand human misery by enabling a rapid rise in human populations.

Our species, *Homo sapiens,* has lived on planet earth for perhaps a million years. Until recently, there was virtual balance between the rates of birth and death. Around 8000 B.C.—about the time food gathering shifted to food cultivation—there were an estimated 5 million people living on earth (and probably about the same number of lions). With the development of agricultural practices, though, there began a hefty upturn in population numbers. By the time of the birth of Christ, there were an estimated 300 million people on this earth. There were no marked technological changes affecting population numbers during the subsequent sixteen or seventeen centuries, so the number of humans on earth increased slowly until about 1650.

Then began the second major increase in world population, at a rate that approximated 0.5 percent annually from 1650 until about 1900, and nearly 1.0 percent annually from 1900 to 1950. As we approach the twenty-first century, the rate of population growth approximates 1.7 percent annually, and in the poor countries—the nations that can least afford it—increases of up to 3 percent are now commonplace! World population is projected to double in the next thirty-five years. Such rapid population increases cannot be sustained indefinitely. Realizing that population growth and the lag in economic and social development are interrelated in poor countries, and that each exacerbates the other, land-grant colleges and universities can help developing countries increase food supplies as well as in many other humanitarian ways.

Marked improvements in human diets and infant survival rates may help lower birth rates. In many poor countries—as demonstrated by surveys of attitudes, especially among rural people (who comprise most of these populations)—parents are willing to procreate many children just to ensure that some will survive to become adults. They know that more than a third of their offspring will not reach adulthood. Thus, this form of old-age security is perpetuated.

Preschool children comprise over 25 percent of the population of developing countries as compared with less than 10 percent in more technologically advanced nations. There, too, the frequency of child deaths due to disease is more than 300 times greater than that in Europe and North America. Of course, malnourished children are much more susceptible to disease. Moreover, prolonged food deprivation in infancy can cause irreversible cognitive, emotional, and neuromuscular retardation.

In addition to a lack of food and health care, there are insufficient schools and teachers to assure adequate access to education in many developing countries. This author has observed schoolchildren in Africa going to and coming from schools throughout the day, and learned that since there were inadequate school facilities and teachers, students attend school for only a short period each day. The public policy supporting this approach was based on the belief that it is better to provide a modest amount of education to the masses than to thoroughly educate a select few and leave the majority uneducated.

Political leadership and public policy influence the degree to which many developing countries are attempting to resolve the challenge of assuring adequate amounts of food. India—the world's most populated democracy—was fortunate when, in August 1947, Jawaharlal Nehru became the first Prime Minister and Minister of Foreign Affairs of the newly constituted Republic. Nehru was born into an aristocratic family in 1889. Like Mohandas Gandhi, he practiced law for a period before joining Gandhi in the struggle for India's independence.

Nehru worked hard to establish a democratic state and increase the people's living standards. He carefully studied the most pressing needs of his people and concluded that the greatest need of all was food. Beneath the portrait of Prime Minister Nehru in the administrative headquarters of the Indian Council of Agricultural Research in New Delhi is the following quotation from his inaugural address to a spirited but hungry people: "Most Things, Except Agriculture, Can Wait."

By participating in numerous nationalistic initiatives over many years—activities that frequently resulted in his being imprisoned by the British—Nehru had learned firsthand that his nation's top priority was to better utilize the natural resources of India to feed the people. He was painfully aware that his country had only 2.4 percent of the world's land mass, but more than 15 percent of the world's people to feed. To accelerate the process of increasing food production, Nehru and other leaders of India turned to the world's most successful food and agricultural enterprise—the agricultural and food system of the United States—for help. We responded by sharing the concept of the highly successful land-grant model of teaching, research, and extension which—working together in a free-enterprise system with farm organizations and commodity groups and other entities—had accomplished wonders in producing food and fiber during the first half of the twentieth century.

This nation's assistance was made available through the U.S. Agency for International Development (USAID). More than 300 staff members from U.S. land-grant universities accepted assignments in India, and more than 1000 Indian faculty members and graduate students studied in the United States. Federal funds were awarded to six land-grant universities that cooperated with the Republic of India in establishing nine Agricultural Education and Research Institutions throughout that nation. Eleven more were authorized by July 1973 when the last U.S. university advisors returned home. The organization, missions, and goals of these establishments closely paralleled the land-grant institutions of the United States. At the same time, the Rockefeller and Ford Foundations and other international organizations also provided assistance.

This included the support of Dr. Norman E. Borlaug, who received the 1970 Nobel Peace Prize for his monumental work with wheat that had contributed so much to the Green Revolution, an outgrowth of post–World War II efforts to alleviate hunger and improve human nutrition in developing countries. Moreover, the Green Revolution fueled significant improvement in other sectors of the economy, thereby enhancing economic development and alleviating poverty. Introduction of high-yielding, fertilizer-responsive varieties of wheat and rice paved the way for massive increases in cereal grain production. With these advances came new hope that hunger, malnutrition, and economic deprivation could be essentially eliminated in developing countries. Indeed, the manifold increase in the production of wheat, rice, and other food crops helped avert the mass starvation that had been predicted. The declaration of Mohandas Gandhi was partly realized: "Pure milk from healthy animals is a luxury of the rich, whereas it ought to be the common food of the poor."

9.3 International Development and Technical Assistance

We must share our knowledge and give people the skills they need to take charge of their futures. Developing human potential is the most important thing we can do.

ROBERT L. THOMPSON

Technical assistance and international development are essential tools in the task of building a more peaceful world. For affluent nations, providing assistance to developing countries has come to be recognized as a modern-day moral imperative. Fortunately, the basic principles of research, extension, teaching, and industrial partnering can readily be exported.

In his January 20, 1949, inaugural address, President Harry S Truman set the stage for expanding this nation's commitment to international development:

> More than half the people of the world are living in conditions approaching misery. Their food is inadequate. They are victims of disease. Their economic life is primitive and stagnant. Their poverty is a handicap and a threat both to them and to more prosperous areas.
>
> For the first time in history, humanity possesses the knowledge and the skill to relieve the suffering of these people. ... The material resources which we can afford to use for the assistance of other people are limited. But our imponderable resources in technical knowledge are constantly growing and are inexhaustible.

I believe we should make available to peace loving peoples the benefits of our store of technical knowledge in order to help them realize their aspirations for a better life. ... Our aim should be to help the free peoples of the world through their own efforts, to produce more food, more clothing, more materials for housing and more mechanical power to lighten their burdens. ... Such new economic developments must be devised and controlled to benefit the peoples of the areas in which they are established. What we envisage is a program of development based on the concepts of democratic fair dealing.

Greater production is the key to prosperity and peace. And the key to greater production is a wider and more vigorous application of modern scientific and technical knowledge.

President Truman's Point Four Program made the benefits of scientific advances and industrial progress available for the improvement of developing countries. Technical missionaries orchestrated irrigation and hydroelectric-power projects, programs to increase agricultural productivity, and disease-eradication campaigns in thirty-three nations during the early 1950s. We devoted substantial energy and financial support to help these countries flourish in freedom; technical development emerged as a vital component of foreign policy.

Characteristics of successful international development programs include: (1) continuity—a framework of continuous financial and physical support as well as technically qualified people is essential to a productive and successful program; (2) high-quality facilities and research; (3) an ongoing spirit of cooperation; (4) a package approach, including the inputs needed for successful proactive programs; and (5) development of all-important human resources—the education of scientists, teachers, and outreach personnel.

Since the early days of President Truman's Point Four Program, agriculture has been central in America's international assistance programs. Some question the wisdom of sharing agricultural technology with developing countries that represent prospective customers. But refusing to share agricultural know-how with developing countries is as thoughtlessly selfish as would be advocating the spread of pathogenic microbes with the hope that we could sell medicines. Further, the very poorest nations cannot afford to be our customers anyway.

9.4 International Institution-building and Educational Partnering

The benefits to land-grant universities from involvement
with international students and overseas assistance programs

have been important and numerous. Professors have received new and broadening experiences. American students have had the opportunity to live and work in other countries—to learn new cultures. International students, in turn, have expanded and enriched the outlook of the university itself, while making valuable contributions in research. Food crops and breeds of livestock developed during exchange and assistance projects have resulted in improved agriculture in the United States, as well. Mutual cooperation has resulted in mutual understanding.

KENNETH L. TURK

Land-grant colleges and universities have had a long, sound partnership with USAID. Institution-building is slow in most developing countries. Ways and means of making the changes in cultural patterns necessary for development without destroying important human traditions are not well-understood. We do not fully appreciate the impact of cultural background on one's willingness to change or even to accept change.

When we interpret other cultures, we may perceive that the habits and biases of others are odd, that their ideas and ways are less advanced than our own, that customs and beliefs are isolated elements, not parts of a pattern. We should instead appreciate that a new idea for those of any culture faces vigorous and often extreme challenge before it can replace an accepted cultural practice. This is especially so for persons who are barely clinging to the edge of life, to whom so much depends on time-tested fundamentals.

Land-grant institutions are now being asked to help resolve certain problems around the globe similar to those they have been so successful solving in the United States. If properly supported, these institutions can provide the human resources and technology needed to accomplish these tasks. But to do so, they will need to commit the professional expertise of the entire institution, not merely those of one department or college. Solving food and poverty problems requires an interdisciplinary approach.

If properly financed, land-grant universities can expand on-campus teaching programs for foreign nationals. They can assist with overseas institutional development. Their staffs can accept short-term assignments abroad. And programs along these three lines can be combined to provide experience at overseas locations for students interested in resolving global food-supply and related problems.

Since many of these challenges are complex, requiring a broad mix of professional expertise, consortium arrangements—where several institutions collaborate—can be effective. Consortia can make significant contributions through overseas research and educational centers of excellence, such as the International Wheat and Maize Improvement Center (CIMMYT) near Mexico

City and the International Rice Research Institute (IRRI) in the Philippines.

Land-grant universities have the proven ability to undertake such ambitious projects. Their contributions to the productivity and efficiency of American agriculture and the well-being of our people are legend. But distributing available food resources to the ever-expanding populations of the many developing countries will require dedicated efforts in disseminating agricultural and food technologies. The world does not have at hand all of the knowledge needed to resolve current challenges, but this knowledge can be generated through the team efforts of consortium-founded centers of excellence.

9.5 Globalization of Land-Grant Institutions

> *We welcome the privilege of ... training foreign students on our campus, and of studying and learning in institutions abroad. It is not a one-way street, for we profit greatly from our associations with peoples of other lands.*
>
> **CHARLES E. PALM**

We must vigorously pursue the globalization of land-grant and other institutions of higher education and thereby establish worldwide institutional cooperative programs that will enable our people to function more effectively and efficiently in the international community.

Internationalism is increasingly a priority for higher education. We must educate our students to be citizens of the planet. We must engender in them an appreciation for cultures that may differ markedly from our own. The experiences which will bring that result can be gained in a variety of ways. For example, U.S. engineers and their students are working with the people of Egypt on long-term developments for the Nile River; natural-resource professors and their students are helping Latin American countries develop their agriculture; business professors and their students are in Eastern Europe teaching emerging free nations there how to start credit unions. Each of these programs involves people helping people—people setting aside personal differences in order to achieve a common good.

The academic community has become more global in nature, and is sharing basic interests, values, and standards as well as fundamental curiosity about the nature of life and the universe. A shared quest for knowledge knows no limits. We learn from these experiences, and these lessons frequently prove beneficial to the citizens of our states and nation.

As land-grant institutions plan and prepare for the twenty-first century, they have the ever-expanding challenge of modernizing and strengthening the curriculum to better prepare students to fulfill societal demands on both domestic and international fronts. Education should be conducted in a global context.

Overall, the U.S. higher education system is recognized as the world's soundest. Our research is matchless in both quality and scope. Our institutional doors open to more people, over more of their lifetimes, than ever before anywhere. So each year they attract tens of thousands of students from other countries, and the number is increasing. For example, the number of Japanese students enrolled in U.S. institutions of higher education more than doubled between 1988 and 1992, to more than 40,000. By contrast, in 1992 only around 2000 Americans were studying in Japan. The total number of Americans studying for credit outside the United States is only about 71,000. This is in comparison with more than 420,000 international students at U.S. universities in 1994.

Each year international students bring—in addition to their rich cultural backgrounds, educational experiences, and friendships—more than $6 billion to the U.S. economy. Moreover, when people who have studied here return home, they commonly become professional colleagues and good customers of this nation's businesses. Many continue to conduct research cooperatively. In 1991, 11 percent of the world's scientific articles were internationally co-authored, double that of a decade earlier. Of the doctoral degrees awarded in the United States in 1991, students from abroad received more than 25 percent of those in the natural sciences, over 40 percent of those in mathematics and computer science, and more than 45 percent of those in engineering.

Newly industrialized countries have sharply increased their investment in science and engineering. One result: The 1991 combined number of natural science and engineering baccalaureate graduates of six Asian nations exceeded those of North America and Europe combined. Still, overall, the industrialized nations have nearly ten times as many scientists and engineers per capita, invest approximately twenty-four times as much money in research and development, and see their children spend about three times as long in school as the balance of the world.

9.6 The Competitive Global Marketplace

The development of an international outlook—being able to function well in and with different cultures and countries—is more essential than ever in this era of global competition.

DONALD PETERSON

International competition is a national issue. It must be approached from a national perspective. Science and technology will drive competitiveness in manufacturing.

Developing nations should be encouraged to concurrently develop agriculture and other industries. Unfortunately, some have been pushing industrialization but neglecting agriculture. Rapid industrialization often is associated with rapid urban expansion and rising urban incomes. People in these countries spend a major portion of any extra income on food. Thus, a policy of pushing industrialization while neglecting agriculture—particularly in the face of a rapid population increase—is dangerous; foreign exchange is unavailable to pay for growing food imports.

Some question the wisdom of sharing our technology with developing countries because it might reduce demand for American products. In the short run, this might well occur in the case of certain commodities and products. But in the long run this nation would benefit from exchanging our top products for those of other nations. One area in which the United States enjoys clear competitive advantage is food production. Factors constraining our competitors in agriculture include the facts that:

• Asia—the area where the demand for improved diets is growing fastest—has approximately ten times more people per acre of cropland than does North America.

• Australia, Canada, Eastern Europe, South Africa, Thailand, and the former USSR have more climatic constraints on agricultural expansion than does the United States.

• Prime areas for food production in Ukraine and Russia remain under marginal management and lack certain aspects of infrastructure.

• Countries such as Argentina, Brazil, and Turkey have sizable amounts of arable land but lack infrastructure, which—although crucial—is expensive to develop.

• The nations of the European Union, Eastern Europe, Korea, and Japan would experience a serious decrease in agricultural production if their governments were to cease subsidizing their producers at the rate of two to ten times world-market prices and to continue using expensive inputs.

• We should note that each country, including the United States, should produce crops for which it enjoys a comparative advantage. This will lead to increased trade among nations. It also will result in greater production efficiency. For example, you cannot produce bananas in Russia, but wheat can be efficiently produced there.

Global trends are toward greater emphasis on free-market economies. International markets for agricultural commodities ultimately will be won by the most efficient producers. The greatest losers in a market environment of tariff and other trade barriers are the low-cost producers—those who, in a free market, would be able to take advantage of open competition.

The Asia-Pacific region is home to approximately 60 percent of the world's population, and its economies are growing faster than any other. No such large group of people has ever gained so much affluence so quickly as Asia is doing today. Encouraged by the free-trade rules of the General Agreement on Tariffs and Trade (GATT), capitalists are investing billions of dollars in Asian factories that make shoes, clothing, electronic equipment, and many other labor-intensive products.

To Napoleon Bonaparte, China was a sleeping giant that should be left to slumber lest it wake and **move the world.** In the next century, capitalists and industrialists hold the key to the wisdom of the French emperor's foreboding. China is already awake and sitting on the edge of its capitalistic bed, yawning, stretching its muscles, peering through the window at the promise of a beautiful economic sunrise heralding a new day for its 1.2 billion people.

In 1992, the city of Shanghai approved 2012 foreign-capitalized projects, absorbing contracted international capital of some $3.6 billion, more than that over the previous twelve years combined. The next year, Shanghai granted approval to another 3650 projects, garnering an additional international investment of more than $7 billion. Also in 1993, capitalists from forty countries signed contracts worth more than $100 billion to build new factories and open new markets across China.

As a result, per-capita gross national product (GNP) in China increased by nearly 8 percent annually in the 1980s and early 1990s. India's GNP has been growing by more than 3 percent, Indonesia's by nearly 6 percent annually. China, India, and Indonesia have three of the four largest populations in the world. Moreover, the GNP of Malaysia is increasing by 6 to 7 percent annually, and that of Thailand by 5 to 6 percent.

This per-capita income growth is rapidly translating into a powerful demand for improved diets. The Chinese demand for meat has increased by roughly 10 percent annually in recent years—more than 8 million tons of additional meat consumption per year. India's consumption of milk is increasing by about 2 million tons annually.

As countries such as China and India—the world's two most populous nations—develop their off-farm earning power, it will make sound economic sense—and good environmental policy—for them to acquire a significant portion of their upgraded diets through imports of farm products from countries, such as the United States, that are efficient producers of food and other agricultural products. Asians now consume approximately 12 grams of animal protein per capita daily. Comparable figures for the United States and Japan are 71 and 55, respectively.

Future studies of various regions of the world will focus more on the culture, history, and language of a region, for these are the factors that shape a region's responses to global changes, including the evolution of market-based economies.

9.7   An International Commitment

If we are to be truly successful in promulgating and defending the democratic principles we hold so dear, we must strive to make men free from hunger, as well as free from political intimidation.

The United States cannot become the granary of the world. If the specter of famine is to be banished from the globe, the underdeveloped countries themselves must greatly expand their food production. To do this they need our help. If our pledges of assistance are to be kept and our continued domestic agricultural productivity assured, we must act now to provide training necessary to ensure an adequate supply of agricultural specialists in the demanding years ahead.

GEORGE MCGOVERN

We must stop living in a world of starving people. Not doing so would be neither moral nor pragmatic. An empty stomach is deaf to conscience, and as recorded centuries ago in the following Old Chinese proverb, revolutions are the companions of poverty and starvation: **When the price of rice goes higher than a common person can pay, Heaven ordains a new ruler.**

Since the United States is incapable of feeding the world, we should expand our efforts to assist food-deficient nations in developing the capacity to increase their production, processing, and distribution of food. Indeed, it is incumbent upon this nation to significantly contribute in this way to the advancement of world civilization.

In international affairs, the year 1989 was historic. It saw the final withdrawal of Soviet troops from Afghanistan, an unparalleled retreat by the Soviet empire. The remarkable spectacle of the Tianamen Square revolt in China, with television cameras showing the world a brave dissident facing down a tank. Totalitarian regimes falling like dominoes in Eastern Europe.

And those of us whose lives had been affected for decades by the Cold War could not have predicted the free fall of the Berlin Wall in September that year. But we recognized this event as symbolic of the end of an era. A new era began shortly thereafter when communism in the former Soviet Union was replaced by embryonic democracy.

Also in 1989 we learned anew that technology is a liberating force. Totalitarian powers could not keep up with or stop the computer, the telefacsimile machine, or the television. These powers unraveled in the face of powerful, instant communications.

It is knowledge that has the power to equalize nations—weak and strong, poor and rich, unfortunate and fortunate. The United States is a strong, rich, fortunate nation. In the ethical spirit of peace with fellow human beings all over the world, we should share our knowledge and our technology.

9.8   Summary

The most grave health problem of the world remains hunger and malnutrition. We have long recognized that an insufficient food supply is a leading contributor to human misery and political instability. More recently, we have begun to recognize that it is also a major deterrent to economic and social development.

JOHN F. KENNEDY

Recent events of historical note indicative of the flowering of freedom in Eastern Europe and the former Soviet Union were envisioned more than forty-five years ago by President Harry S Truman who, in his January 20, 1949, inaugural address said:

> In due time, as our stability becomes manifest, as more and more nations come to know the benefits of democracy and to participate in growing abundance, I believe that those countries which now oppose us will abandon their delusions and join with the free nations of the world in a just settlement of international differences.

The increasingly well-accepted interdependence of the world's people and economies mandates that land-grant colleges and universities embrace a renewed commitment to an expanded international perspective throughout their teaching, research, and public-service functions. These institutions already have played important roles in international development during the past half century. They have contributed immensely to the education of the sons and daughters of developing countries. The knowledge transferred to these young people subsequently has been applied to improve living conditions in the respective countries. Importantly, as well, these students have acquired an understanding of American culture and values which will remain with them for the rest of their lives.

Land-grant universities also have performed scientific analyses of the problems of developing countries. In many cases, this has been done in partnership with institutions of higher education in those countries. Our land-grant schools also are important sources of greatly needed expertise in agricultural production, health care, family planning, and other facets on which developing nations are striving to improve. Moreover, these institutions have greatly assisted in building and strengthening institutions of higher education in developing countries, especially in cooperation with USAID.

Through personal involvement in international projects and programs, faculty members and students discover firsthand that what happens in faraway places is important at home as well. Members of the land-grant network are co-workers with people around the world and contribute immeasurably to improved foreign relations through international studies and foreign-language programs, the exchange of faculty and students, and worldwide research programs aimed at applying science and technology to combat hunger, disease, and poverty. Land-grant institutions also provide educational opportunities to foreign nationals—individuals who have distinguished themselves following graduation in fields spanning government and diplomacy, business and agriculture, science and education, among other disciplines.

Few if any developing nations can solve their problems by themselves. They need the technical assistance exemplified by people of the land-grant colleges and universities who spend years conducting research in collaboration with American students as well as students from developing nations. It is folly for developed countries like the United States to be accomplices to keeping developing nations in poverty by excluding them from our markets and denying them the benefits of technology and technical assistance and then providing billions of dollars worth of financial aid in attempts to palliate the consequences. We must assist these nations as they go about developing their economies, so they can shift from receiving aid to engaging in trade.

In the twenty-first century, domestic and international policy will be inextricably bound. It should be our policy to assist developing countries to become more self-sufficient. This can be accomplished by exporting our experiences with the world-renowned land-grant college and university system, as was embraced by Nehru's India nearly a half century ago. While it still has many problems, India has made great strides in solving its greatest challenge—it has improved the diet of its hungry but determined people.

Lack of adequate food remains the major problem in many developing countries. The two most basic ingredients required for agricultural development in poor countries are knowledge and capital. The primary characteristic of modern market-oriented agriculture, in contrast to subsistence agriculture, is that it is a highly technical business—one based on scientific knowledge. This is where land-grant institutions can make a major twenty-first century impact: contributing to the further development of underdeveloped countries. As for capital, this challenge is secondary to the lack of knowledge, and when ready with respect to knowledge, developing nations can count on the World Bank and other organizations as important partners.

The humanitarian dimension of international development remains strong in the hearts of many people, including many who are the fortunate holders of citizenship in a prosperous developed nation. For the good of the human race, it is important that the admonition of Albert Schweitzer be embraced and implemented:

> Whatever you have received more of than others—in health, in talents, in ability, in success, in a pleasant childhood, in harmonious conditions of home life—all this you must not take to yourself as a matter of course. In gratitude for your good fortune, you must render in return some sacrifice of your own life for another life.

Agricultural and Food Sciences Initiative

I know of no pursuit in which more real and important services can be rendered to any country than by improving its agriculture.

GEORGE WASHINGTON (July 20, 1794)

10.1 Introduction

And he gave it for his opinion that whoever could make two ears of corn, or two blades of grass to grow upon a spot of ground where only one grew before, would deserve the better of mankind, and do more essential service to his country, than the whole race of politicians put together.

JONATHAN SWIFT, *Gulliver's Travels*

Lest we in the United States forget in these times of plenty and obesity: agriculture—and the values inherent in our nation's agrarian tradition—holds a respected place in American history. Thomas Jefferson, one of the most enlightened of our founding fathers, viewed rural life as the origin of true citizens—independent, resourceful individuals who seem to cherish hard work, whose lives are guided by reason and common sense, who respect God, country, and the inherent dignity of all humans. Indeed, rural people embodied the democratic virtues Jefferson extolled so fondly and so eloquently.

Cultivators of the earth are the most valuable citizens, the most independent, the most virtuous and tied to their country by the most lasting bonds.

THOMAS JEFFERSON

163

Two centuries ago this nation's soil, water, and climate comprised a virtually unexploited asset, seemingly awaiting development. Agriculture was the primary source of our nation's early growth. It fed the tremendous industrial expansion that accompanied late nineteenth and early twentieth century immigration.

Still the real wealth of any nation lies not in its material resources but rather in its people. The principal agricultural assets of a nation, then, are people and land. The quality of both proved to be superb in the United States, and our nation continues to be the world's land of opportunity in agriculture as on other fronts. It is strengthened by a rich heritage of determined immigrants, our inherent desire for competitiveness with fairness, and incentives of the free-enterprise system. There have been and will be minor setbacks from time to time. But members of the agricultural and food family have the ingenuity and spirit to overcome them so long as they maintain their vision. The agricultural community's commitment to the future will largely determine the future of this nation's food enterprise. Fortunately, history is replete with the courageous actions of Americans who dared to tackle tough challenges.

Farmers and ranchers and their advocates hold the view that the economic health of the business and industry sectors is closely linked with that of the agricultural enterprise. In other words, agriculture and business are interdependent. To move toward a more healthy overall economy, there needs to be greater public recognition of this crucial state. Each sector of society must come to better appreciate the needs and views of all others, and this must be an objective shared by all.

Among the most striking reasons for the remarkable success of American agriculture has been the working partnership among private citizens, business and industry, government, and the land-grant college and university system. Science and technology have been the driving forces in this nation's impressive strides in agricultural productivity.

The history of land-grant institutions is replete with examples of people in agriculturally related disciplines focusing on clientele needs. They have demonstrated to other programs in the university how research and public service are interrelated, how they can improve the quality of human life.

From the mid-nineteenth century through the mid-twentieth century, land-grant colleges and universities pioneered the models that ultimately shaped the whole of higher education. Agricultural experiment stations served as the model for public encouragement of scientific research. The Cooperative Extension Service served as the prototype for applying research findings to relevant practical problems. The university became a catalyst for public service, an unrivaled engine for change.

As agriculture enters the twenty-first century, additional change is inevitable. New products will potentiate quantum leaps in productivity, and this will be reflected in the consumer's food bill as a portion of family income continuing to shrink. At the same time, the quality of our food will increase and the structure of agriculture will continue to change as there will be fewer but larger farms and ranches.

10.2 Agriculture and Its Mission Defined

The real question for today is whether American agriculture can fulfill its potential as one of America's premier growth industries in a world about to triple its demand on farming resources.

DENNIS T. AVERY

Agriculture employs and exploits biological processes to produce food, fiber, and other useful products. It involves application of scientific and technical knowledge.

As Abraham Maslow recognized in his hierarchy, food ranks among the most fundamental needs of human beings. It is easy to take a continuously adequate food supply for granted. But anxieties about where the next meal is coming from are as old as history. Famines are described in the twelfth chapter of the Book of Genesis, when Abraham went down to Egypt "and there was a famine in the land." In 1125, famine reduced the population of Germany by half. The people of Hungary experienced serious famine in 1505. England suffered a terrible famine in 1586, and between 1870 and 1872 Persia lost a fourth of its population to starvation. Some 10 million Chinese died of starvation as recently as 1877–1878. Famines in India claimed some 3 million lives in 1769–1770, 1.5 million in 1865–1866, and 0.5 million in 1877. In 1891–1892 a Russian famine brought severe hardship to an estimated 27 million people. Of all ills afflicting humans, none is more solvable—yet seemingly less tractable—than hunger. The fear of famine still looms large and regularly among people in many parts of the world. And indeed it is not outside real possibility that devastating famine could strike the whole world with little warning.

The availability of certain crops affects the size of populations in the long run by averting famine in the short run. A classic example: the white potato in Ireland. The impact of the white potato was sensational. Late in the seventeenth century, Ireland had a population of nearly 2 million, most living in hunger. Then the white potato was introduced from the New World. The Irish soil and climate were ideal for its production. The white potato yielded more food per Irish acre than had ever before been produced. In half a century, the population of Ireland had increased from 2 million to 8 million persons, largely because of the potato-increased food supply. The Irish depended on the white potato. Then came the potato crop failure, resulting in a great famine, and more than 2 million Irish literally starved to death. Another 2 million emigrated. Since then, the population of Ireland has been stable at approximately 4 million, and the white potato remains an important food crop there to this day.

One of the great historical events in Europe during the twentieth century was the Russian Revolution of 1917. On its banner was inscribed "Bread and Peace." The two words are related and always have been. Even today, hunger and malnutrition claim the lives of far more people than do wars. Yet we invest thousands of times more federal monies in national and allied defense than in food production and processing.

Again, feeding the world's people better must be a shared responsibility. And land-grant colleges and universities have or can have the technologies to be applied to feeding the world. The rationale for participating in this humanitarian cause was appropriately summarized in the following words of David Rockefeller:

> We cannot live in a world divided between, on one hand, two-thirds who do not eat properly and, knowing the causes of their hunger, revolt, and, on the other, one-third who eat well—sometimes too much—but who can sleep no longer for fear of revolt on the part of the two-thirds who do not have enough to eat.

An important challenge to land-grant colleges and universities is to redefine their mission so it relates more clearly to improving the quality of life in contemporary United States of America as well as in other countries. Many thoughtful proponents of change call for greater focus on programs that address the full human food and fiber system, including health care and safety, energy use and efficiency, and environmental qualities and considerations.

10.3   Food and Agricultural Sciences Research

The primary aim of research must not just be more facts and more facts, but rather more facts of strategic value.

PAUL WEISS

Excellent research provides the basic building blocks for excellent teaching and outreach. Improvements in the efficiency of producing food and fiber attributed to land-grant colleges and universities have been well documented. The people of the United States—and indeed the world—have greatly benefited from an abundant supply of safe, nutritious food.

Most farms, many agricultural businesses, consumers, and others who benefit directly and indirectly from publicly financed research conducted at land-grant colleges and universities do not have the human and financial resources needed to support their own research endeavors. They depend on the land-grant system of Agricultural Experiment Stations.

The Connecticut Agricultural Experiment Station was founded in 1875 as the first in the United States. Then in 1887, Congress enacted the Hatch Act, which provided federal funds to establish an Agricultural Experiment Station at each land-grant college. Its mandate was clear:

> To aid in acquiring and diffusing among the people of the United States useful and practical information on subjects connected with agriculture, and to promote scientific investigation and experiment respecting the principles and applications of agricultural science.

America's bountiful harvests have in large measure been a legacy of the Hatch Act's nurturing of scientific agriculture. If the United States is to be competitive in the global marketplace, the search for new technologies must continue. Moreover, twenty-first century agriculture will not limit itself to food. It will increasingly grow feedstocks for fuels and new materials.

Alas, a gap does exist in the system, and it must be closed. It has to do with information transfer, and is electronic in nature. It is a gap between the slow and speedy adopters of new information. There is reason to conclude that, while early adopters capture monetary returns associated with new technologies, ultimately it is consumers who are the primary beneficiaries of public investment in agricultural research. Over the years, farm profits have been derived from reducing per-unit costs of production by employing output-expanded technologies. This has resulted in the long but dramatic downturn in the number of farms in the United States over the past century. With the industrialization of agriculture, the population living on farms as a percentage of the total population declined from 53 percent in 1820 to less than two percent in 1994. However, the *rural* population has remained in the 20 to 25 percent range of the total population. People enjoy living in rural America.

> *There is a certain privacy and mystique that mounts to a glory when one stands and beholds his field stretching away to the edge of the woods or to the creek or onto the brow of a hill. One is also conscious of the birds and creatures who make their homes here. They are part of the tenancy—living off the kingdom that is your land.*
>
> **CLARENCE MITCHELL,** *River Hill Soliloquy*

Once heralded as human conquest of Nature, research and the resultant technologies are now under scrutiny by numerous severe critics of agriculture. Noting surpluses of certain agricultural commodities, many critics advocate declaring a moratorium on production-related agricultural research. But to stop conducting research aimed at greater efficiency in producing agricultural products would be as foolish as accepting the rationale that we should abandon health-related research and technologies because the fruits of modern medicine already enable people to enjoy healthier lives and live longer than ever before. We are a graying society. In 1900 only 3 percent of the U.S. population was sixty-five years of age or older, whereas in 1980, 12 percent was and by 2000 the number is expected to be around 20 percent. But it would be fatuous to slow, let alone stop, the conduct of health-related research. In neither agriculture and medicine nor the general scientific community will ploys to protect the status quo by restricting research prove useful or productive in the expenditure of intellectual and financial efforts.

Most agricultural research and outreach in the past has focused on increasing productive yields and efficiency of production. The consequent cost savings have quickly been passed on to consumers, so it is proper that the public pay for these programs. In 1994, agriculture received only 2 percent of all federal research and development dollars, and only 4 percent of that spent on basic research. Now research is needed to learn **how plants grow** not merely **how to grow plants**.

Much of the basis for Americans' extremely high standard of living derives from the low price of food in the United States. The importance of inexpensive food to the overall national economy and personal affluence was noted in the 1976 U.S. Department of Agriculture publication "The Secret of Affluence":

> Man's economic activity starts with food. You need food every day; ... with the money and time you have left after obtaining your food, you can do other things. It is these other things that ordinarily measure wealth and affluence. So the easier you get your food, with the least amount of time and income, the more wealth and affluence you have.

The continuing debate on the proper disposition of intellectual property and patentable technologies derived from publicly funded research is nothing new. In 1924, Professor Harry Steenbock of The University of Wisconsin published research results showing that vitamin D could be activated by irradiating food with ultraviolet radiation. His discovery led to vitamin D-enriched milk and the eradication of rickets as a childhood disease.

It also helped launch one of the nation's most successful university-affiliated research foundations. Spurred by the desire that his university share in the economic benefits of his work, Steenbock offered his patents to The University of Wisconsin. But the Board of Regents turned down his offer, saying the university could not "be expected to allot money for a patent application when it is not certain that it will receive something for such an expenditure." Moreover, the Wisconsin attorney general ruled that the university did not have the legal capacity to defend a patent, so the patent would have no monetary value. There also were questions about the propriety of a university controlling something that had been invented through the use of public money.

Alumni of The University of Wisconsin, bothered by the prospect of losing potential income and upset further by a restriction on private gifts by the Regents, established the Wisconsin Alumni Research Foundation (WARF) in 1925. The WARF was created specifically to receive gifts to the university, and the Steenbock patents were its first assets. Ultimately, the patents returned millions of dollars to WARF, which apparently was the first autonomous organization of its kind. Over the decades, WARF has supported important research studies and other projects at Wisconsin, including construction of the Steenbock Library. In 1993 alone, WARF received $15.8 million in patent royalties and licensing fees.

Similar questions have arisen about the propriety of agricultural researchers receiving funding from for-profit firms. Should a researcher—whose salary is derived primarily from public monies—perform research that results in pecuniary gains by a firm providing research support? Or serve as part-time consultants to private businesses? It is in agriculture, home economics, forestry, and veterinary medicine—typical units of Agricultural Experiment Stations, often collaborating with scientists of the U.S. Department of Agriculture's Agricultural Research Service stationed on land-grant campuses—that much of the pioneering research in the agricultural and food sciences is conducted. Most scientific breakthroughs result from collective efforts of several researchers, often over many years.

Let us consider an example. Hybrid seed revolutionized the production of corn as a nutritious food and feed, and at the same time dramatically impacted the breeding of other cereal grains. But it did not happen overnight. The development of hybrid seed corn came in the early 1900s through the collective efforts of many scientists at several Agricultural Experiment Stations. The first hybrid seed is believed to have been produced about 1865 by an Austrian botanist, but not until the twentieth century were its benefits confirmed and farmers persuaded to use it.

Mexico City's magnificent Museum of Anthropology displays corn recovered over several centuries, primarily from old ruins and tombs. One ear dating back several thousand years is barely two inches long and has tiny kernels. Others become progressively larger over time, presumably in response to improved agricultural methods. Observing this display reminds one of the importance of maintaining comprehensive corn, soybean, and other crop germplasm repositories—seed collections which serve as important resources for plant breeders. They contain the genetic materials that control the amounts of amino acids, sugars and starches, fats and oils, and vitamins and minerals in the plants, as well as resistance to disease, drought, herbicides, salt, and other important economic characteristics, not to mention the efficiency with which nutrients, soil moisture, and sunlight are used in the photosynthetic process.

Of course, food and agricultural research findings are of little use until they are made available to users. This is where the teaching and outreach functions come to bear. They complement food and agricultural sciences research, making it a sound public investment.

10.4   Agricultural Efficiency and Exports

Far more than most people realize, the United States owes its eminence in world markets not to its industry, but rather to its incomparably efficient agriculture.

JOHN KENNETH GALBRAITH

In the early history of U.S. agriculture, the draft for plowing was furnished by oxen. Horses were used mostly for riding and as pack animals. Later, lightweight wagons were designed for horses. But the buggy did not appear until about 1840. Important early agricultural inventions that enhanced the trend toward increased efficiency of producing food include the cotton gin in 1793, mowing machine and mechanical reaper in 1831, and steel plow in 1837 (Chapter 1).

Since World War II, U.S. agriculture has increased productivity by over 100 percent in feed grains, by more than 500 percent in food grains, and by more than 100 percent in meat. Annual milk production per cow increased from 5842 pounds in 1955 to 15,554 pounds in 1994, a 166 percent increase.

Nobel Laureate T. W. Schultz has noted that the annual rates of return to public investments in agricultural research have ranged from 30 to 170 percent. These are based on estimates of investment (cost of all nonprofit agricultural research) and estimates of return each year (value of agricultural inputs saved by advances in the agricultural sciences—i.e., cost reductions).

As for quality of life during the past century, the percentage of our workforce employed in food and fiber production, processing, and distribution has decreased by more than half to only about 15 percent. And the percentage of the national population directly engaged in farming has decreased from more than 40 percent to less than 2 percent. Now U.S. consumers spend only about 11 percent of their disposable income for food—by far the world's lowest food bill.

A major challenge facing the agricultural and food enterprise of the United States is to find ways and means of increasing food production while decreasing the demand on oil and gas. New fuel-saving and -producing technologies are needed.

The horrible floods in the Midwest and drought in the South in 1993 notwithstanding, U.S. agriculture exported about $43 billion worth of goods and achieved a trade surplus of more than $19 billion that year. We are by far the world's leading exporter of agricultural products. Fortunately, much of the rest of the world is becoming more affluent, and many of these nations are upgrading their human diets. This will continue to provide a great opportunity for our agricultural enterprise. History has shown that as people move up the income scale, they increase their consumption of high-protein or otherwise highly nutritious foods such as milk and milk products, meats, fruits, and vegetables.

Dennis T. Avery estimates that, if current trends of increased incomes and improved human diets continue in Asia, consumption of meats and other products of animal origin could increase by as much as 500 percent over the next twenty years. And the world's grain farms will need to produce an additional 200 million tons of grain annually to support the anticipated increase in demand in Asia alone. Consumption of milk, cheeses, fruits, and processed foods is expected to grow commensurately. Consumption of pork has increased recently by some 3 million tons annually among China's 1.2 billion people. Milk consumption has increased by 2.0 million tons annually among India's 830 million people. Latin American markets also are growing as income levels increase there. Mexico, with a population of approximately 90 million, is already the world's largest market for nonfat dry milk.

Between 1982 and 1992, world consumption of grain and oil seeds increased by more than 400 million tons, and this growth is expected to accelerate. Worldwide consumption of meat—a high-value product with which the United States can successfully compete—is growing at about 6 percent per year. If these trends continue, they will for the United States add as much as 20 million tons of agricultural commodity exports annually, increase food prices in world markets, and add billions of dollars of added value in processed farm product exports.

Population growth, once considered to be insurmountably inevitable, is now viewed by many as an opportunity for the agricultural enterprise of the United States to increase food and other agricultural exports. Export-based jobs in this country are growing faster than average and pay 17 percent more than the national average in wages.

Around 100 million people are being added to the world's population annually—approximately equivalent to a new Bangladesh each year. Before worldwide Zero Population Growth is achieved (projected around the year

2040), Asia is expected to be approximately nine times more densely populated than North America. We can expect the increasingly more affluent Asian nations to import significant portions of a higher-quality diet from nations, such as the United States, that have more open land. An Asia self-sufficient in food would be virtually bereft of wildlife habitat. Indonesia, for example, is clearing tropical forests to grow soybeans for broiler chickens—a food product other nations could supply more efficiently.

10.5 Agricultural Biotechnology

What sets biotechnology apart from other innovations is the unparalleled speed and magnitude of the expected productivity gains.

ROBERT KALTER

Biotechnology offers shortcuts in plant and animal breeding, since identifiable genes comprise the central component. Once those genes are identified that determine resistance to diseases, pests, cold, heat, drought, salty soils, and herbicides as well as increase photosynthetic efficiency in plants and parallel traits in animals, the tools of biotechnology make a cut-and-paste approach to breeding possible. For example, if a crop is threatened by weeds, the sensible thing to splice-in genetically is not the ability to repel weeds but rather the genetic resistance to herbicides that kills weeds, thereby enabling farmers to spray as needed.

Applications of biotechnology are not new. Babylonians and Sumerians were exploiting yeast in making alcoholic products 6000 years B.C. But today its potential holds great promise to make profound contributions to humanity because of sophisticated research techniques as well as a wealth of basic knowledge. The number of innovations involving biotechnology has been startling in recent years: transgenic manipulations of plant and animal species; superovulation; use of bovine and porcine growth hormones and beta-agonist compounds in animal production; development of environmentally safe biopesticides; and use of genetically engineered microorganisms in the production of foods, medicines, and industrial chemicals. The new techniques make possible the producing of vaccines for livestock in huge quantities for pennies. They also promise to lower the costs of seeds, feeds, pesticides, and other agricultural inputs.

Tools of biotechnology may be used to increase photosynthetic efficiency, decrease the length of the growing season, and dramatically increase crop production. Aside from procreation, photosynthesis is the most important phenomenon in the living world. Without it there would be no nutrients from plants for use by people or the animals that provide foods and other products and services for humanity. Researchers at the University of Illinois recently learned that the photosynthetic efficiency of wild wheat is double that of commercial wheat, holding promise for genetic improvement in wheat production by using modern biotechnology to synthetically equip commercial seed wheat varieties with the genetic complex responsible for the remarkable growth potential of wild varieties.

While technological advances may be blamed for overproduction of some agricultural commodities, they still represent the best assurance of a competitive agricultural advantage for the United States in the global marketplace. The lessons of history are clear. For a nation's agriculture to provide a viable economic base there must be a reliable flow of new technology that increases the efficiency of the agricultural enterprise.

The National Agricultural Biotechnological Council (NABC) was formed to examine the implications of agricultural biotechnology and to develop policy options for local, state, and federal officials. The Joyce Foundation established a think tank to implement the NABC's goals and funded postdoctoral fellows in such social sciences and humanities disciplines as economics, political science, public and business administration, philosophy, law, and sociology to study implications, impacts, and alternatives associated with developments in biotechnology.

10.6   Food and Agricultural Policy

Throughout World War II and the Korean Conflict, the farmer produced to intense demand and reaped fair returns and grateful recognition. But the technological advances that enabled him to meet wartime demands betrayed him once the emergencies were over.

ORVILLE L. FREEMAN

With relatively few exceptions, the United States is now a nation whose people never have been hungry, and whose people for the most part are two or three generations removed from agriculture. The agenda of most U.S. citizens today focuses more on issues such as health care, crime prevention, economic competitiveness, job security, global change, and environmental quality than on agricultural diversity and food security. Contemporary society perceives little need to continue emphasizing the cornucopia that gave the United States its bountiful supply of wholesome, inexpensive food. The common question is, Why worry about food and agriculture so long as we have an abundance of supermarkets? Interestingly, most nations of Europe—where a significant segment of the population personally remembers the serious food shortages of World War II—still give high priority to public support of agriculture and a reliable supply of wholesome, affordable food. Food and agriculture should be taken neither lightly nor for granted anywhere. To maintain a reliable supply of food—produced at costs competitive in the world marketplace—it is important that our research, teaching, and outreach enterprise be kept strong.

Dairy farmers know firsthand the importance of removing from cows two or three times a day all of the milk possible if lactation is to be sustained. This principle was learned the hard way by a city dweller who purchased a farm—and a cow—and moved to the country. In only a few weeks, the cow completely stopped giving milk. When he complained to the fellow from whom he had bought the cow, the seller expressed surprise, as the cow had always been a good milker. The new farmer expressed his surprise, as well, because to his way of thinking he had been especially considerate of the cow. For example, he revealed, if he needed only one quart of milk, he took only one quart. And if he needed none he removed none. He simply had not known one aspect of the basic physiology of milk secretion—to keep lacteal cells active, the milk secreted and stored in the cow's udder must be removed regularly. Otherwise, the pressure of accumulated milk causes these cells to regress, and the cow quickly stops lactating. This is an example of the tremendous wisdom of Nature: do not produce milk if it is not going to be used.

And so it is with the agricultural enterprise: use it or lose it. It is not a faucet that can be turned on and off as needed, but rather it represents a huge investment in human and financial capital that must be managed wisely in concert with the guidelines of a prudent food and agricultural policy formulated by the U.S. Congress.

Until a few decades ago, our nation's food and agricultural policy was regularly set in large part by agricultural organizations and related groups through the Farm Bill. Now this bill—revised in 1995 for the seventh time since 1970—draws attention and input from many other special interest groups, as well: environmentalists, food-safety interests, wetland ecologists, animal well-being activists, wildlife preservationists, anti-biotechnology advocates, food-stamp users, farm-labor supporters, rural revitalizers, and many more. In addition to the Farm Bill, of course, agriculture must abide by provisions of other federal legislation, such as the Clean Water Act, Coastal Zone Management Act, Endangered Species Act, Safe Drinking Water Act, among many.

Globally, the term "American agriculture" evokes images of abundance and economic success. The strategic importance of our food, agricultural, and natural resources system will increase as we enter the twenty-first century. This will require strong leaders, imaginative scientists, greater international business understanding, and increased sensitivity to the interests of consumers and the environment.

The future level of success and competitiveness of our food and agricultural sciences will be planned and implemented by people. New discoveries will be brought about by people. Teaching and outreach services will be rendered by people. Applications of science and education are made by people. Management—good or bad—depends on people. In the equation where the success of our food and agricultural enterprise is the dependent variable, the most important independent variable is human capital—people. Therefore, any futuristic plan for maintaining the strength and competitiveness of American agriculture must include human capital development as the major parameter in the formula.

To provide global leadership, the food and agricultural sciences must recruit and develop bright young minds to the highest level appropriate, in sufficient numbers, and from all segments of the population. And they must then be challenged by competent faculty members having access to modern educational facilities. Thus, as new farm policy is formulated, it is especially important that provisions be made to assure a steady supply of capable people for employment throughout the food chain.

Many federal programs have been important in developing the infrastructure needed to make U.S. agriculture strong. Examples include rural electrification, all-weather roads, soil and water conservation, and pollution control. These efforts would have been virtually impossible on a state-by-state basis. A national effort was needed.

Let us briefly digress here. For many years, the poor quality of rural roads was a serious problem. Ultimately, this problem was taken on in a way that helped systematize relations between farmers and land-grant colleges of agriculture. Rural roads, often closed by winter snows, by spring turned into impassable mud wallows that also kept farmers from their markets. Comparing the county road system to "arteries and veins in the human body through which blood circulates," farmers established state "good roads" conventions in the late 1880s and a national "good roads" convention in 1893. The national convention was funded by A. A. Pope, a leading bicycle manufacturer, and it brought together those dissatisfied with undependable rural roads and those having great enthusiasm for bicycle riding in scenic rural America.

These conventions brought special public attention to the need for an improved network of rural roads. It was land-grant college engineers, especially those in the Midwest, who capitalized on the good-roads sentiment to assert their primacy in rural road design and construction. Leading this important land-grant partnering were staff members of Iowa State University, who studied the rural road question carefully, tested various construction materials and drainage techniques, and built experimental examples. They also published recommendations and construction guidelines (e.g., compared with their urban cousins, country roads required superior drainage and very firm beds), which were disseminated by the land-grant college's county extension agents. The Iowa model quickly became the training school for other states' engineers, and this tended to standardize rural road construction nationwide.

Public policy makers are challenged to formulate food and agricultural policy that is in the long-term best interests of the public and also in concert with the fiscal constraints under which the federal government operates. Of course, the needs and opportunities to expend public monies far exceed the amount of funding available. But the kind of infrastructure just discussed is an important priority that clearly is in the best interests of the general public.

10.7   Environmental Aspects of Food and Agriculture

> *Our land is more valuable than your money. It will last forever. It will not perish as long as the sun shines and the water flows, and through all the years it will give life to men and beasts. It was put there by the Great Spirits and we cannot sell it because it does not belong to us.*
>
> **CROWFOOT**

There was a time not so long ago when scientists and other knowledgeable experts were trusted by the public. Most people and institutions were presumed to be well-meaning and honest unless and until proven otherwise. It also was a time of unprecedented increases in the world's knowledge base, a time of belief in ourselves and our abilities through understanding and logic to resolve technical problems, a time of improvement in living conditions that made our nation the envy of the world. Ironically, the present too is that kind of time. But I suspect few of us often take time to appreciate this fact. Many of us have switched from confidence to despair, and many have been persuaded to fear and even to resent technology. Despite the overwhelming evidence documenting our physical well-being—far beyond the dreams of earlier generations—we have become a nation of people who are easily frightened. "The world's healthiest hypochondriacs," as one has put it well.

What has precipitated all this irrational conduct? What has made us lament rather than rejoice? Why are we so quick to believe the worst about ourselves and so reluctant to recognize and appreciate the good? Perhaps much of the answer lies in our having done a poor job of communicating an understanding of science to the general public. Most students will not study science or engineering as a professional. But if they do not learn about the wonders of science and the important applications of technology in modern society in school, where will they learn it? In the United States today, mainly from television. And who decides the content of today's television programs? Not scientists or other scientifically knowledgeable experts. It is thus critical that scientists find palatable ways to communicate more with representatives of the media.

Rachel Carson was among the first to bring public attention to bear on the indiscriminate use of agricultural herbicides and pesticides. A fish and wildlife biologist, her classic 1962 book *Silent Spring* alleged connections between pesticide abuse and the killing of natural predators that normally control pests; development of pesticide resistance in pests; death of certain wildlife species unable to reproduce in sufficient healthy numbers; and increases in cancer, leukemia, hypertension, and cirrhosis in persons living in areas of heavy pesticide use or eating foods contaminated by pesticides. Her protest led, among other things, to the banning of the pesticide DDT.

Scientific evidence generated in the 1970s and 1980s suggest that improper use of agricultural chemicals can indeed result in undesirable health risks and environmental damage. Now environmentalists and others have accused agricultural researchers of failing to consider potentially harmful consequences of introducing certain chemicals to the food chain, and have claimed further that researchers are insufficiently receptive to the potentials of and the need for selecting nonchemical alternatives. Similarly, agricultural extension workers have been accused of promoting chemical use while failing to properly educate users about untoward consequences and alternative techniques.

There is a kernel of truth to some of these allegations, but to its credit agricultural science has responded responsibly to the criticism. Unfortunately, though, these accusations—some of which have been outrageously in error—have caused a general loss of public confidence in the professional integrity of the agricultural research and extension system. The challenge is to use agricultural chemicals properly, so more food can be produced to feed a hungry world, and to communicate the merits of doing this, in contrast with the other alternatives, to the general public.

In a paper published recently by scientists at Texas A&M University, it was reported that approximately 5.83 million acres of land are currently being used for fruit and vegetable production in the United States. Because the use of pesticides results in higher yields, less land (an estimated 50 percent less) is required for farming. In the absence of pesticides, fruits produced for the fresh market would experience yield reductions of about 80 percent. For all the crops and regions analyzed, the weighted average yield reduction would be 70 percent. In addition to a marked increase in the cost of production if pesticides were not used, few consumers want their sweet corn to come with worms or their apples with scabs. Moreover, spoilage and waste would increase because perishability would rise and product turnover in the supermarket would drop. Exports of fruits and vegetables would decrease dramatically with lower-quality products. Clearly, we need to proceed with caution on policies involving the elimination or even the substantial reduction of the use of pesticides in agricultural production.

Since calm reason and alarmist environmentalism do not commonly co-exist, it is becoming increasingly evident that significant changes in the food and agricultural system, expanding public interest in environmental quality and food safety, competition for natural resources, and the pressure of an ever-expanding population call on the land-grant college and university system to address a broader interface of agricultural issues—issues of special importance to the general public.

An interesting approach to educating the public on environmentally related matters was initiated under the leadership of Gerald W. Thomas. The state of New Mexico established an Environmental Improvement Agency. *Improvement* implies research and an intentional examination of alternatives to improve the environment, not merely the opposite of the negative connotations of *protection*. Universities in general and land-grant institutions in particular have both challenge and opportunity to better educate the public on matters related to assuring the preservation of a safe and healthy environment while concurrently supporting a safe and abundant food supply.

10.8 The Dynamic Agricultural Paradigm

The importance of agriculture to our national economy has little to do with the number of farmers we have, or the share those farmers and others who work in agriculture make up of our total work force.

G. EDWARD SCHUH

In early American history, farmers were producers, processors, marketers, and consumers of food. Agriculture meant farming. The food distribution system was rudimentary. Value-added processing occurred in the homes of farmers and nonfarmers alike, and farm equipment and machinery were produced by blacksmiths rather than by an agricultural implement industry. In the founding of many towns in the Midwest, the first business to be established often was the grist mill. Grain for grinding was transported by wagon, so the mills were established in enough locations that customers could make the round trip in one day.

When most land-grant institutions were chartered, three-quarters of the U.S. adult population was engaged in agriculture. The tremendous number and magnitude of changes that have impacted the food and agricultural sciences over the intervening years notwithstanding, one fact remains: food will be needed forever.

> *The painter paints, the author writes, the athlete throws the ball, the builder builds, the soldier fights, the farmer feeds them all. No book without the farmer's wheat to make the author's bread, no landscape without the farmer's meat for artists must be fed. The strong rough hand that holds the plow controls the situation, then let the greatest make their bow to him who feeds the nation.*
>
> **ANONYMOUS**

Our paradigm today is to undergird production agriculture with a social objective of sustainability, environmental compatibility, and stewardship of the natural resource base upon which both agriculture and our urban-rural society depend for sustenance, economy, and ecological well-being. We must not abandon our roots of production agriculture, but rather we must manage agriculture as a component of the natural-cultural ecosystem in which it operates. This includes respecting, protecting, and conserving the nation's rich soil, as noted by Clarence Mitchell in *River Hill Soliloquy:*

> It is my belief that the land is our first and final line of defense. Land is the greatest single, tangible asset of any society. As long as we cherish and protect it, its value will increase and outlast the "paper securities" that are so popular today. The preservation of its value should have a top priority in our national security. When "the cards are down," good, productive earth could well mean the difference between power or weakness and between an affluent or an impoverished society.

Thanks in large part to the successes enabled through the research and services of land-grant colleges and universities, American agriculture is poised to enter a period of sustainable growth and become an even more powerful, export-driven industry well into the next century. This growth opportunity will come from the challenge of meeting the ever-expanding demand for food to accommodate improved human diets in developing countries—the increasing affluence of Asia, Latin America, and other parts of the world; new markets opening as a result of the Uruguay Round of discussions that spawned the General Agreement on Tariffs and Trade (GATT) and the North American Free Trade Agreement (NAFTA); and increasing competitiveness of America's technologically sophisticated agriculture. Added to these favorable economic factors is the advantage of recently developed environment-friendly American agricultural techniques—technologies that support U.S. farming in meeting the growing world demand for food and fiber without significantly degrading the environment. Indeed, our nation's farmers can expect to export more fruits, vegetables, grain, meats, and milk products, partly in the form of value-added products.

For thousands of years, the world has recognized that, because of soil erosion, farming was not fully sustainable. Ever since people learned to grow crops, they accepted the fact that a certain amount of soil erosion is part of the price paid for producing food. The recent development of **no-till** and **conservation tillage**, accompanied by proper application of herbicides, can reduce soil erosion by 50 to 98 percent compared with farming systems that use moldboard plows and mechanical cultivation. Additionally, earthworm and soil microbial populations increase greatly in no-till and conservation tillage systems. These changes in tillage practices corroborate an observation of John F. Cunningham: "The real wealth of our nation—food, minerals, and fiber—comes from the soil, and conservation practices, which are prolonging the soil's usefulness for decades, even centuries."

Sustainable agriculture, to become a reality, must be ecologically sound, economically profitable, socially acceptable, and politically supported. Much discussion on sustainable agriculture has been generated in recent years.

New **precision farming** systems will enable farmers to apply the inputs their soils and crops need—and no more. This will protect the environment as well as reduce per-unit costs of production. Precision farming uses a Global Positioning Satellite (GPS) system to locate the tractor or other machinery within a few feet of its real position on the planet and in the field. Radar then guides the machine. An on-board computer recalculates several times per second exactly how much fertilizer, seed, lime, and chemicals should be applied to each square yard of soil. The key database comes from intensive soil sampling (the soil samples also must be located using the GPS). Soil sample data are entered into an electronic field map, along with information on soil hydrology, slope, past cropping history, expected plant population, nearness to waterways, and many other factors. This new system will greatly reduce chemical use and thus production cost without significantly sacrificing crop yields—a win-win practice for farmers, consumers, and the environment alike.

American agriculture today differs dramatically from that of yesteryear.

Today's agribusiness complex includes not only producers but also suppliers, processors, and distributors; managers of natural resources; and an array of other activities and services as well as consumers and their needs and desires. On average, farmers today receive about twenty cents of each consumer food dollar (proportionately more for animal products—meat, milk, and eggs—and proportionately less for more extensively processed foods made from food grains and other plant products). They spend more than half of this gross income purchasing inputs. So farmers realize as pre-tax net income considerably less than ten cents of the consumer food dollar.

Farmers are major customers for numerous basic commodities such as rubber and steel, purchased in the form of buildings, equipment, tires, trucks, and farm machinery. Developments that affect the purchasing power of farm families have tremendous impacts on the overall national economy, as well. Farmers not only are quick to put their money back into circulation, but basic farm production takes on the economically beneficial added value when processed into food and fiber products either purchased by the public or exported.

Benjamin Franklin envisioned this when he said, "The great business of this country is agriculture." And Booker T. Washington—the great visionary who organized Tuskegee Institute—shared the following philosophy in his famous 1901 autobiography, *Up From Slavery:* "No race can prosper until it learns that there is as much dignity in tilling a field as in writing a poem."

10.9 Summary

Those who labor in the earth are the chosen people of God, if He ever had a chosen people, whose breasts He has made His peculiar deposit for sustainable and genuine virtue.

THOMAS JEFFERSON

Today we stand at a new frontier in agriculture. We live in the age of high technology. Our objectives remain the same: an abundant, safe, wholesome, inexpensive food supply for consumers; a profitable, sustainable business enterprise for farmers and those who provide services to production agriculture; and the application of production practices that preserve the soil, respect the animals, and are environment-friendly.

The agricultural symphony we are attempting to orchestrate requires every facet of the agricultural and food chain to exemplify Dutch philosopher Baruch Spinoza's noble affirmation:

> For myself I am certain that the good of human life cannot lie in the possession of things for which one man to possess is for the rest to lose, but rather in things which all can possess alike, and where one man's wealth promotes that of his neighbors, as well.

Research—gaining new knowledge and discovering new relationships—is essential to agricultural productivity and efficient food production. The programs of land-grant institutions form the nation's base of agricultural research and reflect our capability to address national needs.

American agriculture is as productive as it is today primarily because for decades our nation has made sound investments to create both a precious reservoir of knowledge and a pool of educated people. We are now enjoying the dividends of these investments.

But future American agriculture will be secure only to the extent we continue to make such investments. Unfortunately, a sizable segment of the American public believes that all is—and always will be—well with agriculture, that our productive capacity is so great that agricultural research may rationally be scaled back. This is not so. Consequently, we face the challenge of educating the general public of the continuing need to secure for the future this all-important component of our national economy and national security. Agriculture is not an economic island. It is a major and basic component of the U.S. economy. If we are to have further industrial progress, we must have further agricultural progress. And in agriculture, research is an absolutely essential component of progress.

We can proudly point to the current payoffs from investments made previously in agricultural research. Using less than 1 percent of the world's agricultural labor force, U.S. farmers and ranchers collectively produce over 8 percent of the world's food grains, 27 percent of its feed grains, 21 percent of its beef, and 28 percent of its poultry. Each farmer in the United States provides food for more than 130 people in the world. For healthy, safe, reliable, convenient, inexpensive foods, our nation's consumers spend only 11 percent of their total personal disposable income—the least anywhere on earth.

Agriculture in the United States and the land-grant college and university movement have grown together. Few progressive developments in agriculture can be mentioned in which land-grant research and extension programs have not been directly involved. There also have been major improvements in the lifestyles of country living. Mechanization in fields, farm lots, and farm homes has greatly reduced the drudgery formerly associated with life on the farm. Advances in farm productivity, judged by reductions in the hours of labor required per unit of food produced, have been unmatched in any other industry. This was made possible by applying the technology developed in large part by land-grant colleges and universities.

Major trends in American agriculture today include:

• Agriculture is quickly becoming more global;
• A major surge of new information and technologies is in the pipeline;
• The cost of producing food is decreasing;
• Emphasis on cost accounting, records, and financial management is increasing;
• The home computer is playing an increasingly important role in securing the benefits of ready access to databases, market and weather information, educational programming, and related topics;
• There is high public concern over agricultural chemicals in food and water supplies;
• The export market for food and agricultural products is expanding; and
• Support for rural institutions of all kinds is declining.

Our nation's well-fed public has a high stake in these trends. The nation's well-being is closely tied to that of the food and agriculture enterprise. Thus, the future of land-grant institutions—indeed of all higher education—as it pertains to agriculture should be of deep and continuing concern to all citizens. The United States must not relinquish its world leadership position in the agricultural and food sciences by failing to invest in its ultimate resource—human capital. Major human resource needs, including new initiatives to ensure access to higher education and to prepare students for tomorrow's changes in the workplace, must be met.

If the citizens of the United States continue to prudently use their two most precious assets—people and land—they can expect to continue enjoying the benefits of a highly successful agricultural and food enterprise. Daniel Webster shared his views on this when he had the following chiseled into the granite of his home in Washington:

> Let us develop the resources of our land, call forth its power, build up its institutions, promote all its great interests, and see whether we also in our day and generation may perform something worthy to be remembered.

The Dynamics of
Change Initiative

*There is nothing more difficult to carry out, nor more doubt-
ful of success, nor more dangerous to handle, than to initiate a
new order of things. For the reformer has enemies in all those
who profit by the old order, and only lukewarm defenders in all
those who would profit by the new order. This lukewarmness aris-
ing partly from fear of their adversaries, who have the laws in
their favor; and partly from the incredulity of mankind, who do
not truly believe in anything new until they have actual experience of it.*

NICCOLO MACHIAVELLI (1469-1527)

The Prince

11.1   Introduction

*To improve is to change—to achieve perfection is to change
often.*

SIR WINSTON CHURCHILL

Those who believe there are certain well-established ways of doing
things that will never change should visit the Smithsonian Air and Space Museum in our nation's capital. Change is always a timely topic. All organizations, institutions, and businesses that are successful embrace it, contemplate
its impact, and develop short- and long-term goals and strategies not merely
to ensure survival in facing change but to maximize success because of it.

We have read Washington Irving's rendition of how Rip van Winkle returned home in the 1780s—after a twenty-year slumber in the Catskill Moun-
tains of New York—to find a number of significant changes. But few of these
were of the same magnitude as those we have ourselves seen in the past
twenty years. And soon these too will likely be considered small in compari-

son with the profound changes we shall experience over the next two decades.

We are in the midst of one of the most intense periods of change—politically, technologically, and socially—that has ever occurred in human history. Colleges and universities are central to this monumental phenomenon. Those of us involved in American higher education must respond. To do so we may need to restructure, reconfigure, reallocate, reinvigorate. Higher education cannot address the challenges and opportunities at hand by simply extracting a little blood from everyone. Nor can we afford to lose focus, which tends to spread resources ever more thinly across programs of ever-increasing scope. Tough decisions must be made. And letting go is a much tougher proposition than adding on.

Administrators know that it is extremely difficult in a university environment for leaders to attract broad-based support in such matters because of the many constituencies, groups, and individuals that make their individual or collective interests known, apply pressures to preserve the status quo, and tend to form a gridlock with one another. The all-important question is, Which colleges and universities will have the collective courage to make the decisions necessary to enable them to step forward to become recognized as national leaders?

Change will be the predominant feature as land-grant universities minimize the question, How can we survive? and maximize the question, How can we better serve students and society? New expectations, challenges and opportunities, linkages and partnerships, and resource quantities and origins are critical components of the multidimensional transition through which land-grant institutions are passing as we begin a new century.

The cumulative increase in the rate of change is a major contributor to achieving excellence in academe. Yet colleges and universities are notorious for changing at glacial speed.

Openness to change encourages the emergence of new perspectives, clarified values, strong passions, renewed confidence, and unwavering commitment. Indeed, these are imperative in sustaining individual and institutional passage through the *white waters of change.*

For change to occur in an organization, individuals must change first. Nobel Laureate T. S. Eliot believed "the river is within us and the sea is all around us." Marilyn Ferguson concurred: "No one can persuade another to change. Each of us guards the gate of change that can only be opened from the inside. We cannot open the gate of another, either by argument or by emotional appeal." Yet again real need for change is upon us in higher education.

Fundamental changes needed in land-grant institutions include:

• Making the land-grant mission a university-wide commitment. Central administrators must recognize that a College of Agriculture, for example, cannot address many of today's public concerns and issues by itself. The full resources of the university must be brought to bear.

- Broadening public access to decision-making in land-grant universities by more inclusively defining clientele and user groups.
- Blending distinctive cultures as related to scholarship within land-grant universities.

The culture of autonomous scholarship has long embraced the view that knowledge should not be sought for utilitarian purposes. This view holds further that academic productivity should be evaluated by professional peers on the bases of criteria established by these same peers. The culture of autonomous scholarship has an important place in institutions of higher education, but it alone has not engendered strong public support for land-grant institutions over the years. This conclusion should not be misconstrued as implying that subscribing to a utilitarian motivation for scholarly work results in weak scholarship. But if utilitarian ends are rejected by the community of scholars and autonomous scholarship alone rules, the user-friendly intellectual base that has characterized land-grant institutions over the years will surely suffer.

Another important culture involves outreach, which has tended to develop its own approach to problem-solving and information dissemination. Extension workers must be prepared to address an increasingly wide range of social problems affecting the user group. To do so, they must draw upon a very broad base of information, some of which is regional or even national in scope.

Merging these two cultures will be possible by renewing the philosophies and provisions of the original 1862 land-grant model. But it will require a collective effort to gain input from established and potential user groups as well as the cooperation and commitment of members of the entire land-grant family to identify and resolve important social issues. Such changes well could result in reduced emphasis on the more traditional specialization in research and extension.

The fact that we are shifting from a national economy based on exploitation of natural resources and human muscle power to a knowledge-based economy is illustrated by a sobering story about a medical college dean who told the graduating class, "As you embark on your professional careers as medical practitioners you will, in time, find that half of what we taught you is wrong. Unfortunately, we do not know which half."

Could not the same be said as well for many other professions and trades? Much change is in store for our college graduates. Continuing education and the retooling of graduates will be even more important in the twenty-first century than it has been up to now (Chapter 8).

11.2   Accepting the Philosophy of Change

Change advocacy is a slow process. Patience is an important part of the process.

JACQUES DUBOIS

Change is the process by which ways of doing things are reordered. Hopefully, that will enable universities to better serve students and the public interests. There is a natural tendency in most individuals to resist change, to find security in the status quo. Yet change is the essence of progress, and those who resist inevitable change usually perish. It is not change per se that causes the problems so much as it is the rate of change.

The current level of performance—or being—is a state of equilibrium between the **driving forces** that encourage upward movement and the **restraining forces** that discourage it. Driving forces are commonly positive, reasonable, logical, conscious, and economic. Restraining forces are often negative, emotional, illogical, subconscious, and socio-psychological.

To significantly engender change in an institution, the feelings and philosophies of the people who compose it must first change. This is difficult, if not impossible, to achieve by a single stroke. Change in academe is better facilitated over an extended period via a steady stream of small changes that are viewed by most as being consistent with the direction of a larger change that over time is increasingly found to be acceptable.

To effect change, pressure must be continually applied. Great courage, toughness, and tenacity are required of contemporary administrators. Substantial courage is required to sustain the pressure long enough for people to realize that in academe the days of entitlement and status quo are over. To achieve this typically requires a lengthy period of change during which there will inevitably be a period of low morale, considerable complaining, resisting, and delaying. During times of major change, rumor mills run rampant. Employees are anxious for answers, information, and understanding. Effective communications are especially important to the process; it is practically impossible to overcommunicate during times of major transition.

It is easier to bring about **substantial change** when those affected perceive the change to be grounded in **substantial thinking**. Critical thinking provides advantage to those who seek a firm foundation for deep change. In academe, all groups want to participate in the deliberations that precede and accompany change.

As Oscar Wilde observed, "Discontent with the present is the first step in progress." The challenge is to manage change in the most effective ways possible. Universities cannot remain static in a rapidly changing world or they will be replaced by more adaptive, more useful entities.

How should the process of change in higher education begin? One of the truest axioms of organizational theory is that significant change rarely occurs without an external inducement coincidental with an internal sense of discontent. External inducements abound in (1) an increasing demand for college degrees that emphasize vocational aspects as well as cost considerations; (2) the possibility of alternative, better-capitalized providers of post-secondary education; (3) a shift in public attitudes that is making higher education's funding more subject to market forces and consumer needs and preferences; and (4) a political environment that is increasingly less patient with higher education's sense of itself as an enterprise that should be protected from the forces that have recast most other economic entities in the last two decades (Chapter 2).

When external inducements for change have been applied and communicated, higher education usually has not responded with a sense of urgency. The public perceives in academe an impulse to resist, to attempt to counter the need for change, to stand on the prerogatives of process. Moreover, in actual practice, university leaders who seek to direct as well as to facilitate change frequently find themselves confronting a tall, steep mountain of dilemmas, seeking a walkable bridge between the real demands of the external world and the values of the academy, between day-to-day necessities and long-range visions, between tradition and innovation, between leadership and management (the latter frequently by common consensus), between past and present, between present and future.

11.3 Counter-Reformational Aspects of Culture to Change

Change must be accepted ... when it can no longer be resisted.

QUEEN VICTORIA

Change is generally difficult to bring about because people are resistive, reactive, and closely tied to old habits. Naiveté about change is doing the same things in the same ways but expecting different results.

The processes of change, especially reforming and restructuring, are especially difficult to bring about in academe. Agents of change commonly underestimate the power of faculty and staff to stifle constructive efforts to act against what they perceive as their own best interests. It is important to balance the need to maintain collegiality with the awareness that deferring painful steps associated with marked change is not an option. The untenable consequences of not changing must be recognized. To accept the attitude that *we want to sit this one out* is to willingly permit someone else to both choose your partner and call the tune.

It is only natural and to be expected that employees will view proposed or announced change from the standpoint of how they will be affected personally. Self-preservation becomes the overriding concern and consideration. Indeed, organizational interests take a back seat to personal interests. Employees worry, gossip, and trade rumors, instead of concentrating on their jobs. Anticipated, proposed, and announced changes can and do negatively affect employees' productivity.

Up to a point, resistance to change is understandable and not totally bad. We might think of it as being like a person's body temperature. It can go too high or too low. When resistance is too high, there will be casualties—people may quit, productivity may decrease, morale may sink. If resistance is too low, however, it may reflect a complacent and over-stabilized institution or organization.

When there is a discrepancy between the existing culture and the proposed change, culture usually prevails. This often means that the proposed change must be modified. This may be relatively simple or quite difficult.

Resistance to change sometimes makes no sense. The story is told about a young woman who cut her roasts in half before baking. This aroused the curiosity of her newlywed spouse. "Why?" he asked. "Because that is the way my mother did it," came her response. "Have you ever asked your mother why?" "No," she replied, "but I will." So she asked her mother why she cut her roasts in half. "Because my mother did it that way," her mother said. So the new bride took it upon herself to ask her grandmother why she cut her roasts in half. "Because my pan was too small for the roasts I bought," her grandmother said.

It also is essential to recognize a need to change. If a frog is placed in lukewarm water to which additional heat is very gradually applied, it will typically show little inclination to escape. Being a cold-blooded creature, its body temperature approximates that of its surroundings. But it cannot detect a slow rise in temperature, so it remains oblivious to ensuing danger. It could readily hop to safety but chooses to stay put even as steam fills its nostrils. Eventually, the frog succumbs, a misfortune that could have been avoided had it simply been alert to the very real problem.

Accepting—even honoring—business as usual is a sure prescription for ultimate failure. In academe, as in business, we must become closer to those we serve.

Over a century ago bib overalls and striped caps became the business base of the Oshkosh Company of Oshkosh, Wisconsin, as it aimed its marketing efforts at farmers and railroad men. As the years passed, the numbers of farmers and railroad men dropped and long-term prospects for sales growth appeared dim. That is until a retired farmer came to the corporate office one day and told the management how proud he had been to wear his Oshkosh bib overalls over the decades and now wanted a pair for his grandson. Oshkosh took the hint and launched their successful children's clothing line. We must not be anesthetized and paralyzed by what we have been doing.

Adherence to traditions of the past is a deterrent to progress. For centuries, shoes were made of braided grass or animal hide held to the feet by leather cords. These simple sandals protected the feet against rough stones, hot sand, and cold weather. But for most of history, shoemakers did not make different shoes for the right and left feet. Why did it take so long before left and right foot shoes were manufactured?

11.4   The Challenge of Making Change

Be sure to take change by the hand before it takes you by the throat.

SIR WINSTON CHURCHILL

The challenge of changing is great, the responsibility even greater. Prerequisites of change include education, leadership, commitment, persistence, and patience. To bring about change, educational leaders must manage the inevitable resistance to it. Strategies must be devised to diffuse resistance and at the same time bring about internal attitude changes that permit change in behavior. All players—governing boards, administrative leaders, faculty, staff, students, alumni, and others—must ignore short-term discomfort and commit themselves to critically necessary changes.

Change should be viewed as friend not enemy. George Bernard Shaw once said, "You see things; and you say 'Why?' But I dream things that never were; and I say 'Why not?' "

The common denominator among today's land-grant and other institutions of higher education in the United States is change. The motivation comes in different forms. Abraham Lincoln enjoyed sharing the story of a senior frog who became stuck in the mucky mud of a deeply rutted country road in central Illinois one spring. The frog had many influential friends, and it called on them to help free itself from the predicament. They responded enthusiastically and tried diligently but alas were unsuccessful. The next day, the frog met its friends at a nearby farm pond. "We don't understand," they said. "We tried to help you out of the mud yesterday, but failed. We thought you were destined to die there. What happened?" The happy frog responded that he too thought impending death was to be his lot. But suddenly a wagon approached from down the road, and as he heard the horses' hoofbeats and the wagon's squeaky wheels, he suddenly was motivated to muster the energy to wiggle free. **When the situation develops that is clearly one of self-survival—whether in a frog, a human, or an institution—things can be and are done that were previously assumed to be impossible.**

Many important challenges that will require major changes in land-grant colleges and universities are emerging as these institutions plan and prepare for the twenty-first century. These include budgetary constraints—serious funding shortages as publicly funded universities are being asked to do more with less—and special challenges associated with stretching the breadth and length of educational programs, as disciplinary needs and academic requirements become more complex. In one sense, universities per se have no needs of their own. People have needs. And it is for people to determine whether their publicly supported universities will be employed to fulfill these needs.

In reordering the priorities of land-grant colleges and universities to better demonstrate that they are mission-driven, customer-sensitive, results-oriented enterprises—all attitudes viewed favorably by the public—certain realities prevail:

• Services are more likely to meet customer needs when the user group participates in the design.

• Institutional accountability for outcomes will serve as the basis for public funding in the future.

• Employees and students will respond favorably to a more positive attitude toward employee trust and student services.

Land-grant institutions must respond quickly and strongly to the dramatic changes that are occurring in our society as they prepare for the twenty-first century. The problem is not that these institutions are doing so much wrong but that they have failed to take full account of changes occurring in the society they serve. Indeed, the changes most important to contemporary higher education are those external to it.

Colleges and universities have become less relevant to society because they have not fully understood the complexity of the new demands that are being placed upon them. The institutions that will be recognized as tomorrow's leaders in higher education are those that foresee the changes needed and then promptly act on these needs.

11.5 Conflict Aspects of Change

If there is no struggle there is no progress. Those who pro-

fess to favor freedom and yet deprecate agitation, are men who want crops without plowing up the ground, they want rain without thunder and lightning. They want the ocean without the awful power of its many waters. This struggle may be a moral one, or it may be a physical one, and it may be both moral and physical, but it must be a struggle. Power concedes nothing without a demand. It never did and it never will.

FREDERICK DOUGLASS

The tides of change often cut deeply, and this frequently foments conflict.

Conflict is typical. ... We are currently so busy hiding conflict that we quake when we must simultaneously deal with it and pretend it does not exist. Perpetual harmony is alien to all life; ... conflict and cooperation are usually intermingled in all advances, especially in democracies.

MELVILLE DALTON
Men Who Manage

Overt resistance to change is open, public, obvious, and often involves heated debate as arguments against change are vehemently articulated. **Covert resistance** to change is the more difficult sort for academe as it tends to be private, indirect, even concealed, malicious, destructive. It often takes the form of foot-dragging and occasionally even sabotage.

Not every needed change can be accomplished, but nothing can be changed until it is faced. People are more capable of completing change when working as a team than when acting as a collection of individuals. Synergy draws out the combined strengths of team members while protecting their weaknesses. The team relies on a common goal—the desired change will be beneficial.

In his book, *The Structure of Scientific Revolutions,* Thomas Kuhn discusses the difficulty of changing a scientific paradigm and how such revolutions often involved fierce controversy, name-calling, and dissolution of long friendships.

The Chinese philosopher and orator Confucius compared accomplishing change to cooking soup: "You should apply high-intensity heat in the beginning until the soup begins to boil. Then you can let up on the amount of heat applied. But if you start out simmering, your soup will never get done."

Managing change—and its inevitable accompaniment, conflict—is a highly complex assignment for those involved in administering higher education. Increasing the driving forces often brings progress in the short-run, but if restraining forces are strongly at work, it becomes increasingly difficult to ultimately effect change. The harder one pushes on a coiled spring, the harder it is to push, until the power of the spring suddenly takes over.

The result sometimes resembles a yo-yo, reflecting the difficulty of bringing about sustained change. The natural tendency is for all players to submit to the institution's culture and traditions, and in the process lose the capacity to take the risks essential to effect critically needed change.

11.6   Strategic Planning and Change

> *Resistance to fundamental reform has been ingrained in the American collegiate and university tradition, and except on rare occasions, the historic policy of universities has been one of drift, reluctant accommodation, belated recognition that while no one was looking, change had, in fact, taken place.*
>
> **FREDERICK RUDOLPH**

Rarely do universities die dramatic deaths. Instead, they stagnate and fade away. Failure to establish new goals and priorities continues until the institution finds itself not up to the competition. For it to move toward a higher level of academic excellence, the right choices must be made. These involve deciding which programs to continue and support, which faculty and staff to recruit and retain, which students to recruit and teach, and which fiscal resources to pursue and manage.

Strategic planning is a hallmark of progressive organizations. It deliberately and methodically addresses missions, goals, emerging needs, and opportunities as it determines institutional priorities. This is serious business. As noted by futurist Peter Drucker, "Long-range planning does not deal with future decisions, but rather with the future of present decisions." Careful strategic planning provides institutional leaders the opportunity to maximize the lead time for making prudent decisions. An important prerequisite to strategic planning is **strategic thinking**, the process of consensually acknowledging, articulating, and achieving a vision of future values and institutional missions.

It is difficult to begin new programs in academe by substitution instead of addition. Universities are doing today much the same things they were doing three decades ago. If corporate America behaved the same way, it would not be doing anything today; it would no longer be in business. For American business, becoming and remaining competitive has meant computerizing, customizing, streamlining, increasing productivity, and eliminating waste. It has meant becoming more focused, being more conscious of quality, giving more attention to product design and production technologies. It has meant reducing overhead, limiting fixed costs, reducing personnel. Now it is higher education's turn. Difficult choices must be made. We need stronger—and not necessarily bigger—colleges and universities.

Today's students and other clientele of the land-grant system expect of it what they demand elsewhere: improved services, lower costs, higher quality, and a proper mix of educational experiences and services—things that satisfy their sense of what constitutes excellent education.

Public institutions of higher education tend to argue, trying to refute public perceptions and charges that students are paying more but receiving less. Threats of external regulation are nonchalantly dismissed as violations of academic freedom. In defending tradition, colleges and universities often act as if they are unaware that the world has changed, that higher education is increasingly accountable to market pressures, to government regulations, to competition from alternative providers of educational services.

If the nation's colleges and universities do not wisely choose priorities for the future and courageously make the tough but necessary decisions, outside forces will do these things for them. As highly labor-intensive organizations, it is impossible for universities to bring costs under control without confronting two of the most divisive issues in academe: (1) faculty teaching loads and (2) institutional productivity. Heretofore, most attempts to address these issues have been stymied by politicized debate over academic prerogatives instead of leading to creative ways of more efficiently providing instruction, scholarship, and public service.

The need for dynamic academic leadership owes its urgency to budgetary restraints. To reduce recurring costs means collapsing personnel lines subsequent to a rethinking of the scale and shape of the teaching, research, and outreach missions. This reality is extremely unpalatable because colleges and universities are employment-centered and resort to the tactic of personnel reduction only as the last resort.

Strategic planning for twenty-first century colleges and universities requires twenty-first century leadership now. Leadership that is creating and communicating a vision and concurrently offering strategies for achieving both short- and long-term goals. That is building bridges among people and ideas. That is challenging what is and taking the necessary risks to bring about changes for the good of the institution and those it serves so as to achieve what ought to be.

Change tends to be more acceptable when it is evolutionary, when it occurs at a pace with which people can comfortably deal. But as Bruce Barton has observed: "When you are through changing—you are through."

A major challenge for administrators, then, is to provide the leadership required to persuade faculty and staff to abandon status quo inertia and enter the state of transition from desired to necessary. This is risky business in terms of an administrator's position longevity. Change agents must be prepared to accept and keep criticism in perspective as they pursue institutional goals. The insightful sixteenth president of the United States, Abraham Lincoln—one of the world's greatest leaders of all time, a person who derived tremendous personal strength from his firm convictions and iron will—offered stabilizing words of encouragement to visionary leaders when he said:

> If I were to read, much less answer, all the attacks made on me, this shop might as well be closed for any other business. I do the very best I know how, the very best I can, and I mean to keep doing so until the end. If the end brings me out all right, what is said against me won't amount to anything. If the end brings me out wrong, ten angels swearing I was right would make no difference.

Transforming an ice cube into a new shape can take on special challenges. If the process is not managed correctly, too much heat can be applied and the ice cube will melt and turn into steam. If, on the other hand, too little heat is applied, the outside of the cube melts while the core remains solid. Facilitating change in an institution takes on similar challenges. Changing too fast may steam things up, especially when accompanied by a lack of support from weak upper administrators or governing boards, whereas changing too slowly will never bring about the necessary results.

11.7   The Role and Responsibility of Faculty in Change

The conservative ... I have often described as a person who thinks nothing new ought ever to be adopted for the first time.
                                                        FRANK A. VANDERLIP

Any faculty comprises a group of individuals who beg to differ. Faculty members are well known for defending the status quo. Change occurs in academe, but it often comes painfully slowly in the minds of administrative leaders who are in tune with urgent realities. If faculty consensus is possible, it should be exploited. But after a reasonable period of debate and deliberation, choices must be made. J. S. Mill has noted: "Institutions of higher education are usually regarded as conservative, as strongholds of reaction, and as tending to lag behind the life which they express and further."

Having said these things, it must be said now that the most important people in higher education—aside from students—are the faculty members who carry out the teaching, research, and public service functions of the institution. While commonly considered as having the least formal power in the university in conventional terms, faculty members actually have the greatest overall impact on the level of institutional excellence. Indeed, they are the true custodians of academic excellence.

Faculty members tend to become more conservative as they grow older. They become less flexible in adapting to new situations as they are more fully tenured-in. And as faculty become more entrenched in tenure, internal changes become harder to effect. Tight budgets mean that new programs often must come from substitution, but it is difficult to replace anything in academe.

On average, there is one faculty member for every sixteen college students in the United States. Nationwide, between 1975 and 1985, the number of full-time faculty members increased by 6 percent and student enrollment by 10 percent, but the nonteaching staff increased by 60 percent. Today there is one nonteaching staff employee for every eight students, so they outnumber the faculty two to one.

Aware of these trends in faculty, student, and staff numbers, many faculty members are critical of administrators for allowing such increases in staff numbers. They have perceived this as resulting from a growing vacuum in institutional leadership and have responded predictably. They consider themselves to be independent professionals responsible primarily to themselves and their professional colleagues rather than to their institutions. Faculties want presidents and chancellors to face inward, resembling their own more vocal membership in style and manner, unrealistically expecting that these qualities will be found acceptable by alumni and friends of the institution, legislators, and other external constituents (Chapter 12).

Faculty members have been trained to excel as individuals not as groups. And the primary loyalty of the faculty frequently is to their respective academic disciplines. Their reputation among professional peers determines their marketability, access to competitive funding, and numerous other perquisites. The need to engage in productive scholarship is one of the chief pressures in faculty life. Being aware of these professional realities, faculty members frequently ask, "Why should I want to change when I can expect no professional or personal benefit from the change?"

Because most faculty members, once granted tenure, are virtually immovable for the rest of their lives (tying up valuable funds, facilities, and equipment for decades), the decision to grant tenure is the most important decision made in academe. It is crucial to recruit and retain only those who are highly allergic to mediocrity.

Great faculty members often succeed spontaneously, frequently using methods peculiar to themselves. Fortunately, most professors respond to more than the lure of fame and fortune. It is important to maintain an environment in which academic excellence is expected and properly rewarded. Only then can administrators expect faculty members to support change.

11.8 Summary

Progress is always controversial, because it requires doing something different in order to move ahead.

WINTHROP ROCKEFELLER

Directed change is hard to bring about in any organization. It is especially difficult in academe. Universities are staffed by highly educated, articulate individuals who have been trained to challenge new ideas and priorities as part of the scholarly process. But unfortunately this usually results in defense of the status quo. They say, "That is what we have always done in the past—and even before that!"

Change is an important dynamic of democratic capitalism, the core of a free society's energy. The culture of higher education must be nurtured to accommodate and embrace change more rapidly and more fully—even to the extent of aggressively initiating it. Either we shape the future or the future will shape us. Stephen Baker said, "Dissatisfaction with the *status quo* leads to improvements and then we have progress."

While an eighteenth-century physician would find the practice of modern medicine befuddling, a teacher from the same century would probably be comfortable with many of the practices of contemporary teaching. The learned professions are undergoing profound changes as they adapt to the realities of competition, developing technologies, and economic scarcity. Faculty members may be the last to be shaken from the tree of established practices. Many simply presume that the services they provide and actions in which they engage are in the best interests of the public, and that there will always be need for and thus demand for their services simply because they are good for people. Few faculty members envision the changes, for example, that distance education is destined very soon to make in education at all levels and on all fronts (Chapter 4).

Let us hope that some future C. P. Snow will have no basis to feel compelled to write of any university that "it had one of the wisest faculties on the American educational scene—the majority of whom lacked the gift of foresight." Only people with vision—empowered with ideals and ideas and the courage to implement both—can make lasting change.

Land-grant institutions have a splendid opportunity to serve the public.

The changes most critical to higher education today are those external to it; new societal demands are reshaping the academy. The danger is that universities have become less relevant precisely because they have yet to listen to and understand the new demands being placed on them. As we look ahead we must ask if higher education will embrace the well-known winds of change and focus its substantial resources on matters most important to society today—people, education, technology transfer and economic development, global competitiveness, environmental concerns, food and water safety, and ethics, among others.

Higher education must demonstrate more willingness to search for new ways to implement innovation where needed and to capitalize on the opportunities at hand. Cybernetics will drive change in the decade ahead just as manufacturing did during the industrial period, and it will provide the foundation for a greatly expanded, easily accessible international information superhighway.

History is replete with stories of giants that did not adapt. Now is the time for higher education to examine its portfolio. How can it contribute more to the betterment of society? Do higher education's leaders and policy makers have the courage to make basic reconfigurations rather than incremental changes in these times when the challenge is to improve quality and services concurrent with reducing costs?

From time to time in a university's history, opportunities arise to rededicate its commitment to excellence in teaching, research, and outreach. An important part of this task is to gain a fuller appreciation of who its particular customers are—their backgrounds, educational goals, and other expectations.

Education changes individuals, and individuals in turn change society. Change is a continuing process, although, as Charles Kettering said, "the world hates change, yet it is the only thing that has brought progress."

Many works of art are valued for their balance and harmony, their creativity, their originality. A university is no different, although administrators who have had responsibility for coordinating the various entities of the university family in changing and financially restricted times know that it is often similar to trying to take a dozen kangaroos for a walk, all at the same time.

The art of progress is to preserve order amid change and to preserve change amid order.

ALFRED NORTH WHITEHEAD

These thoughts are intended to serve as a wake-up call to the various groups that comprise the university family. All are important to the dynamics of change. The responsibility to make changes in land-grant universities in keeping with the needs and expectations of society is awesome. But just as surely as those who went before proved that they had the vision, commitment, and courage to respond to societal needs, those of today's generation can once again demonstrate the extraordinary potential of ordinary people. Notwithstanding the criticism often expressed that faculty and others associated with higher education remain comfortable with the status quo, there is nothing **wrong** with public universities that cannot be repaired using parts of what is **right** with public universities.

C H A P T E R   1 2

Financing Land-Grant and Other Higher Education Initiatives

Education is not a priority to compete with defense, deficits, drugs, or AIDS. It is the solution to those problems.

DAVID KEARNS

12.1 Introduction

The idea has been widely accepted that higher education produces benefits for individuals in the form of personal development, economic opportunity, rich satisfactions, and benefits for society in the form of political, economic, and cultural advancement.

HARVARD R. BOWEN

Funding is the lifeblood of a university's existence. It nourishes programs in the arts, humanities, and sciences, and enables land-grant universities to fulfill their comprehensive missions of teaching, research, and public service. To be serious about fostering academic excellence, a university must be assertive in seeking ways and means of increasing funding from state, federal, and private sources.

While the nation's gross national product has increased dramatically since 1940, expenditures at public universities have increased proportionately even more. The total budget for all colleges and universities in the United States was approximately $7 billion in the 1960s, but surpassed $170 billion in the early 1990s. During the same period, the number of institutions in higher education doubled, from approximately 1700 to more than 3400, and that of faculty members increased from 147,000 to 783,000. Student enrollment in college expanded from about 1.5 million to nearly 14 million, and the number of doctoral degrees awarded annually multiplied over tenfold, from some 3300 to 35,000.

These trends in higher education paralleled major transformations in the whole society. These included (1) a greatly enhanced role of science and technology, including dramatic developments in the biomedical sciences; (2) the flowing and ebbing of the Cold War; (3) global mobilization of capital, people, and technologies; (4) the coming of the technology driven Information Age; (5) the changing nature of women's roles, of families as well as demographics; and (6) increasing public concern for environmental issues.

Budgetary needs in higher education far exceed the financial resources available. And when this equation is out of balance, when urgent public concerns are perceived as being overlooked or the fiscal investment controversial, debate about priorities in academe is certain to follow.

All stakeholders in the academic community have concerns about rising costs and the availability of financial resources to support needed education, research, and public service. The funding feast for higher education is a thing of the past. For the foreseeable future, ever-expanding budgets in higher education are of the past. Our public financial resources are finite, our taxpayers surly. Across the nation, budget-scrubbing for higher education is fashionable. We must learn to manage available resources better.

People outside academe are saying, *Do more with less, just as we are doing.* A tall order? Yes. But this is an opportunity for universities to work more closely with the public in remedying a higher education cost:benefits ratio generally perceived as being too high (Chapter 13). The principal customers of higher education—students and parents—want to be shown (not told) that universities have responded to calls for attention to costs, access, quality, and services. Land-grant and other institutions of higher education must either get better and get more efficient or get less (Chapter 2). They owe it to the citizenry to do just that.

12.2 Setting Funding Priorities

In the middle of every difficulty lies opportunity.
ALBERT EINSTEIN

One fact upon which virtually all in the land-grant system agree is that there are more needs and opportunities than available money to address them. When demands exceed resources, spending priorities must be set. No university will ever be fully funded, and institutional administrators must become assertively realistic in addressing the situation. Now is the time to be serious about priority-setting. If we are to reallocate resources, however, a commitment is needed from as many entities within academe as possible. Without commitment, any such plan is destined to fall prey to factionalism, favoritism, internal dissension and friction—in short, to fail.

The current fiscal plight of this nation's colleges and universities has been analogized to a simple parable. One warm summer, a close-knit family fulfilled a major dream by working together to build a grand house, a sturdy structure with many rooms and fine leisure areas. Then came an especially cold winter, and the family needed wood to fuel the fireplaces. As the bitterly cold weather continued, the need for additional firewood became ever more pressing. Eventually, the family looked at their grand house and agreed to pull a board here and a beam there to burn as fuel. As the winter went on, more and more boards and beams were pulled to stoke the fireplaces. As it was a large house with thousands of pieces, all concluded surely a few would not be missed. But indeed, before the winter ended, the roof and ceilings began to sag, showing the effects of the missing boards and beams, which together were critical to the structure's strength. Because of budget reductions, many universities are dismantling their programs piece by piece. The damage goes unnoticed at first because the system enjoys the momentum of strength and success.

But education cuts never heal. Persistent underfunding and deferred maintenance already are taking their tolls. The result: a gradual erosion of quality and effectiveness plus subtle distortion of institutional missions. Piecemeal and across-the-board budget cuts alike resemble soil erosion; the effects do not show up right away, but after many years the ability to sustain crop production becomes impaired and eventually may be lost altogether.

Universities must be realistic. Geldings can not respond to the command to "be fruitful and multiply"! Budgets can be reduced by only some finite amount. At some point, choices must be made among program breadth, program quality, and student numbers.

Given current budgetary constraints, refocusing and reprioritizing should be guided by an urgent sense of parsimony: *There are tough choices to make. How can we do the job better, assure quality in the face of diminishing resources, do as much or almost as much but with fewer resources?* We must not emulate a fellow described by Mark Twain:

> A stubborn patient with inadequate circulation developed gangrene in his toe, but refused to seek remedy till it reached his knee. He instructed his surgeon to amputate the toe. Of course, this did not stop the spread of infection. When gangrene reached his hip, he requested that the leg be removed just below the knee. In time he died, an ending that might have been prevented if proper action had been implemented sooner.

Alas, this situation can lead to cynicism and sarcasm among faculty, staff, and students. A common question at Oregon State University with regard to merged and eliminated programs was, *What's the difference between the* Titanic *and Oregon State?* Answer: *The* Titanic *had a band.* (The Oregon State University band was one of the programs eliminated. Approximately two years later it was reinstated as a much smaller program.)

Abundance breeds magnanimity; scarcity breeds competition. Higher education now faces scarcity in fiscal resources. Many business people have experienced powerful creativity being born out of scarcity and adversity. Many budgetary problems can be satisfactorily resolved by developing more ideas and innovative approaches. But administrators must accept the great challenge of persuading faculty and staff that (a) higher education already is well into a period of markedly evident fiscal crisis, (b) efficiency and productivity must be the responsibility of every member of the academy, and (c) academic innovations generally must be funded through substitution not addition. When the ship encounters rough seas and the captain's best plan is to lighten the load by throwing crew members overboard, it is time to ask each and every crew member to suggest alternatives.

Unfortunately, higher education's greatest asset is also its greatest expense. In times of extreme budget reductions—the kind universities are now experiencing all around the country—it must be acknowledged that the payroll by far comprises an institution's largest cost of doing business. Education is the most labor-intensive enterprise extant. Roughly three-fourths of higher education's cash flow goes into salaries, wages, and benefits. In reality, major budget reductions require a downsizing in the number of employees; contrary to the belief of many, administrators have no substantial funds stashed away for a rainy day.

Budgeting in universities amounts to much more than bookkeeping. It comprises a basic tool chest for setting priorities and then adjusting programs to fit the needs and opportunities embraced by the plan. Universities now must invest very selectively in high-priority areas. These include academic programs, library, human resources, maintenance, and cost-saving student services and administrative systems. This selectivity must focus on ways that best achieve institutional goals.

There are two approaches to reallocation and reform. One: employ an across-the-board incremental approach. The other: deal directly with fundamental structural and philosophical matters. In the end, the segmented, incremental approach often exacerbates the problem. A holistic vision—one in tune with domestic and global realities—is what is needed for the twenty-first century.

When asked to help determine the most prudent budgetary reductions, the knee-jerk reaction of most faculty members is to zealously protect their own disciplinary turf. This frequently leads to the politically weaker programs and units being discontinued, regardless of needs, opportunities, or for that matter program quality.

To cope with devastating fiscal realities caused by decreasing real budgets, many universities have reduced student enrollments and course offerings, increased class sizes, reduced library acquisitions (exacerbated by steep increases in the cost of acquisition for all media), frozen salaries, reduced faculty and staff numbers, and deferred maintenance of physical facilities. More than a third of the nation's universities experienced real-dollar budget reductions between 1991 and 1994.

12.3   Fiscal Aspects of Administration and Faculty Governance

Bad administration can destroy good policy, but good administration can never save bad policy.

ADLAI E. STEVENSON

University administrators come in three types: (1) bureaucrats—ineffective but harmless; (2) political operatives—too interested in advancing their own careers to grapple with difficult issues; and (3) true leaders—those who can articulate a vision for the institution and have the courage to make tough decisions on budgets and personnel, follow through on them, and live with the consequences.

In the present climate, assertive university presidents of the true-leader type are in the peculiar position of knowing from the moment they arrive that their days as chief executive officer are numbered. Even those who prove to be most successful recognize that their effectiveness starts to wane during the first year. Indeed, every time an administrator makes a decision, someone—and sometimes everyone—can construe that decision as unfavorable. Consequently, as presidents make decisions that displease various individuals and groups, the core of dissidents grows ever larger as the months and years roll by. Some say, "Friends come and go, enemies accumulate."

Most institutions are over-managed but under-led. Managing involves productivity and efficiency. Leading involves vision and effectiveness. Management is about systems, controls, procedures, policies, structure. Leadership is about prioritizing, innovating, and initiating. Management is about copying and maintaining the status quo. Leadership is about creativity, adaptivity, and agility. Leadership looks at horizons and the long-term big picture, not merely day-to-day activities and the bottom line.

The nature of leadership at the university level is fast changing. Now there is a more delicate balance of interests and a polite tug-of-war and a blending of emphases. The presidency is an office fraught with perils, shot through with ambiguities; an office that is many different things to many different people. There are more elements that need to be conciliated, but fewer amenable to being led.

To quote, paraphrase, and supplement the distinguished former University of California president Clark Kerr:

> The university president is a many-faceted character, in the sense that he or she must face in many directions concurrently while not contriving to turn his or her back on any individual or group. Indeed, comprehensive research universities have many doors and windows to both the inside and outside communities.
>
> The university president is expected to be a friend of students; a working colleague of the faculty; a close partner with local business and community leaders; a supporter and cooperator with the institution's alumni, friends, and supporters; a sound administrator with the institution's governing board and the state's coordinating board; an inspiring public speaker—and willing to do it often; an astute bargainer with foundations and federal agencies; a politician and close friend with the governor and other elected state and federal officials; a friend of business and industry, labor, and agriculture; a persuasive and effective diplomat with donors, prospective donors, and friends of donors; a champion of education generally, and of higher education in particular; a supporter of and regular contributor to his or her academic discipline; a spokesperson to the media; a well-published, highly respected scholar in his or her own right; a public servant at the state and national levels; a devotee of opera, sports, and other publicly visible university programs and activities—equally; a decent human being, a strong family person; an individual always ready and willing to travel domestically and internationally on short notice; and an active member in local civic clubs, chambers of commerce, the religious community, and country clubs. He or she must also enjoy eating most meals in public, and attending (often offering impromptu remarks) public ceremonies and functions.
>
> He or she should be firm, yet gentle; compassionate and sensitive to others, and insensitive to self; a person with unlimited vision who can look to the past and to the future with equal authority; be aware of and appreciate the rich heritage and culture of the institution; be visionary while being responsible, sound, and prudent; affable yet reflective; know the value of a dollar; inspiring in visions and perceptions, yet cautious in acting; a person of high character, integrity, and principle, but capable of negotiating a deal; a person with broad perspective who will follow through with details; a patriotic American, but ready to question and criticize the status quo; a seeker of truth; a motivational leader; a lamb at home and a lion when fighting for the budget and betterment of his or her institution; a well-dressed, well-mannered person who always wears a smile and displays a positive can-do, will-do attitude; a person who remembers names, birthdays, and sends bundles of thank you and congratulatory notes—both on and off campus. Who could ask for anything more?

Administration is a means, not an end. Yet the ends of education cannot be well served without effective administration, particularly during periods of change, conflict, and budgetary constraints. University administration is essential in arranging for the conduct of institutional affairs. Administrators confer with people, handle paper, and make decisions on a continuing basis. The tasks look much the same from one institution to the next, but the moods and tempos of the efforts rise and fall as they reflect the attitudes, personal experiences, and work ethics of individuals.

A major challenge facing institutional leaders today is to provide the forceful leadership required to move higher education through these difficult times and simultaneously transcend the constraints associated with diminishing resources, athletics-oriented and meddlesome governing boards, and legislators as well as the incessant, often conflicting demands of various other well-meaning constituencies.

There is great need for trust between faculty members and administrators. It is important for administrators to make institutional goals compatible with individual goals. The faculty should be involved in establishing institutional objectives. When those who will be largely responsible for achieving the goals help set them, greater understanding, acceptance, and widespread support results. Moreover, faculty members need to be engaged in the process of institutional change, because they are perceived by the public to be the greatest single impediment to institutional change and progress.

Governance of higher education is becoming less by higher education and also less of higher education. A major administrative challenge is to preserve governance of higher education by higher education. To do this, there must be an awareness of societal purposes so as to be externally accountable while maintaining internal governance. While the trend toward shared governance is in some ways commendable, it often is too slow, too consumed by process—sometimes to the exclusion of substance—so the results lack the boldness characteristic of significant change (Chapter 11). Creative ideas frequently die not because they lack merit, but rather because their sponsors grow weary of the tedious process and prefer to invest their resources in more immediately productive pursuits.

12.4 Importance of Institutional Image in Achieving Public Support

A leader is a dealer in hope.

NAPOLEON BONAPARTE

In today's fiscal climate—when public support is absolutely essential for the survival of land-grant universities—both high-quality and cost-effective programs must be provided. One of the most important and difficult challenges for a publicly supported, comprehensive university is to develop and communicate a shared vision of mission with its various publics. Such a vision should be clear and focused enough to provide a useful, conceptual framework for objective planning. It should assist the institution in deciding what it can and cannot expect to accomplish with available resources. Moreover, it should enable the institution to clearly identify and regularly communicate with its customers (mostly students), clientele groups, partners, and support groups.

Public perceptions and institutional images are critical to increasing public support of higher education. Public institutions should strive to send a nonstop message to the public about the products of their many exemplary education, research, and public service endeavors. Increased emphasis on positive image building is greatly needed as land-grant universities seek additional resources from all sources. Examples of direct results of basic research conducted in universities include: computers, nuclear power, synthetic vitamins, polio vaccine, hybrid seed corn, and oral contraceptives. It is impossible to assign precise dollar values to the impacts of these and other important research developments, but their contributions to national and global productivity as well as to the public welfare surely fully compensate public investments in higher education and its research endeavors.

12.5 Role of Institutional Alumni in Achieving Public Support

Nothing is ever completed, least of all, education.

VICTOR A. RICE

America's colleges and universities are struggling to survive the impact of a new set of values, a new set of social and economic challenges. Approximately 20 percent of citizens over the age of twenty-five—some 33 million Americans—hold a baccalaureate or higher degree. This large group has the potential to dramatically change the present course our country is on. There is an opportunity for higher education to initiate various volunteer alumni programs, designed to make a difference for many segments of society, while enhancing its own image and ultimately financial stability. Alumni leadership and support in public and private fund-raising is critical.

Since higher education seems to have no readily identifiable national champion outside academe—no strong, unflinching, vocal advocate to regularly speak up in support of colleges and universities—alumni and former students can play this role.

Major public universities have traditionally relied on around 5 percent of their alumni to raise 3 to 5 percent of their respective annual budgets. This support is always greatly appreciated. But the fact is, alumni and friends of public universities comprise a potentially much greater resource than this. Unfortunately, for the most part they have not been adequately mobilized to accomplish sustained fund-raising for alma maters. These people represent one of the academy's greatest, but still largely untapped, resources.

If we empower our alumni to have a greater positive impact on social and economic problems, both they individually and collectively and the society at large will envision a new role for higher education. When alumni learn they can make a difference through and for their alma mater, they embrace new values that give them greater reason to personally contribute to the common good.

Astute indeed are those institutions that have organized their alumni on state and national bases to serve as advocates in legislative lobbying efforts. Properly versed on program strengths and contributions to the public as well as on institutional needs, opportunities, and priorities, these representatives—many of whom are close friends and supporters of elected officials—can be highly effective. They tend to be perceived as being less self-serving than university leaders themselves. Similarly, state and national networks of influential, persuasive alumni are critically important in identifying prospective donors and working with institutional and foundation leaders in private fund-raising efforts. Many alumni also are leaders in business and industry and can impact corporate giving there, too.

12.6   Fiscal Aspects of Intercollegiate Athletics

In several cases, board members have declined to support the efforts of presidents to clean up their athletic programs. But rather, have aligned themselves with popular coaches, athletic directors, or booster groups—in effect, declaring by their actions (or lack of them) that athletics are more important than academics or integrity. The fiduciary responsibility of trustees makes it imperative that they be involved in all matters that can affect stakeholders' confidence and trust in their institution.

JOHN B. SLAUGHTER

Issues facing intercollegiate athletics mimic those faced by universities in general—institutional control, academic integrity, student well-being, fiscal responsibility, and gender and cultural equity. Because athletics is the main window through which the public views universities, restoring faith in the integrity of the intercollegiate athletics program is a must. Public questions about the ethical integrity of higher education have increased in step with the publicity about various abuses in intercollegiate athletics.

The most important responsibility of a university faculty is to ensure the soundness of its academic programs. Therefore, it is imperative that faculties be actively engaged in determining policies for the conduct of intercollegiate athletics. In their 1989 book, *The Old College Try: Balancing Academics and Athletics in Higher Education,* John Thelin and Lawrence Wiseman summarize the effect of college athletics on the public's trust in higher education:

> The national publicity associated with scandals at a handful of universities with big-time varsity sports programs has a disproportionate influence on public images and opinions of **all** colleges and universities. The media attention afforded big games and big scandals dominates and distorts the popular image of what American higher education is all about. The most serious concern is that flagrant, sustained abuses in college sports programs lead to the erosion of public faith in institutions of higher education.

A cursory reading of the national press or a spot check of radio and television newscasts will reveal that right now college sports are passing through another of their periodic public launderings. At the root of the problem lies intense economic pressure that breeds an emphasis on winning by any and all means. This attitude is frequently amplified by pressures from alumni and booster groups. These are not problems the solving of which should be left to the discretion of the National Collegiate Athletic Association and the athletic conferences alone. They are matters of institutional responsibility.

Apart from heritage, there are strong arguments for a healthy competitive athletics program being closely connected with the university—one that functions as an integral part of the institution. In an already fragmented university world—one that frequently dwells more on nostalgia than on reality—university athletics teams provide a common rallying point that can enhance the esprit de corps of students, faculty, alumni, and the general public. Those who will never be excited by a great library, computerized student services, profound and far-reaching research projects, or even nationally prominent master teachers, will find in a winning team the roots of a sense of pride that can pay off in a multitude of ways, including financial support for university needs outside athletics. One former Big Eight Conference president told this author that he raised several million dollars for his university in one night—the night before his team competed in the Orange Bowl.

Great universities and winning athletic teams are compatible, although institutions such as the University of Chicago give clear evidence that the former can exist without the latter. For a large public university, however, the grassroots support that athletics prowess can provide cannot be ignored. We should stress excellence in all we do, and that includes a broadly based athletics program for men and women in both revenue- and nonrevenue-generating sports.

In the end, the attitude that should prevail is this:

> I like to win, both in the academic rankings of departments, schools, and colleges, and on the courts and in the stadia, because by nature I am a competitor who abhors being viewed as second-rate. But I would rather lose after a vigorous struggle and play by the rules than win by cutting corners and smearing the reputation of a distinguished university. Recruiting and retaining athletes must be open and above board, following both letter and spirit of the law set forth by conference and national regulating bodies. Above all, we must make certain that our athletes are bona fide students and have every opportunity to receive a high-quality education, and we must expect and insist that they conform to the academic standards established for all students. Student athletes are under intense additional pressures, especially during the season of their particular sport, as well as being asked to represent the university at alumni functions, in high school appearances, and in special programs such as "Say No to Drugs," so some may need special academic assistance and understanding. But they are students first, athletes second. We owe them education—not exploitation—for only a minuscule few can realistically look forward to a lengthy professional career in athletics. Their college education will serve them long after the glories of the contest have faded on the local or even national sports pages. Implicit in this is the belief that we can do all three: play by the rules, provide an excellent educational experience, and have winning teams. If this is not possible, then adjustments consistent with the institution's firm commitment to academic excellence and integrity must be made. (*Adapted from remarks shared with the University Faculty/Student Senate by John E. Cribbet, distinguished former chancellor and law dean of the University of Illinois at Urbana-Champaign.*)

Operating an athletics program that complements but does not dominate the university sends the right message to the public: student athletes are provided the opportunity to gain a balanced academic and athletic experience.

Indeed, the primary reason for college athletics should be to complement the educational process, not merely to entertain alumni and others. Participating in a sports program provides most athletes a scholarship to continue their education; provides wholesome recreation; develops physical strength, agility, and stamina; and instills the virtuous qualities of leadership, character building, teamwork, respect, and self-discipline. Moreover, athletes participate in the most ethnically diverse sector of the university. People from highly diverse family backgrounds and cultures work together to achieve common goals. These attributes are diminished when the enterprise becomes part of the entertainment industry and college teams become farm clubs for professional teams.

Many view university athletics programs as open spigots in the cash till. They wink at a major component of the institutional revenue stream that chronically overestimates revenues and underestimates expenses, resulting in deficits. Unfortunately, governing boards tend to condone such situations, consequently putting pressure on administrators to effect remedies. The administrators then must decide from where to reallocate the funds to accommodate the budgetary shortfall. Should it be from reducing library acquisitions? Providing fewer class sections? Deferring maintenance of facilities? Or from other important institutional needs?

Revenues directly realized from intercollegiate sports exceed expenses at some major universities, enabling them to transfer badly needed monies into other important student-oriented programs and services. For example, Notre Dame University commits the revenues from its New Year's Day bowl appearances (averaging about $3 million annually) to student financial aid for nonathletes. Also, more than $20 million from the first five years (1991–1995) of its NBC contract was devoted to Notre Dame's financial-aid endowment. A total of $34 million in NBC, bowl, and licensing revenues was directed to academic support from 1990 through 1995, almost all of it as student financial aid. At Notre Dame, only athletic ticket sales, a portion of the television income, and proceeds from the athletics department apparel catalogue are categorized as athletics revenue. Other income generated directly and indirectly by athletics—including parking fees, income from stadium concessions, bowl-game proceeds, the bulk of national television revenues, and the university's substantial annual licensing income—is directed to other academic and student-life needs. For many years, the athletics program at the University of Nebraska has given a major portion of its sports income to support the university library.

12.7   Public Support of Higher Education

In the conditions of modern life, the rule is absolute: The race which does not value trained intelligence is doomed. Not all your heroism, not all your social charm, not all your wit, not all your victories on land or sea can move back the finger of fate. Today we maintain ourselves. Tomorrow science will have moved forward yet one more step, and there will be no appeal from the judgment which will be pronounced on the uneducated.

ALFRED NORTH WHITEHEAD

No investment of public monies offers higher potential long-term payoff than education and research. They may not immediately bear fruit, but they will bear fruit. The olive tree commonly requires about seven years before it bears olives, but it remains productive for a long time. Some of the trees that were bearing olives in the Garden of Gethsemane outside Jerusalem at the time of Jesus are still fruitful. If our nation fails to invest in education and research now, it will not be assured a well-educated citizenry, a forfeiture by default of future economic growth and development opportunities.

The proportionate share of state-appropriated money going to higher education has been decreasing in most states for several years. There are numerous reasons for this, not the least of which is the public perception that the funds going to higher education are not being administered as effectively as they should be. Also, many believe too much public money is going to support programs for which the institutions were not originally created. Universities basically are out of touch—and thus out of favor—with taxpayers. It is time once again for universities to be more public service oriented.

According to a report by the National Conference of State Legislatures, the states appropriated more state monies to correctional agencies than to higher education during fiscal years 1993 through 1995. Adjusted for inflation, spending on public welfare during the thirty-year period 1960 to 1990 increased by 630 percent, whereas that on education increased by only about 225 percent.

The 1991–1992 academic year was an especially difficult one for university budgets. For the first time in thirty years, total (uninflated) state appropriations for public higher education dropped from that of the previous year. Consequently, teachers are now teaching more courses and more students with fewer teaching assistants; tuition is increasing, and salary increases are smaller and less frequent. Moreover, since overall college enrollments have not decreased, a significant portion of the cost of funding higher education has been shifted to students and their families. During the past decade, the annual tuition bill for students has more than doubled at public institutions and more than tripled at private schools. The situation is very serious indeed, and most in higher education believe that it is not an anomaly but rather will likely continue into the foreseeable future.

There is a fundamental shift afoot in public policy related to the funding of higher education. If those responsible for the fiscal affairs of colleges and universities fail to address in organized, meaningful ways the realities of reductions in public monies appropriated for higher education, the institutions will succumb to the forces of fiscal gravity and eventually be forced to give up programs and sacrifice services. This challenge must be faced with the courage and determination needed to emerge as strong public service-oriented institutions that can recapture the public trust and translate that into the support needed to emerge as educational partners with the twenty-first century public.

Approximately 38 percent of all federally appropriated nondefense research funding went to universities in 1991. Federal dollars such as these leverage much larger amounts of the state funds needed to drive change and make progress. The same is true of private monies that go to leverage state and federal funds.

An important challenge to members of Congress is to craft federal policy that will result in strengthening linkages between federally funded research programs and national goals such as national security, ample energy at reasonable cost, maintaining a sound economic infrastructure, adequate environmental protection, enhanced human health, innovation in high-technology manufacturing, expanding the overall knowledge base, increasing economic competitiveness, educating future scientists and engineers, assuring an abundant supply of wholesome and inexpensive food, and creating a scientifically and technologically literate citizenry and workforce.

One means of addressing specific research needs that relate to such national goals is through competitive grants. The idea of competitive grants is to "seek excellence wherever it is." In general, however, competitive grants favor stop-and-go type research projects (Chapter 7). This can be good in that new, high-priority, or urgent projects can be funded. But this method of funding research does not lend itself to assuring the crucial continuity of long-term programs. Additionally, another inherent consequence of most competitive grant programs is that the process tends to exacerbate disparities among universities. Often the large, most prestigious, and already well-financed universities are best positioned to compete. They have a critical mass of reputable faculty and thus can demonstrate disciplinary breadth and depth. Also, because of reputation and funding, these institutions have been successful over the years in attracting many of the strongest and most productive faculty members. They also typically have superior research facilities, laboratories, and equipment—much of which was purchased with funds from earlier grants. Less-well-off institutions will become even less able to compete in such an environment, except in those areas where they develop special niches of research expertise.

Important issues confronting our nation—and, therefore, our institutions of higher education—include (1) how to most effectively retool our workforce to meet the manufacturing and other needs of a service-based global economy; (2) how to best face the challenges of living in a multicultural, ethnically diverse society; and (3) how to best enhance the values of individual citizens so they can effectively deal with a wide array of social issues. Adequate funding on a recurring basis is essential to addressing these multiple criteria if institutions of higher education are to maintain global educational leadership and high research productivity.

For this nation to achieve the per capita income level needed to adequately support public education and research, it is important that productivity increase further. Labor productivity is a critically important factor affecting national income. Education affects individuals' productivity by (1) imparting greater discipline and reliability, (2) assuring improved health, (3) increasing efficiency, (4) enabling faster adoption and reaction to new information, and (5) heightening mobility. It may also alter the amount of available physical capital by boosting rates of saving and investment, prerequisites of economic development.

The level of educational preparedness among entering college students is determined primarily in school grades K-12. Unfortunately, great variation and much inconsistency exist. Educational reform is needed in the United States. We cannot expect to compete in a world which is decentralizing power and freeing up economic wealth if we cling to an educational system that is choking on centralization and lack of discipline.

Some believe the system simply needs more money. But several studies indicate a low correlation between public spending per student and student performance. Such countries as South Korea and Spain rank low in terms of spending, but their students outscore ours on mathematics and science examinations. Class size is often emphasized, but class sizes in France, Japan, Korea, and Spain average more than fifty students, yet their test results are commendable.

To more accurately evaluate per-student cost it should be noted that in the United States this figure is driven up by high administrative costs. Spending on administration here is approximately twice that of European countries. Learning does not occur at the hands of administrators. Instead, it is facilitated in an environment of autonomy where teachers have the freedom to carry out their responsibilities with minimal administrative oversight (Chapter 6).

12.8 Enhancing Private Funding for Public Higher Education

Philanthropy is an American habit and the modern foundation is an American invention—to make human beings healthier, happier, wiser, more conscious of the rich possibilities of human existence and more capable of realizing them.

CHARLES DOLLARD

As land-grant universities pass the midpoint of the 1990s and prepare for the twenty-first century, they are faced with a twofold challenge: (a) static or declining real dollars resources and (b) a pressing need for higher levels of educational, research, and public-service programming for citizens of their respective states and the nation. Today and in the foreseeable future, it is important that land-grant institutions look more to the private sector for funding to supplement public support. This is the key to financial support sufficient to redirect energies from the struggle for survival to the pursuit and attainment of greater institutional excellence.

Private gifts are essential for the extra ingredients that determine the level of educational, research, and public-service excellence attained. Most institutions have minimal discretionary authority over expenditure of publicly appropriated monies, but they can exercise much discretion over university development efforts and the private gifts that accrue as a result.

Over the years, this nation has been fortunate in having a large number of resourceful individuals who cherished hard work and the opportunity to help others, those whose lives were guided by reason and common sense, people who respected God, country, and the inherent dignity and self-worth of others. Many of these same stalwart citizens embraced the philanthropic spirit—an attitude of making a difference in the quality and character of the lives of their fellow human beings. This commendable commitment to others has found expression in a myriad of socially constructive ways—expanded educational and cultural opportunities for fellow citizens, improved health care and community services, forward-looking civic projects, and development and dissemination of new scientific knowledge. Whatever the particular charitable cause, citizens of the United States have traditionally volunteered to give generously of their time, ingenuity, and personal funds to meet emerging societal needs.

There are those in academe and elsewhere in this country who read the signs of the time and gloomily shake their heads, concluding that we are entering an accelerating phase of the demise of the excellent quality of life enjoyed in recent decades in this magnificent country. But this is not the first time the doomsayers have delivered their message. The year 1809 began with headlines of gloom and doom. Napoleon was marching across Europe with his ruthless army, and no nation seemed safe from his power-hungry ambition. In the midst of this preoccupation with political developments, other important events passed virtually unnoticed. Indeed, in 1809, people were worrying excessively about battles and forgetting about babies; their future leaders; people who would advance ideas, ideals, philosophies, and even philanthropies; those destined to better humanity. Without question, a new generation of leaders was born in 1809: Gladstone and Tennyson in England; Mendelssohn in Germany; Abraham Lincoln and Oliver Wendell Holmes in the United States. Together, these and other newborns were destined to help shape the course of modern history in positive, meaningful, lasting ways.

Throughout human history, what often seemed exceedingly important in the short run turned out to be less so in the long run. And what seemed insignificant or was even ignored at the moment proved to dramatically change the world over time. That might well be the situation in the United States today. So as higher education concentrates on its admittedly pressing problems of today, it is important that we not overlook the basic strengths and potentials of alumni, friends, and the general public to respond favorably **if the right message is communicated.**

It is important that we keep matters in proper perspective and not forget what brought the land-grant system to this point, importantly including tremendous national commitments to educating the masses (Chapter 1) and to the welfare of all citizens through various philanthropic and voluntary activities. Nor should we forget that this nation—ensuring the precious freedoms it has given us to enjoy—has long prided itself in the fact that neither family background nor cultural background nor adverse circumstances of any kind limits the educational achievements of our citizenry.

We admire people who, though apparently handicapped by adversity, succeed at making significant contributions to society. Perhaps it is an even greater marvel that there are those who, blessed by prosperity and plenty, succeed in the selfsame achievement. For example, as already mentioned, Abraham Lincoln and William Ewart Gladstone were born in the same year, 1809—one in a cabin, the other in a castle. The former was so poor he considered the first day he earned a dollar to have been one of his proudest days. The latter—rich from birth to death—never for a moment gave anxious thought to his monetary fortune. While the former gleaned his learning from borrowed books read before an open fire, the latter took the best education Christ Church College, Oxford, could offer. The former was so homely a cabinet member once called him a gorilla, while the latter was regarded as one of Europe's most handsome men. The former started (some would say) with nothing, the latter (as they say) with everything. Yet both came to be the top political leaders of their respective nations.

It is noteworthy when those who possess much are motivated to be generous toward the less fortunate, which is precisely what makes the raising of private support for students and their education a highly rewarding experience. Philanthropy—in the form of individual, collective, and corporate support for education and social betterment—can be traced back to the Middle Ages, when early European universities relied heavily on income derived from rent on land holdings donated by wealthy patrons. Still, it has distinctly American characteristics and roots. Philanthropy in the United States provides major educational, cultural, and leadership opportunities for our citizens. In colonial America, philanthropic efforts were directed toward establishing Harvard and Yale and molding the colonies' future leaders to realize the wisdom and profound impact of such efforts.

Many Founding Fathers, including Thomas Jefferson and Benjamin

Franklin, espoused a philanthropic concept of enlightened self-interest, believing that the staunch individualism which pervaded the new democratic society could be melded with a recognition of the practical and philosophical worth of philanthropic activities. It is not surprising, therefore, that the modest philanthropic projects of the colonial and federalist eras focused on the development of schools, lending libraries, and societies for the advancement of learning, in addition to such essential community services as fire protection and health care.

An early private gift of special note was made in 1829 when British chemist James Smithson gave the U.S. government a then-generous bequest of $500,000 with the provision "to found at Washington, under the name of the Smithsonian Institution, an establishment for the increase and diffusion of knowledge among men."

Hence, voluntarism—the spirit of community cooperation and participatory involvement in philanthropic causes—has flourished since the earliest colonial days. Benjamin Franklin has been described with accuracy as "a kind of one-person volunteer conglomerate in establishing, and in getting people to join, private organizations to serve public needs." At age forty-two, Franklin sold his printing house and devoted the second half of his life to public service. Rather than patenting and seeking profit from his many inventions, he willingly gave the products of his ingenuity and labor to the world.

Alexis de Tocqueville, the noted French social historian who studied American social institutions during the 1830s, commented glowingly on the spirit of volunteerism and social commitment in this then-new democratic society. He lauded the American propensity to organize philanthropic associations of all sorts to meet demonstrated societal needs as well as the tendency to "make really great sacrifices for the common good." These desirable social traits, he concluded, were attributable to the free democratic institutions prevalent in the United States:

> The free institutions of the United States and the political rights enjoyed there provide a thousand continual reminders to every citizen that he lives in society. At every moment, they bring his mind back to this idea, that it is the duty, as well as the interest of men to be useful to their fellows.

The American spirits of philanthropy and volunteerism are alive and strong today. Those closely associated with the nation's land-grant and other institutions of higher education are keenly aware of the importance of philanthropic giving in support of higher education and scientific discovery. Private and corporate giving to land-grant and other universities sustains numerous scholarships, fellowships, and endowed professorships as well as faculty research, teaching, and public service programs, student study tours, internships, and many other types of worthwhile educational enrichment programs.

As our nation's Founding Fathers so astutely observed, philanthropic support for science and education remains a highly effective means of enhancing and promoting social progress—developing useful new knowledge, applying that knowledge to emerging societal problems and needs, and above all in preparing future leaders for all facets of society. In the face of mounting budgetary pressures among public institutions of higher education, private funding truly provides the desired margin of excellence in many educational, research, and public-service programs.

Enlightened alumni and community leadership are critical ingredients in stimulating private contributions to higher education. Analysts of philanthropy in the United States have observed that individual and collective participation in charitable causes may be motivated by numerous things—moral and religious upbringing, enlightened self-interest, economic benefits, self-gratification, a personal sense of altruism, and simply an aversion to social nonconformity. Others have observed that individuals (approximately 83 percent of all private donations are pledged by individuals) give with their heart, based on their respective value systems, whereas corporations give with their mind, based on economics and taxes. Collectively, private and corporate gifts currently provide about 8 percent of all higher education revenues.

Factors important to private fund-raising include (1) the strength and reputation of academic programs and faculty; (2) plans for future academic-support activities; (3) strong internal and external goals clearly supported by leadership; (4) the institutional mission and projected changes; (5) public confidence that the gifts will be used wisely; (6) a widespread belief all other sources of support are being pursued; and (7) a general public attitude that private gifts really are needed.

People do not commonly contribute in accordance with their ability to give but rather with their understanding of the need and the worth of their giving. Based upon the foregoing, it is clearly evident that public perceptions are highly important in raising private external monies for a publicly supported university. Level of giving is greatly affected by level of commitment, which in turn correlates with belief in program needs. People give most to the projects, programs, and activities they helped create.

Mark Twain once said, "If you want money, ask for advice. If you want advice, ask for money." Those who have enjoyed the pleasure of communicating the need for private monies with donors and prospective donors are keenly aware of the importance of personalizing the process. A cow will not give milk in response to a letter. The surest way to get milk from a cow is to sit down next to her, give her your undivided attention, be kind and considerate of her, and do not forget her when she shares some of Nature's most nearly perfect food. Mark Twain—and millions before and since—astutely observed the power of listening. Most prospective donors will tell you what they are most interested in supporting. For some, it is undergraduate scholarships, for others, research—often on some topic that touched their own life or that of a family member. Money is given **by** good people **to** good people in the best interests **of** good people.

Gifts may be quite specific. For example, one donor included in his will a provision that the gift be used to assure that all future students at the recipient institution be given the opportunity of having all the milk they wanted to drink. Another provided for one Irish white potato per student daily. Frequently, the decision to make gifts designated for a highly specific purpose or with special provisions is motivated by an experience in the donor's life. Some want the awarding of scholarships tied with need, others with part-time work, still others with both need and work.

Raising significant sums of private monies for routine repairs and maintenance is extremely difficult. Donors want their names or those of family members immortalized on buildings and endowed professorships, scholarships, and other important programs, not on plumbing or air conditioning or electrical systems. It is a bonus for the institution when a gift for capital improvement includes endowment provisions for perpetual maintenance.

In soliciting private support for land-grant institutions, it is well to peremptorily describe the uniqueness of the institution. Otherwise, the question, Why should these institutions be funded uniquely? may soon need to be answered. Good communications between institutional representatives and prospective donors cannot be overemphasized. Familiarity with needs begets involvement, which in turn begets commitment, which in turn begets private giving. In all, it is important to stress partnership with donors as well as being ever aware that people want to be associated with programs that help deserving people. Thomas Jefferson summarized it well: "I believe that every human mind feels pleasure in doing good to another."

12.9 Financial Aid Aspects of Financing Higher Education

A free and comprehensive education is the birthright of each child.

HORACE MANN (1837)

One of the toughest fiscal-policy issues in higher education is financial aid. These policies will shape not only the future of institutions, they will shape the future of higher education as well. The national system for financing the higher education of students is in disequilibrium. Federal policy now provides inadequate financial assistance for capable students from low-income families and underrepresented groups (decreased from 80 percent in 1982 to 74 percent in 1992).

The cost of higher education increased almost four times faster than family incomes between 1982 and 1992. State student support accounted for about 6 percent throughout the decade, whereas academic institutions increased their share of total student financial support from 12 percent to 19.5 percent. Most of the balance of increase in student financial support came from the parents and families of students.

In recent years (in addition to increases in other college costs) tuition has increased nearly three times as fast as inflation, twice as fast as the cost of living. This has made it extremely difficult for many students and their families to afford the cost of a college education. This situation explains in large part the findings of a recent study, which showed that approximately 28 percent of college freshmen indicated that financial assistance was an important factor in their selection of a college, whereas ten years ago the figure was only about 15 percent.

Results of another recent study showed that college graduates' inflation-adjusted incomes increased by 33 percent during the decade of the 1980s, while the incomes of those with only a high school diploma decreased by 11 percent. Moreover, during their lifetimes college graduates earn more than twice that of those who did not graduate from college. With the trend to more "high-tech" jobs, we can expect these numbers to become even more convincing. Not merely is the future of the next generation of individual Americans on the line—the future of the United States itself is on the line (Chapter 3). Our ability to provide high-quality higher education will be a critical factor in determining this nation's place as a world economic and political leader in the twenty-first century. Affordable tuition is good, common-sense public policy for this nation.

All this notwithstanding, a major force reshaping American higher education is increasing substitution of market revenues for public appropriations. As the need to restrain state budgets has forced reconsideration of public priorities, state legislatures have revisited expenditures for higher education and other public services, such as public schools (grades K-12), social welfare, correctional agencies, and health care. The trend has been to regard higher education as more of a private good than a public good. Having heard the message that a college education translates into the higher earnings associated with a good job, several legislatures have concluded that a college education contributes more to individual advancement than to national progress. One result: students enrolled in public institutions are being asked to pay increasingly larger portions of the cost of attaining a college education.

12.10 Responsibilities of Coordinating and Governing Boards

Few governing boards have the competence or the inclination to be innovative, to be experimental, to chart new courses. By their very nature governing boards tend to conserve what is and seek new paths only when a crisis is clearly at hand.

JOHN MILLETT

Throughout the United States, there exists a sense of uneasiness on the parts of governors, legislators, members of the academy, and others about the effectiveness and level of responsiveness of state coordinating boards and institutional governing boards. It is important that these entities demonstrate strong leadership in understanding and focusing on the economic, cultural, educational, social, and political environments in which universities operate. They should set forth the visions for higher education in their respective states and then serve as proponents of the system.

If asked how a land-grant university should be managed, this author would begin with the board of trustees, sometimes known as regents or curators. Each and every board member should be sincerely interested in education: persons who put academics ahead of athletics—those who clearly understand and support the role and purpose of land-grant institutions. They set the tone for a university, so it is incumbent upon them to give the president or chancellor all the support needed to carry out board policies and decisions, whether academic, philosophical, or other.

It is not necessary for every board member to always agree with the president (although, because of the deviousness of some board members, unanimity is the preferred vote). It is instead the role of the board to reach decisions by a majority vote. After the vote has been taken, however, that decision should be university policy until it is changed, and then only by another decision reached by majority vote. There need be no acrimony over differences. Responsible people should be able to express their views in such a manner that even though sharp differences may be held and vigorously expressed, they should be aired and then left in the boardroom. An important responsibility of the president or chancellor is to maintain continuous, effective communication with members of the governing board.

To attain the goal of achieving greater levels of excellence in service to students and other stakeholders, particularly in times of tight budgets, priorities must be set for the expenditure of monies. This often will include eliminating academic programs that have become obsolete or redundant. Governing boards must be prepared to make, support, and stand by tough decisions when thorough analysis—and not merely sentiment or vague discontent—indicates that current policies or procedures interfere with or impede the most effective use of an institution's fiscal resources. Serving on a board of higher education is a highly responsible honor. It should not be a position for individuals who need, in order to be able to function, a continuously high comfort level. Moreover, governing boards should communicate and deal with the president, not with deans, athletic directors, coaches, faculty and staff members, and others. When communications of any kind are received from persons other than the president, board members should refer them to the president for disposition.

Coordinating boards, governors, legislators, and other state officials share in the responsibility of searching for new and creative initiatives that will advance the values of both the state and higher education. Coordination of higher education is intended to achieve these common goals throughout the system and to sustain public support through accountability and efficiency.

Unity and effective coordination of higher education has been a common objective of state policy makers throughout the United States during the past four decades. During the 1950s, many states created coordinating boards to serve the dual purpose of protecting the autonomy of institutions while ensuring public accountability. The role and scope of these boards has expanded—as have their bloated budgets—as various issues have created the challenge of ensuring access and quality in view of state needs and fiscal resources. Among these are admissions and graduation standards, assessment of student learning, role and mission statements, the need for improvements in teacher education preparation, high school preparation for college, and equitable funding of operating and capital budgets.

As with many other state agencies, state coordinating boards tend to grow, to expand staff and administrative personnel, and thereby to siphon off precious appropriated monies urgently needed for libraries and academic programs in the institutions where the students are being taught. Powerful, overgrown coordinating boards often weaken individual institutions. Programmatic decisions should be made by institutions, not by coordinating boards. In the long run, dynamic institutions flourish best when they enjoy considerable autonomy—that is, when central coordinating boards are small or nonexistent.

In these times of tremendous stress on publicly appropriated monies, it is time to revisit the most cost-effective means of providing the coordination needed among institutions of higher education within a state. The recent New

Jersey experience of dissolving its higher education coordinating board has merit. The principal role of such a board should be to foster compatible, diverse, yet complementary approaches to meeting the state's educational needs in the most cost-effective manner possible. The board's job is to promote harmony among different and often competing institutions. Coordination should result in greater cooperation, not greater competition. It should not mean compelling institutions to accomplish goals through regulation and coercion, but unfortunately this increasingly is the case.

The recent case in New Jersey reportedly was that the coordinating board had focused mostly on resolving problems and conflicts created by their own lack of visionary policy on budget, tuition, and governance. They tended to emphasize regulation and compliance rather than a shared vision and plan for statewide higher education.

All too often, coordinating boards fail to move beyond the command-and-respond philosophy of an entrenched bureaucratic hierarchy geared for central control. Instead of producing justifiable, legitimate coordination among institutions, coordinating boards have tended to exacerbate tensions, polarize stakeholders, and lavishly consume precious public resources. Unfortunately, they usually have first "dibs" on newly appropriated state monies.

A common myth about state-level coordinating boards is that they buffer institutions from political interference. This simply is not the case in most states. The tendency is for statewide boards to cause enormous amounts of paperwork to be generated (much of which will never be used). In addition, they tend to usurp authority for long-range planning, budgets, and tuition that have been vested instead with individual institutional governing boards. The main motive of many coordinating boards seems to be preserving their own existence, expanding their staff and payroll, and expanding and exercising their authority.

Perhaps worst of all, most coordinating boards fail to provide the state a long-term vision for the value of higher education and a realistic plan for fulfilling such a vision. Coordinating boards could play a useful role if they would (1) stress maximal institutional-level autonomy and accountability with minimal state regulation, (2) reduce staff and size of operation, (3) develop a statewide higher education vision statement, (4) help develop and coordinate comprehensive statewide distance education programs, and (5) develop and promote a realistic plan to properly finance higher education and the programs and services needed by students, businesses, and citizens.

It would be well for political leaders of every state to review the excellent "1993 Report to the General Assembly of Virginia" submitted by that state's Council of Higher Education, which recommended: (1) decentralization of authority for operating institutions; (2) investing in new teaching technologies; (3) curricular streamlining; (4) competency-based credentialing; (5)

interdisciplinary approaches to learning; and (6) reconception of faculty roles and rewards.

12.11 Summary

If you are planning for one year, grow rice. If you are planning for twenty years, grow trees. If you are planning for centuries, grow and educate people.

CHINESE PROVERB

Higher education in the United States—still considered the best in the world—needs moral as well as financial support to meet the challenges of a changing world in the twenty-first century. Colleges and universities cannot live on loaves and fishes.

Recognizing that we live and function in a world of limited financial resources, steps must be taken to make the painful decisions related to rational priorities. In the past, resource acquisition has been top priority. Now, resource utilization needs first consideration. Increased emphasis on resource allocation and fiscal planning must be stressed in order to more effectively use the resources we already have. If these choices are made properly and promptly, land-grant institutions will be better positioned to deliver much-needed public services in the twenty-first century.

Institutional priority-setting and overhaul are needed, which will enable colleges and universities to offer new services by substitution, not merely by increased budgets. Outmoded services must be replaced by new, more useful ones. Certain basics are obvious in setting financial-expenditure priorities. These include scholarships, fellowships, and graduate assistantships to assure a steady stream of well-prepared human resources; research grants to assure the continued spawning of new science and technology; the resources needed to assure a high level of timely public services; and a strong library and other means of supporting information services.

As public funding for land-grant institutions has waned, philanthropic giving by individuals, corporate entities, alumni and friends, professional associations, and foundations has assumed a proportionately greater importance in the mix of funds required to sustain excellence in education and research programs, capital projects, programs for the enrichment of faculty, staff development, and support of students who depend on scholarships and fellowships. Institutions must never find themselves captive to single-source funding. Beyond publicly appropriated monies, the critical margin for excellence in land-grant and other colleges and universities is that provided by private gifts—an endorsement of the philosophy espoused by Thomas Jefferson: "The duty of every man is to devote a certain portion of his income for charitable purposes and ... his further duty is to see it applied to do the most good."

A Challenging Future for Land-Grant Institutions

At a time unlike any of the past, we must envision the future.
ABRAHAM LINCOLN

13.1   Introduction

The future belongs to those who believe in the beauty of their dreams.

ELEANOR ROOSEVELT

This is a time for land-grant colleges and universities to remember and reflect upon the past. A time to take inventory of the challenges and opportunities facing them today. A time to chart new courses as they plan and prepare for the twenty-first century.

It is sometimes useful to look back, but it is critical to look ahead. Some prefer to dwell on the past, to rest by the roadside swapping tales of yesteryear, to postpone change until the weather cools, the crops are in or out, the moon in a certain position. Former Michigan State University president John A. Hannah put it this way:

> I have never been much interested in the past except as one may avoid mistakes by not repeating them. To me, tomorrow is the important day, not yesterday. Tomorrow, today will be yesterday, and one cannot live it over again. I never learned much looking backwards, and I never wasted much time wishing that things might have been different.

We dare not retrace the long road of yesteryear. To honor it is one thing, but to prefer the past over the future will cost us the future. We should decide which parts of the past should be preserved, but more importantly we must

227

identify the needs and opportunities that lie ahead and commit ourselves to fulfilling them.

The future can be addressed in three ways: (1) by reacting to changes after they occur, (2) by resisting changes as they are occurring, or (3) by anticipating trends and opportunities and helping bring about needed changes. Progressive universities follow the latter course. But as they come to realize that difficult choices must be made, they must be certain that these choices are made purposefully, with inputs of as much information, insight, and imagination as can be mustered.

In large part, the future is ours to create. But we must provide the vision, the focus, the direction needed to deliver it. Moreover, there will be special moments when the doors will open and let the future in. Fortunate are those wise enough to recognize and capitalize upon such opportunities.

For well over a hundred years, land-grant institutions have demonstrated the ability to evolve to meet new challenges. Today they comprise a priceless resource. W. H. Cowley helped put this in perspective when he said:

> Colleges and universities are much more than knowledge factories; they are testaments to man's perennial struggle to make a better world for himself, his children, and his children's children. This, indeed, is their sovereign purpose. They are great fortifications against ignorance and irrationality; but they are more than places of higher learning—they are centers and symbols of man's higher yearning.

We must provide our children the opportunity to fully develop their intellects. We have an obligation to leave them an effective means of preparing for the future.

13.2 Preparing for the Future Through Strategic Planning

If you do not think about the future—you cannot have one.
JOHN GALSWORTHY

Abraham Lincoln once said that if he had eight hours to cut down a tree, he would spend seven hours sharpening his ax. This leads to the story of a robust woodsman who was furiously engaged in sawing down a huge tree. A friend passing by paused to observe that the woodsman looked worn out and asked, "How long have you been sawing?" The woodsman, with heart racing and breath short, responded, "About four hours." His friend commented,

"Maybe you would save time and energy if you sharpened your saw." The exhausted but determined woodsman replied, "I don't have time to sharpen my saw."

Strategic planning has to do with focus. It begins with development of a plan. This plan is not entirely based on past trends and future predictions, although they are important. This planning has to do with focusing so as to control destiny. Strategic planning involves identifying the things that matter most, determining what to do about them, and then setting a course for doing them. It includes sharpening institutional missions and goals, sharpening institutional focus, and sharpening individual commitments, as well as sharing ideas on ways and means of bringing about productive internal renewal.

It is especially important that we do extensive planning today lest future leaders reflect on our era as one in which what was everyone's business proved in the end to be no one's—a time when each looked to the other to take the lead and opportunities were lost. The shared vision, knowledge, and insights gained by participants in the process of strategic planning is as valuable as the ultimate plan per se. A major purpose is to inculcate a commitment to strategic thinking that in turn creates and sustains an environment of strategic management and decision making.

Sound planning looks outward. It focuses on keeping the institution in step with changing times, needs, and opportunities. Strategic focus is devoting intellectual energy to the areas that have real effects on our nation and the daily lives of its people.

Strategic planning involves formulating succinctly stated operational aims. It is based on what is expected of the institution—teaching, research, and outreach—and certain most probable conditions—the vitality of the economy, population demographics, priorities of the public, as well as the institution's traditions, strengths, and stability. Strategic decision-making in academe means the leaders are active in securing their position in history. It embraces the notion that one can help shape one's own destiny while at the same time being shaped by external forces.

Strategic planning is predicated on the reality that more of the same will not enable an institution to achieve the needed results. New ways must be found to more effectively and efficiently deploy the resources needed in education, research, and public service. This process has been underway in American industry for more than a decade, and the results have been noteworthy: productivity has enjoyed an average annual increase of nearly 4 percent.

Without strategic planning and sound fiscal management, because of internal institutional politics, resources well may be shifted from excellent programs to less deserving ones. Tensions may develop between those advancing the agenda of a particular sector and those responsible for developing the entire institution, so strategic planning must have holistic focus.

In all, when establishing priorities that will determine resource commitments it is important to have bona fide participation of all involved. Mere input refers to what happens when individuals or groups give their recommendations to policy makers who express thanks and proceed to do what they believe is best. Participation occurs when all interested parties discuss and develop alternatives on which there is general agreement to proceed.

13.3 Revitalizing Relevance and Reality in Land-Grant Institutions

Has not the famous political Fable of the Snake, with two Heads and one Body, some useful Instruction contained in it? She was going to a Brook to drink, and in her Way was to pass thro' a Hedge, a Twig of which opposed her direct Course; one Head chose to go on the right side of the Twig, the other on the left, so that time was spent in the Contest, and, before the Decision was completed, the poor Snake died with thirst.

BENJAMIN FRANKLIN

Land-grant institutions today face many challenges of consequence. How to prepare generalists as well as specialists in an age of specialization longing for more useful generalizations. How to make the university seem smaller as it inexorably grows larger. How to properly recognize faculty teaching, student counseling, research, and other scholarly efforts. How to develop courses and curricula that serve the needs of students as well as the scholarly interests of teachers. How to personalize instruction as more teaching is accomplished through educational technology. How to bring educational policy to the forefront of faculty concerns. How to position administrators so as to better relate to individual students, faculty, and staff. How to encourage the perception that administrators serve and stimulate rather than rule and regiment. How to achieve a recognizable margin of excellence in a populist society.

The ways we think about the past influence our destinies. As we reconsider, rediscover, reread, rethink, rechart, rewrite, reteach, recommemorate the past, we continuously rearrange the foundations upon which we operate as well as the dynamics that are ushering us into the future. Yet in this tumult of change it must be remembered that some things endure. Reason remains a constant force. Civilization and culture are cumulative and are rebuilt neither easily nor quickly. Work deserves reward. Progress relies on honesty and virtue.

Land-grant initiatives for the twenty-first century should be those known to benefit society through their ability to address timely public issues, facilitate public discourse, provide relevant knowledge, and increase the probability of collaborative solutions. Needed most today is the rediscovery and reimplementation of the fundamental concept underlying the original land-grant concept: a commitment to combine extension with research. The needs of our knowledge-based society of today are similar to those of the agricultural-cum-industrial society of a century ago. Now as then there is need for scientific and technical advances and means of bringing them to the workplace (Chapter 5). Commitment to public service by land-grant institutions has never been needed more than it is today.

A task as essential as it is difficult is to persuade administrative and disciplinary units that they are the basic building blocks of land-grant institutions. That it is impossible to put together a mosaic for the good of the whole without the strengths of the individual units being available to one another and to the whole. As Rudyard Kipling said, "The strength of the pack is in the wolf, and the strength of the wolf is in the pack."

Synergy is the essence of principle-centered leadership. The whole is greater than the sum of the parts, and each part is improved by being a part of the whole. The spirit of this attitude was shared by Helen Keller:

> I long to accomplish a great and noble task, but it is my chief duty to accomplish humble tasks as though they were great and noble. The world is moved along, not only by the mighty shoves of its heroes, but also by the aggregate of the tiny pushes of each honest worker.

13.4 Mission and Academic Trends in Land-Grant Institutions

We must begin by reconceptualizing the core academic mission. Most universities describe their mission as involving teaching, research, and extension with each of these mission components being treated as separate and conceptually distinct forms of professional activity.

JAMES VOTRUBA

The primary purpose of the land-grant system is to provide an environment in which faculty and students can discover, critically examine, organize, preserve, advance, and transmit the knowledge, wisdom, and values through teaching, research, and public service that will enhance and sustain survival of present and future generations as well as help improve the quality of human life. Cardinal John Henry Newman put it this way:

> A university is the high protecting power of all knowledge and science, of fact and principle, of inquiry and discovery, of experiment and speculation; it maps out the territory of the intellect, and sees that ... there is neither encroachment nor surrender on any side.

Academic trends include widespread agreement that teaching will remain the central mission of land-grant universities. But student choice of courses and curricula will increasingly challenge faculty prescriptions. The traditional residential campus will give way to more off-campus living. Service to the public will increase in many new directions, such as urban affairs, ecology, race relations, and internationally oriented organizations. The democratic impulse will dominate systems of governance leading to enhanced faculty, student, and staff representation, election, and consensus, rather than appointment and decision-making by institutional authorities. The locus of power to plan and allocate financial resources will gravitate toward managers of systems and centers of excellence.

Challenges facing undergraduate education include:

1. Preparing students for an increasingly wide range of opportunities and responsibilities offered by a changing society. Here, one can argue the need to sharpen curricula to ensure that students receive a meaningful mix of learning experiences. An equally pointed reason to simplify the curricula is to reduce costs and thereby realize savings that can be invested in new high-priority programs and other emerging needs.

2. Improving the preparation of students for college. Too much money is being spent on remedial courses at universities. This problem needs to be fixed in grades K-12.

3. Increasing the proportion of high school graduates who continue their education. Universities are gateways to many professions. Numerous high-technology fields require an increasingly better-educated workforce.

4. Meeting the educational needs of an increasingly diverse student population.

5. Improving ways and means of assessing student and institutional performance. The public is demanding this (Chapter 2).

6. Motivating faculty members and rewarding them properly for improving undergraduate education.

7. Increasing public awareness of the importance of undergraduate education.

8. Seeking comprehensive feedback from alumni about the effectiveness

of their undergraduate learning experiences.

9. Strengthening programs for accurately assessing the educational needs of new and returning students.

Although vacant faculty positions are at present not plentiful, demand for professorships is expected to increase significantly during the late 1990s and continue to increase into the twenty-first century because:

1. College enrollment is expected to increase as the progeny of the baby boom generation reach college age and as high school graduates increasingly realize that (a) modern technology forces workers into worldwide competition and (b) there is less room in the workforce for the less well-educated. The new world order includes acute competition in the workplace for the unskilled and less well educated.

2. Faculty members first hired in the 1950s and 1960s are retiring and thereby creating a large number of vacancies.

3. The number of U.S. citizens obtaining doctorates in the sciences each year has not increased appreciably for two decades, and there is no indication it will do so in the foreseeable future.

13.5 The Challenge and Importance of Vision Among Land-Grant Institutions

Sometimes institutions are simply the sum of the historical accidents that have happened to them. Like the sand dunes on the desert, they are shaped by influences but not by purposes; ... they are the unintended consequences of millions of fragmented purposes.

JOHN W. GARDNER

In the fifteenth century, China may well have been the most culturally and technologically advanced nation in the world. It owned great fleets of oceangoing vessels. In 1433, a fleet of Chinese ships sailed to Africa to trade, explore, and advance Chinese culture. But the Ming Empire had other priorities—problems at home, pressing needs elsewhere. They recalled the fleet and burned it, concluding it was time to end "wasteful" exploring.

About the same time China was burning its fleet, a small European nation's farsighted leader, Prince Henry of Portugal, Henry the Navigator, sent ships up and down the coast of Africa. Soon another European nation—

Spain—just emerging from centuries of war and internal turmoil, also launched a program of exploration. For a period, geographical neighbors Portugal and Spain competed to explore and use the new world Spain had discovered.

While Portugal did not abandon exploration as China did, it soon gave way to Spain through its gradual loss of sea-exploration capabilities. Spain went on to reap the benefits of two continents, ushering in a golden age for its people, an exciting period that lasted almost two centuries. With the destruction of the Spanish Armada in 1858, the British seized the leadership position with such expeditions as Sir Francis Drake's world voyage and Captain James Cook's Pacific excursions.

Nations lose their leadership position when they give up research, exploration, science, discovery. The question at hand for land-grant universities is this: Which pathway to take with regard to the oceans of needs and opportunities in the twenty-first century? Throughout the recorded history of humanity, the technological challenges have never been so great, the opportunities never so promising, but in some cases reaching the goals seems so distant. The world is rapidly changing, and to remain competitive and maintain global leadership in the twenty-first century the United States of America will need the best-educated and -trained workforce, the most advanced technology, and the strongest leadership in academe, business, and government. The challenge is before us—providing the opportunity to accept it and prove once again that there is in ordinary people an extraordinary resolve to be the best.

Who heads the Office of Vision for higher education? It is important to create a vision that projects beyond the local service area, one that recognizes major statewide and national trends. Through history there have been points in time when decisions set an institution's course for decades. The long-term legacy the land-grant system leaves to future generations may well be decided in the next few years.

The task of prophecy is complicated, and it is made more difficult by the internal and external crosscurrents to which universities are exposed. But first a university needs a purpose, a vision of its end goals. If it is to have an expressed vision, the president or chancellor must be identified with it. Successful leaders for the twenty-first century will be those who embrace the future, those who value continuous learning for themselves and their institution, those who are well-grounded in beliefs and values that provide an empowering educational environment for the university family. Beardsley Ruml summarized it this way:

> The president of a college or university is the highest personal symbol. He is the one who must develop and articulate a compelling vision that will unite the students, alumni, faculty, staff, donors, and trustees and lead them to set aside at least some of their parochial concerns and conflicts.

13.6 Individual Commitment to Excellence in Teaching, Research, and Service

We are what we repeatedly do. Excellence, then, is not an act, but a habit.

ARISTOTLE

The quest for excellence is truly a democratic rather than an elitist pursuit, inviting the involvement of men and women of widely diverse capabilities and talents. Excellence is often best realized in an environment where both ordinary and exceptional individuals are inspired to strive for and accomplish the extraordinary. This is neither predestined nor does it occur by accident. People must make it happen through their vision and commitment. Moreover, excellence is a fleeting state of existence. Never permanent, it must be fervently pursued on a continuing basis.

Excellence is a matter of purpose, of commitment, of resources, not of size. It is so precious and highly respected that it is well worth the extra effort necessary to achieve it. Achieving excellence in academe fulfills faculty, staff, students, alumni, and friends. The pursuit of excellence per se provides its own intrinsic rewards.

When the university family is individually and collectively committed to attaining ever higher levels of academic, professional, and institutional excellence, when they possess a common thread of uncommonly strong commitment to these goals, when institutional strategies and priorities have been developed and necessary underpinnings of academic programs with high standards of performance and public accountability are in place, the stage has been set for inspired and resourceful individuals to achieve high levels of excellence in teaching, research, and public service.

Resolute commitment, sincere and persistent effort, intelligent direction, and skillful execution are paramount in achieving excellence. Consider Andrew Jackson, who—although a natural runner—was considered too light to be a successful wrestler. Yet Jackson could not be defeated. As one of his classmates put it: "I could throw him three times out of four, but he would never stay down. He ... never would give up." Like Jackson, individuals committed to excellence have a positive attitude, a commendable outlook on life, a strong work ethic, an unwavering determination to utilize the spirit of competition to demonstrate excellence. They are dedicated, intense, motivated, formidable professionals!

Many distinguished individuals have shared their philosophies, experiences, and observations related to the topics of excellence, work ethic, and contributions to others. Selected examples follow:

All things excellent are as difficult as they are rare.

WALTER O. ROBERTS

Wealth, notoriety, place, and power are no measure of success whatever. The only true measure of success is the ratio between what we might have done and what we might have been on one hand, and the thing we have made and the thing we have made of ourselves on the other.

HERBERT G. WELLS

I want to be thoroughly used up when I die, for the harder I work, the more I live. Life is no brief candle for me. It is sort of a splendid torch which I have hold of for the moment, and I want to make it burn as brightly as possible before handing it on to future generations.

GEORGE BERNARD SHAW

Quality is never an accident; it is always the result of high intention, sincere effort, intelligent direction and skillful expectation; it represents the wise choice of many alternatives.

ELBERT L. JONES

Standards are contagious. They spread throughout an organization, a group or a society.

JOHN W. GARDNER

Lord grant that I may always desire more than I can accomplish.

MICHELANGELO (1475–1564)

One contributes most in life when he spends it for something that will outlast it.

JAMES BELL

13.7   Impact of Public Policies, Issues, and Priorities

> *... that education should be regulated by law and should be an affair of state is not to be denied, but what should be the character of this public education, and how young persons should be educated, are questions which remain to be considered. ... Neither is it clear whether education is more concerned with intellectual or with moral virtue.*
>
> **ARISTOTLE**

As we approach the end of the twentieth century, the people of the world are reaping rich benefits from a half century of broad-based investment in science and technology. The knowledge generated by scientists, mathematicians, and engineers has dramatically increased agricultural production; created new industries, such as semiconductor manufacturing and biotechnology; connected all parts of the world through information networks; and created the means for a healthier and longer human life span.

With the close of the Cold War, United States policy makers will likely focus more attention on economic and social concerns. Through the first decade of the twenty-first century, we will confront public policy issues that require the integration of accepted scientific knowledge, scientific uncertainty, and conflicting ethical, economic, and political values. Proliferating social problems are outpacing the wisdom needed to resolve them.

What major changes in communications, geopolitics, and technology can we expect the next millennium to bring? Recent trends indicate that substantial emphasis will be given to three "E's"—education, environment, and ethics. The public is going to place high priority on these broad areas of concern. While the public will is sometimes slow to work its way through the political process, in time it does do just that, and elected officials respond accordingly.

Additional emerging public concerns that will influence the near-term future of higher education include three "A's"—accessibility, accountability, and affordability. Included in these are economics, the new demographics, and racial and cultural tensions resulting from the dilemma of providing equal access and educational opportunity to underserved minority groups as well as the quality of undergraduate education. And then there is the matter of ethics, both as a subject for learning and as practiced by the professoriate. Taxpayers, parents, and students alike are demanding much greater accountability.

In a democratic society, it is often difficult to agree on the importance of a particular issue. There are multiple perspectives as to what is in the best interest of the public. Challenges this brings include: short-term focus, inability to demonstrate immediate results, and fierce competition for governmental funding. Many have concluded that during the past century we have focused on the problems of rural America more than on those of urban America. In any case, problems of urban cultures are manifold and must be comprehensively addressed. Only institutions that rethink their roles, responsibilities, and structures in light of contemporary mandates, opportunities, and priorities will be prepared to compete successfully and contribute meaningfully in the twenty-first century.

13.8   Increasing Contributions of Women to Higher Education

The true measure of life is not its duration, but its donation.
NAOMI MUNCY

The notion that women should have unfettered access to a college education is a relatively recent development in the United States. It was not until late in the nineteenth century that the concept of educating young women beyond elementary school was embraced. Even as women were gradually permitted to enter high school and college, the guiding principle for a long time was separate and unequal.

In 1833, Oberlin College became the first in the United States to admit women. But for many years these female college students were offered less rigorous courses and moreover were required to wait on and wash the clothes of the male students! It was only in the aftermath of the Civil War that co-education became more prevalent on campuses across the country. But even then, economics not equity was the driving force. Since casualties of war meant the loss of male students and their tuition dollars, many colleges and universities turned to women to fill classrooms and replenish coffers. Still in 1870, more than two-thirds of American universities barred women. By 1900, however, more than two-thirds admitted women.

Today most female and male students attend the same institutions, sit in the same classrooms, read the same books. But the legacy of inequity continues beneath a veneer of equal access. Female students rarely see mention of the contributions of women in the curriculum, and most textbooks continue the practice of reporting predominantly male worlds. To complete the agenda for equity, educational institutions must empower female students to fully participate in society.

As recently as thirty years ago women had few professional career choices. Most went into teaching or nursing. Today, women truly have unlimited career options. And while they have been slow to enter engineering, physics, and geology, they now represent approximately 40 percent of the biological scientists, 30 percent of the chemists, and nearly 60 percent of the psychologists. In 1992, 5500 women earned medical degrees in the United States, but only eighty-six women were awarded doctorates in physics.

Women are contributing greatly to the movement toward increased emphasis on undergraduate education. Since Congress enacted Title IX of the Education Amendments of 1972—legislation that outlawed sex discrimination in colleges and universities receiving federal monies—there have been numerous notable advances in gender equity. For example, U.S. Department of Education data show that:

- Women now comprise about 59 percent of all undergraduate students.
- For the first time in U.S. history, women are more likely than men to seek all major types of advanced degrees—master's, doctoral, medical, and law, among others.
- Women now receive approximately 44 percent of all doctorates awarded to United States citizens—up from only 19 percent as recently as 1973.
- The proportion of women receiving master's degrees in business administration has increased almost ninefold (from 4 percent in 1972 to nearly 35 percent in 1994).
- Women now constitute approximately 25 percent of all newly employed assistant professors—nearly double the figure in 1972.
- The proportion of full-time faculty members who are women increased from 27 percent to 35 percent during the last decade (many of these are temporary positions, however).
- Women now comprise about 12 percent of college and university presidents—up from only 5 percent two decades ago.
- Since 1972, women's studies curricula have achieved full legitimacy in academe—from only a few dozen in 1972 to thousands now.

In 1991, women comprised 88 percent of all elementary school teachers and 56 percent of all secondary teachers in the United States. Overall, women represent about 45 percent of the United States workforce, and during the 1990s women comprise approximately two-thirds of the new entrants into the workforce.

13.9 Enhanced Opportunities for Land-Grant Universities

An institution cannot be understood without first understanding the conditions that led to its creation.

JOHN K. GALBRAITH

For land-grant colleges and universities of the twenty-first century, will it be **outlook** or **lookout?** While the future may appear somewhat foggy, the answer to the question depends in large part on the vision, commitment, and focus of members of the land-grant family who can, through proper direction and close communication with the public, create a highly responsive educational system to address public needs (Chapter 14).

The future of the United States depends to a great extent on a responsive, service-oriented land-grant college and university system that can provide vision, leadership, teaching resources, a well-trained workforce, and research and technology to enable the nation to move forward as a strong global competitor and contributor.

Academic institutions are in a state of transition across the land. Land-grant universities have a distinct opportunity to emerge as the best-working higher-education model for the twenty-first century—the institutions best able to meet the educational and public service needs of the future. Indeed, the education and development of those who will lead the world in science and education, in business and industry, in social advances and other important ways is a challenge which land-grant colleges and universities should accept.

In the early history of our Republic, educational levels among the American people were relatively equal: few had much formal education. Then the wealthy became able to attend college, which resulted in an upper tier of substantially better-educated individuals. This untenable situation served as impetus for the 1862 Land-Grant Act that established low-cost, high-access higher education for the sons and daughters of the working class.

There are few greater challenges facing the United States today than that of bringing larger numbers of the poor, the educationally and economically disadvantaged, and the disenfranchised into the mainstream of society. This can best be accomplished through education. Unfortunately, rapidly rising tuition costs at land-grant and other public colleges and universities is pricing many academically capable potential students from low-income families out of an equal opportunity to pursue further education.

At a time when post-high school education is more important to job procurement and lifelong success than ever before, attending college is also more expensive than ever. If the situation is not changed soon, this nation is at risk of losing the potential career contributions of an increasingly large number of low-income and middle-class students and of once again becoming a two-tiered society, with a small privileged group of educated people and a large number of less-fortunate individuals struggling below. Land-grant institutions need to provide leadership in program-cost-containment in order to hold the line on tuition costs and thereby recapture public support as "the people's universities." In December 1994, the Board of Trustees of Michigan State University—one of the nation's premiere land-grant institutions—pledged to limit tuition increases during the next four years to increments no greater than those in the consumer price index.

13.10 Summary

America has the most universal system of higher education of any other nation in the world; ... these institutions have had enormous impact on the growth, culture, and career development of the American people. ... As America's colleges and universities wrestle with present-day issues, ... the land-grant colleges and universities shall survive because they have become an inextricable part of the people and politics of America.

F. W. NICHOLAS, SR.

We are clearly at an important branching in this nation's higher education. Educators are grappling with numerous complex challenges. Waves of economic, demographic, educational, and technological changes demand that colleges reconsider whom they will teach, what they will teach, how they will teach, the degree to which the classroom of tomorrow will change, and even whether learning will occur in classrooms. Of one thing we can be sure: business as usual will not suffice. Either we will shape the future or it will shape us. Either we will change or we will be changed. Act or be acted upon. As successful businesses have had to do, institutions of higher education must look for every opportunity to become more efficient, improve customer services, and reduce costs.

The future vitality of land-grant colleges and universities will be defined by their ability to control costs and promote learning and scholarship and their commitment to access and equity. Strategic planning is a crucial management tool for institutions of higher education interested in service and survival.

The strategy offering higher education the greatest hope is synergism—mutualistic collaboration. Whereas in the past we have had consortia of universities working together, the consortia of the future will be comprised of universities, business and industry, public advisory groups, and government —federal and state—working together.

Rather than dwelling on nostalgia, land-grant universities need to accept contemporary reality. This reality is the widespread recognition that new knowledge is a fundamental factor of economic and social growth. The university's primary product—knowledge—is unarguably the most precious and at the same time the most powerful single element in the culture of higher education. It affects the rise and fall of faculty members' careers just as it does the rise and fall of social classes and nations.

The most important service that can be rendered by higher education is that of fulfilling the educational needs of students. To do this most effectively and efficiently requires overcoming one of the most powerful forces in human nature: resistance to change (Chapter 11). Yet change is utterly essential to assuring a steady stream of crucial new knowledge, and in achieving greater efficiency in the various functions and services of academe.

Institutional excellence does not exist in a vacuum, nor does it operate at some unseen higher level. It touches the daily lives of everyone associated with the university, influencing their every thought and judgment, stimulating their desires—indeed, their drives—to serve in an exemplary fashion. Institutional excellence reflects synergism. It is the enhanced product of professionalism and dedication on the parts of all who participate in charting the university's course. The quest for excellence is a powerful creative process, dispelling apathy and overcoming the natural, comfortable inertia of mediocrity. Maintaining excellence is the best way to attract the most academically talented students and thereby to ensure continuing excellence.

The new millennium will provide reasons for pessimism to those who look for them. But ultimately pessimism is a delusion and a snare. While there will be new problems to confront, there also will be new opportunities to seize. At best, we can only try to peer through the mists to discern the shape of the future which, when viewed from the perspective of an optimist, will be seen as being resplendent with opportunity. Thomas Jefferson portrayed that perception and attitude when he wrote, "I like the dreams of the future better than the history of the past."

Renewing the Public Promise:
A Plan of Action

It was the best of times, it was the worst of times. It was the age of wisdom, it was the age of foolishness. It was the epoch of belief, it was the epoch of incredulity. It was the season of light, it was the season of darkness. It was the spring of hope, it was the winter of despair. We had everything before us, we had nothing before us.

CHARLES DICKENS (1859)
A Tale of Two Cities

14.1 Introduction

We cannot avoid our duty. With the primacy of power is also joined an awe-inspiring accountability for the future.
SIR WINSTON CHURCHILL

Education has always been important to the United States, but never more important than it is today. Our competitors for business opportunity and global market share also are working to better educate their people. If we are to lead the world, we must first lead the world educationally. Education is an absolutely essential feature of our quality of life. It is at the heart of economic strength and security, creativity in the arts and letters, invention in the sciences, and perpetuation of cultural values.

The land-grant movement was originally driven by a broad national consensus that higher education should be available to the poor as well as the rich, to women as well as men, to those of color as well as those of European origin. From the beginning, the land-grant university system has had as one of its objectives the extending of practical education based on scientific knowledge to working people.

The results have been remarkable. The first century following passage of the monumental land-grant act was a golden age for higher education. The United States developed the world's best research universities, enrollments burgeoned, sponsored research increased dramatically, and extension and other forms of outreach came into their own. Civilization and democracy flourished, and people respected and supported higher education. It seemed to many that it would continue forever.

But more recently public discussions have focused attention on the problems and weaknesses of higher education and even minimized its strengths and contributions to society. "Efficiency" and "accountability" have become fashionable words. Those who wish to hold colleges and universities more accountable are demanding that the outcomes of higher education be identified, measured, and compared with the costs.

Of course, outcomes are so complex and varied that they are not easy to identify and measure. The situation is exacerbated by the fact that, for many taxpayers, higher education is not part of their personal experience, and they see no immediate, practical reasons to give priority to higher education over many of the other needs of modern society. Unless and until taxpayers insist on higher education being a higher budgetary priority, elected public officials are unlikely to give it special attention.

As a result of all this, what once was the envy and hope of many nations—a model of excellent, accessible higher education—is losing the favored position it once enjoyed in American life. Higher education no longer finds itself exempt from coming under the intense scrutiny of an increasingly skeptical—even cynical—public (Chapter 2).

As university financial aid decreased in real dollars and tuition charges and other fees have increased, enrollments have been capped at many institutions. As a consequence, accessibility to higher education—especially for students from low-income families—has become more restrictive. Private support has not increased enough to fully compensate for budgetary shortfalls. Morale among university faculties and staffs nationwide has never been lower. This detracts further from the image higher education wishes to present, leading in turn to further loss of the vital public support needed to enable it to play an expanded role in scientific discovery, technology development and transfer, and overall economic development. These circumstances make it especially important that higher education make compelling arguments to taxpayers—particularly those who have never attended college and who have no college-graduate or -bound children—that everyone in society has a vested interest in higher education as an enterprise essential to a high-quality life for all Americans.

14.2   National Association of State Universities and Land-Grant Colleges

Our progress as a nation can be no swifter than our progress in education.

                                                    JOHN F. KENNEDY

The idea that education and research have been great American strengths—entities employed in a democratic setting to effect a civil, prosperous, technologically advanced culture—is valid. Our nation's future is inexorably tied to the success of our education system, thus no other single enterprise so richly deserves or so urgently needs the support of this nation.

The uniquely American land-grant college and university system is without peer. It is the envy and hope of the world. As Peter Magrath, president of the National Association of State Universities and Land-Grant Colleges (NASULGC), has so succinctly noted, "America's state universities and land-grant colleges—all of them truly people's universities—are a marvelous enterprise that has served our nation superbly. They are fundamental to our democratic system and essential to our aspirations for a better, more just future." But past performance will not secure future preeminence. The world has taken note of our technological and cultural success stimulated by effective public higher education and has now begun to copy the system.

As the United States prepares for the twenty-first century, higher education—and its strong research-extension arms—must and will respond to public needs but also to the substantially increased international competition that determines technological and cultural world leadership.

NASULGC is a voluntary association that provides the leadership to evaluate national needs, determine priorities, and communicate with state and national elected officials and the public. This important association represents 182 institutions, including all 105 land-grant colleges and universities located in the fifty states, the U.S. territories, and the District of Columbia. There are now approximately 20 million alumni of NASULGC institutions. In 1995 more than 2.9 million students were enrolled in these colleges and universities. Each year NASULGC institutions award approximately 500,000 degrees, including about one-third of all baccalaureate and master's degrees, 60 percent of all doctoral degrees, and 70 percent of all engineering degrees awarded in the United States.

In November 1991, the NASULGC senate voted to reorganize the association in accordance with principles contained in a study called "A Charter for the Nineties and Beyond." The new structure established councils and commissions as the major operational program units. Councils are groups of persons with similar roles at member institutions, organized for the primary purpose of communication with one another and with relevant groups about issues involving federal legislation and academic issues. Commissions maintain oversight over broad federal legislative and other issue areas of interest to their specific members. They are similar to interdisciplinary centers within a university. All significant insights and information generated through the deliberations of these organs is shared with member institutions in order to provide focus at the national level.

In this manner the land-grant colleges and state universities, working through their revitalized national association, are effectively positioned to deal with the enormous changes—social, economic, technological—that are impacting our nation in general and its higher educational system in particular. Change is essential for our public land-grant universities as they struggle to continue to be vibrant and relevant in the century ahead. A significant reordering of priorities and ways of going about the work of public higher education is already occurring at many universities; and by working through their national association at all administrative levels and involving all academic disciplines, these institutions can demonstrate the system's key priorities and specific needs to be accomplished, thus communicating a reinforcing message throughout the higher education system. Providing prioritization at the national level is a paramount contribution of NASULGC—a function clearly in keeping with an observation advanced by author-futurist Peter Drucker: "Management is doing things right; leadership is doing the right things."

14.3 Directions for Education, Research, and Public Service

Do not look backward on the finite shadows of the past; instead, walk tall and proud into the unlimited expanse of the future.

ZAYD O. AYERS

The education, research, and public-service successes of those who have gone before serve as a challenge to us now to provide present-day vision and leadership, which are essential to building a better future. As Ralph Waldo Emerson said, "This time, like all times, is a very good one if we but know what to do with it."

The future of higher education in the United States should be based on the following propositions and philosophies:

That higher education contributes to the cognitive and affective qualities, and to the practical competence of people as individuals, and is therefore conducive to their full development as human beings. This proposition is underpinned by the benefits of receiving a well-rounded, general education, as noted by Benjamin Jowett: "No man will be a first-rate physician or engineer who is not something more than either, who has not some taste for art, some feeling for literature, or some other interest external to these professions. The great charm of universities, which gives them such a hold in life, is that they form a society in which mind is brought into contact with mind, and there is conversation and enthusiasm for knowledge and united help in study."

That higher education enhances the quality of social life in many ways. As noted by education leader Horace Mann, "Education then, beyond all other devices of human origin, is the greatest equalizer of the condition of men—the balance-wheel of the social machinery."

Alexander Heard shared this thought: "Our largest common goal in higher education, indeed in all education, is to create and stimulate the kind of learning that breeds strength and humor and hope within a person, and that helps build a society outside him that stirs his pride and commands his affection."

And British author-social reformer John Ruskin, in his work *Unto This Last,* wrote: "Production does not consist in things laboriously made, but rather in things socially consumable; and the question for the nation is not how much labor it employs but how much life it produces. For as consumption is the end and aim of production, so life is the end and aim of consumption. There is no wealth but life."

That the number of persons who could benefit from higher education greatly exceeds the number now enrolled, especially if innovative programs suited to diverse clienteles were available. Plato noted more than 2000 years ago that "the direction in which education starts a man will determine his future life."

British mathematician-philosopher Alfred North Whitehead put it this way: "In the condition of modern life, the rule is absolute: the race which does not value trained intelligence is doomed. ... There will be no appeal from the judgment which will be pronounced on the uneducated."

And scientist-scholar Albert Einstein put the whole of the origin of education in perspective—as he did the new concepts of time, space, mass, motion, and gravitation through his theory of relativity—when he wrote, "Bear in mind that the wonderful things you learn in your schools are the work of many generations—all this is put into your hands as your inheritance in order that you may receive it, add to it, and one day faithfully hand it on to your children."

That each person should have the opportunity to develop fully his or her unique personal abilities. Samuel Chapman Armstrong noted in 1868: "In the school room, students have their opportunity to learn the three great lessons of life—how to live, how to labor, and how to teach others."

More than 2000 years ago the Greek philosopher Aristotle wrote, "Education is the best provision for old age."

While strongly encouraging students to pursue a college education, I also subscribe to the following bit of philosophy espoused by John W. Gardner: "An excellent plumber is infinitely more admirable than an incompetent philosopher. The society which scorns excellence in plumbing because plumbing is a humble activity and tolerates shoddiness in philosophy because it is an exalted activity will have neither good plumbing nor good philosophy. Neither its pipes nor its theories will hold water."

Land-grant institutions must continue to address the changing constellation of forces impinging upon individuals and families—and ultimately upon all of humanity worldwide. The psycho-social-cultural-spiritual needs of individuals, families, and groups in global context will require ever more creative approaches in teaching, research, and public service.

Two somewhat diverse influences—the needs of emerging democracies to ensure family well-being and develop requisite competencies for managing resources, on the one hand, and the needs of a greatly expanding service-oriented economy, accelerated by the technological advances of The Information Age, on the other—provide an environment for one of the most challenging and potentially rewarding periods in the history of the land-grant system. Providing visionary leaders and all-important human resources for an age to be characterized by social, political, educational, and leadership empowerment are crucial to maintaining the family as the bedrock of civilization. As we approach the twenty-first century, it is imperative that the land-grant system, in the words of General Omar Bradley,

> steers their ships by the stars ... importantly, the constants of the profession—individuals, families, humanity— ... rather than by the lights of every ship ... —elusive trends, fleeting concepts— ... that passes.

Significant challenges facing higher education include negative public perceptions of higher education that translate into weak public support; significant demographic shifts; financial-shortfall and cost-containment pressures; ever-changing revenue structures; needs and opportunities to work more closely with business and industry; rapid technological advances; deteriorating facilities and increasing capital-expenditure needs; the need to re-place technically obsolete instruments and equipment; noncompetitive salaries for faculty and staff; and an increasingly globally competitive economic environment.

Most of these are related to budget, which should come as no surprise because, as noted by John E. Cribbet, "while dollars alone will not build a great university, no great institution was ever built without material resources."

To meet the projected national needs of the twenty-first century, a substantial cadre of scientists, engineers, physicians and other health-care professionals, social scientists, teachers, social workers, humanists, and other vocationally trained persons will be needed to help find ways and means of conserving resources, cleaning the environment, restoring cities, improving the nation's infrastructure, overcoming racial injustice, improving health and health care, eradicating poverty, and achieving economic stability. There will be no shortage of work to be done as the nation addresses these and other problems in its attempt to build a better life for its citizens.

Addressing these public needs calls for an intensified effort in research and public service. More not less. To achieve these goals, land-grant institutions should be called on (and then supported accordingly) to give increasing attention to the advancement of basic knowledge, the preservation of our cultural heritages, the exploration of means and values in contemporary settings, the evaluation of public policies and societal trends, and the cultivation of the arts.

To what degree should land-grant colleges and universities respond to public expectations for them to address these and other related social, political, and economic priorities? This author believes that helping resolve these concerns should be viewed as important opportunities to regain public trust. Land-grant institutions of higher education and the larger purposes of our society have from their inceptions been inextricably intertwined. It is important to maximize the effectiveness of America's land-grant institutions through institutional bridge-building.

14.4 Important Resources for Renewal of Land-Grant Colleges and Universities

The main fuel to speed our progress is our stock of knowledge, and our brake is our lack of imagination. The ultimate resource is people—skilled, spirited, and hopeful people who will exert their wills and imagination for their own benefit, and so, inevitably, for the benefit of us all.

JULIAN W. SIMON
The Ultimate Resource

Land-grant colleges and universities have long been known for their dedication to serving society. Unfortunately, society has changed faster than have the land-grant institutions. We have a great opportunity to renew and increase our commitment and our value to national and global societies by assertively and confidently moving to bring needed reform to the land-grant colleges and universities.

Land-grant institutions have a great deal of power at their command:

The power of knowledge and information. The global Information Age focuses on the value of knowledge. American science and technology are challenged by extraordinary opportunities to expand the knowledge-based horizons of humankind. The challenging frontier is not to be found to the east or west nor to the north or south. It is to be found in the laboratories and libraries of research universities, where human intellect, curiosity, ingenuity, and skills are unlocking the secrets of Nature at an ever-increasing pace.

The power of diversity. This nation has been made much stronger and more competitive through its import of courageous, determined, and talented people thoroughly representing the nations and cultures of the world.

The power of a distinguished faculty and staff. When an institution of higher education chooses its faculty and staff, it chooses its future.

The power of students and their families. Students, their families, relatives, and friends represent a sizable portion of society. When these people become mobilized, they can significantly influence the institutional support base.

The power of dedicated alumni. Properly educated with respect to their alma mater's needs and opportunities, alumni can have great impact on public policy and support. A large number of alumni hold elected positions of public responsibility at all levels.

The power of a rich heritage. Overall, public confidence in the people who conduct agricultural research and deliver technology applications to farmers remains high. Those who served in the past built a solid reservoir of goodwill among the user group. The well-proven system of agricultural education and research that already exists in land-grant colleges and universities translates into the fact that preserving a rich heritage and expanding the education and research agenda modestly can be accomplished at a marginal cost more modest than the full cost associated with creating new agencies and bureaucracies.

The power of a motivatable citizenry. To help achieve the potential of this resource, higher priority must be given to informing the public, and their elected officials and representatives of the contributions, goals, and needs of land-grant colleges and universities.

Scope for improvement notwithstanding, the land-grant college and university system demonstrates considerable flexibility, great competitiveness, and outstanding productivity. The new can be tested and the old retested with much alacrity and skill. The pluralism of higher education approximates that of American society. The general test of land-grant institutions is not how much is done in mediocre fashion (although some is), but rather how much is done in exemplary fashion (and much is). Indeed, much of that done in exemplary fashion is to the nation's great benefit. The challenges to do more with less are great, and so must be the collective wills and commitments to favorably impact the destiny of America's world-renowned land-grant colleges and universities.

14.5   Renewing the Public Contract

You cannot escape the responsibility of tomorrow by evading it today.

ABRAHAM LINCOLN

A recent statement by the National Research Council defines the situation: "The land-grant system must renew its social contract. The system must respond to a changing student body, a changing clientele, and changing technology for information delivery. Old structures and cultural norms no longer fully meet the demands of these new realities."

In a January 12, 1994, presentation to the Committee on the Future of Agriculture, Board on Agriculture and Renewable Resources, National Research Council, entitled "Preparing for the Next Century: The Land-Grant Universities in a Period of Transition," Emery N. Castle noted three fundamental characteristics of the land-grant system that will continue to have meaning in the period ahead.

1. **Usefulness of social relevance.** Here Castle observed that land-grant institutions were not founded on the principle of knowledge for knowledge's sake. The consequences of education and research make a difference in the lives of people.

2. **Accessibility.** Here he emphasized the philosophy of Thomas Jeffer-

son, who believed something approaching universal access to higher education was important to the future of the Republic. Castle noted further that today many people view land-grant universities as elitist organizations unconcerned with the welfare of disadvantaged groups.

3. **Decentralization.** Here Castle expressed the view that much of the extraordinary productivity of the land-grant system reflects the considerable local autonomy that enabled local conditions to affect the design of research and educational programs.

Land-grant colleges and universities are people. Revitalization of an institution must therefore begin with renewal of the people who comprise it. The land-grant system will never be better than the capabilities and commitments of those involved in it at the various levels.

Today we need to reclaim the visions of people such as:

Jonathan Baldwin Turner, who first envisioned the possibility and potentiality of—as he conceptualized and called it—a university for the industrial classes.

Justin Smith Morrill, who transformed Turner's dream into the reality of the 1862 land-grant colleges and the historically black 1890 land-grant institutions.

Congressman **William Henry Hatch,** father of State Agricultural Experiment Stations.

And Georgia's **Hoke Smith** and South Carolina's **Asbury Lever**, whose legislation in 1914 provided the foundation for agricultural extension as well as technology transfer in the United States.

The focus of the collective foresight of these leaders was expressed by Justin Smith Morrill, whose original bill envisioned the public interest as having everything to do with an education that would be, first, accessible to students of all economic classes; second, practical as well as classical; and third, supported in part by the federal government.

Reclaiming the visions of these visionaries may mean redefining our jobs as we try to fulfill the public's goals and needs. An ongoing vigil aimed at serving the public good must be maintained, and the public must be reminded that land-grant institutions were created to do just that and that they indeed continue to do just that. To accomplish this goal depends on our ability to maintain the public trust. We must articulate clear priorities, uphold standards of integrity and accountability, and inform the public—enthusiastically and patiently—that the primary focus of our activities is and always has been the public good. Whether we succeed or fail in this initiative depends on whether the general public trusts those who comprise the land-grant institutions.

Students must remain the primary focus of land-grant colleges and universities. But not their only focus, as these institutions rightly continue to reach out beyond campus boundaries to assist individuals, groups, and businesses as needed and as they continue to conduct research in the land-grant tradition related to agriculture, engineering, forestry, home economics, marketing, veterinary medicine, and many related disciplines as well as social, economic, and political aspects of the American system of free enterprise.

Land-grant colleges and universities are accountable to their various publics for high-quality, productive, efficient performance on all mission fronts. Yes, they must demonstrate that they teach—and well; that they serve their various clientele groups—and well; and that their research, scholarship, and creative activity—the distinguishing missions of comprehensive universities—buttress teaching and public service—and well.

The future of land-grant colleges and universities will be what its people make it. The future will be shaped by choices people make, structures people choose to implement. Institutional excellence, as with a kite, flies as high as the forces behind it. And those forces include individuals external to the academy who will decide how much public support is to be allocated as well as creative, professionally competent, committed people working internally who will actually accomplish the university's deeds.

14.6 An Agenda for Action

Be ashamed to die until you have won some victory for humanity.

HORACE MANN

The day is short, the labor is long, the workers are idle, the rewards are great, and the master is urgent.

JOSEPH L. BARON

Have you ever thought about the enormous amount of planning that must have been involved in designing the great pyramids of Egypt with precisely the correct angle? If they had been designed to have a greater angle, they would have been vulnerable to winds. If they had been designed with a wider base and flatter top, the base would have moved outward in the sand. It is important today for land-grant colleges and universities to develop a comprehensive, responsive, responsible plan, and then to develop an action agenda to implement this plan.

All members of the land-grant system can take pride in what has been accomplished so far. Now we must recommit our collective efforts to doing more. Past success does not assure future success. It is important to reaffirm our past ideals, our rich heritage and traditions. This is the time to rekindle our pioneering spirit, to prepare to meet the challenges and fulfill the opportunities of the twenty-first century.

Public service means more than doing good things for others. In today's society, public service means that university faculty help apply knowledge to "real" problems. Knowledge must be brought into intimate relationship with the real problems and real concerns of real people: connecting theory and thought to action and practice. Land-grant colleges and universities must be viewed as having rededicated their commitment to improve the human condition. We must make it clear that what we do is relevant to society's concerns and needs. If we fail to clearly align ourselves with public priorities, we shall be low priority with—considered irrelevant and unresponsive by—the public.

Land-grant institutions must keep aware of the fact that sometime early in the twenty-first century, many of the most populous states will have no single racial majority. Recruiting, welcoming, and including students from diverse cultural backgrounds into the higher education community is not a matter of meeting quotas; it is a real imperative! If students from diverse backgrounds are not brought into our classrooms in proportionate numbers, we will fail to serve our public. As a result, of course, higher education would be letting many citizens drift into unemployment and homelessness, because they will not have been provided with the education and skills needed to become productive members of the workforce.

To respond to public concerns and priorities, the land-grant system needs a *Plan of Action*. Recommended components of such a plan are:

Develop a marketing plan. Land-grant colleges and universities should expand efforts to market their services. This means first systematically understanding whom the institution does serve as well as whom it shall be serving. Marketing will improve the institution's communications with outsiders as well as better focus on its public mandates and its comparative advantages.

Form focus groups. These should be comprised of groups representative of the public in all its various demographic dimensions. These focus groups would be brought together to debate public issues, determine needs, and set priorities.

Have an independent moderator interview focus group members. What are their primary needs and concerns? What educational services would they like to have available? What are their perceptions of land-grant institutions?

Balance quality with a service-oriented attitude. W. Clement Stone once said, "There is very little difference in people. But that little difference makes a big difference. The little difference is attitude. The big difference is whether it is positive or negative." The public should know that at all land-grant institutions bureaucracy is being reduced, committee meetings minimized, red tape cut.

Focus on customers. Public support derives from those who are served.

Call funerals for outdated programs. The Edsel was an attractive car, nicely designed and roomy. But it had a short life. Many programs in higher academe likewise should fall victim to the sunset law.

Review trends. What do people want and need in educational services? Lifestyles change. For example, more and more people seek to own five-acre "ranchettes" in rural America. Others want to pursue a college degree while fully employed. These two trends alone open opportunities for distance education (Chapter 4).

Study industry trends. How are business firms adapting to customer concerns, issues, and needs? There is an increasing demand for convenience (for example, for fast food and oil changes). How will demographic trends have impacts? People are more concerned with food safety, environmental matters, and other ethical issues.

Develop a plan for improved communication with the public. It would be wise for land-grant institutions to invite more media staff people to visit their campuses. Press, radio, and television representatives should be invited to witness the quality first-hand as a substitute for some of academe's press releases—to stay a few days, attend classes, observe exciting research in progress, use databases and the electronic library, become acquainted with student, faculty, and staff leaders.

To accomplish the various components of this action plan will require engaging the active support of education leaders representing the land-grant college and university system. This may require reprioritization of the schedules of some institutional leaders. But we can affect how we use our time, and giving priority to a plan of action to help bring about renaissance in the land-grant college and university system would be prudent.

The needs and opportunities for land-grant institutions to better serve the public are great. To ignore this call to action would be self-defeating. Former

President John F. Kennedy summarized it well: "There are risks and costs to a program of action, but they are far less than the long-range risks and costs of comfortable inaction."

14.7 Summary

> *No individual has any right to come into the world, and go out of it, without leaving behind him distinct and legitimate reasons for having passed through it.*
>
> **GEORGE WASHINGTON CARVER**

> *I am only one,*
> *But still I am one.*
> *I cannot do everything, but still I can do something;*
> *and because I cannot do everything*
> *I will not refuse to do the something that I can do.*
>
> **EDWARD EVERETT HALE**

As we approach the end of the twentieth century and prepare to enter the twenty-first, higher education faces a number of enduring conflicts and contradictions. Some are basic challenges that must be confronted and resolved by every generation. These include nationalization versus internationalization in higher education; noteworthy merit in academic pursuits versus equality of treatment; preservation of the past versus improvement of the present versus positioning for the future; differentiation of functions among institutions versus their homogenization in a world of mass access; and commitment to ethical conduct in the pursuit and dissemination of knowledge versus exploitation of the process for individual gain.

As land-grant institutions look to the future, they can be proud of their past. But the fact that they have made countless contributions to these people and the other entities they serve is not cause for contentment. Experiences of the past gives reason to conclude, however, that with proper prioritization the land-grant college and university system can make even greater contributions to those it serves in the twenty-first century. Those of us who share the rich land-grant heritage recognize that ours is a sacred trust in which is embedded profound responsibility to future generations.

Nowhere in higher education does expansion of the tripartite mission of teaching, research, and service find a more experienced and receptive hand than in the land-grant college and university system. This system has a special opportunity to connect with a new wave of change. The land-grant university has all the necessary tools to respond to new public agendas. Now, we must summon and incite the public will.

Banana splits rarely fail to fulfill our expectation of something special because of their ingredients. The same may be said of the 1862 and 1890 land-grant institutions. They are comprised of a fruitful complement of academically talented students; well-prepared, assertive, competent faculty professionals who demonstrate a profound service-oriented attitude; and dedicated staff members and administrators determined to provide excellent service to students and the public. As higher education expands its commitment to improving the quality of life in rural and urban America, the nation is fortunate to have a rich resource available through the land-grant institutions—colleges and universities that have the ability, empathy, and willingness to deliver expanded services provided they are funded adequately.

Dreams enable colleges and universities to move to new levels of excellence. The public's dream is that land-grant institutions might better recognize and more completely fulfill public needs. This is both the principal hope and the basic challenge in reclaiming their lost heritage.

Land-grant colleges and universities must march with history. There will be setbacks to sustain and obstacles to overcome. But the destination is clear, the spirits strong. We must continue to advance the knowledge that great causes, commendable ideals, and important issues are at stake, that we are not merely securing our own futures but rather providing fellow travelers reasonable hope for a better world.

The future of our nation will be shaped by economics, demographics, science, global markets, the strength of the human spirit, the values we hold dear, and the ideals we preserve and defend. Institutions of higher education must share in building new common values including a new sense of community, a commitment to participate more assertively and intentionally in society, in advocating belief in a strong work ethic, in providing educational opportunities for rich and poor alike, in personal efficacy and responsibility, in respect for the principles of diversity, fairness, and opportunity.

It can be hoped that all members of the land-grant college and university family will pledge to give greater emphasis to the educational needs and personal interests of students as well as to providing exemplary service to the public, as we prepare for the future. This must be a resolve we make, pursue, and forthwith follow. The challenge is great. And so are members of the world-renowned land-grant institutional family.

The stream of events related to the land-grant college and university system is so enormous and varied and is flowing so rapidly that no single person can be expected to write a prescription for precisely what is needed to best serve the public interest in the short run let alone the long. But the history of the past 130-plus years is extensive enough for us to observe general patterns and draw useful conclusions. Suggestions and recommendations have been made here in the spirit of continual improvement of a highly respected, world-renowned land-grant college and university system. The explicit plea throughout has been to preserve the faith with, while working to make better, the land-grant system that has brought so much to so many over the past thirteen-plus decades. Each generation since the Pilgrims has known its plagues and privations but found the courage and determination to overcome them.

After all, it is important to remember the tepee. Its poles will not stand individually. But when put together, they gain the strength and stability of unity. And this reminds one of the anecdote told of the Native American who called his three sons to his deathbed. He handed an arrow to his eldest son. "Break the arrow in half," he commanded. The son did so with ease, for he was very strong. The father then retrieved a bundle of twenty arrows lashed together and commanded, "Now break these." The son tried but failed. The father then said, "Now you three remember this, strength comes from numbers and from unity. Always stay together, and you will succeed."

The land-grant college and university family is united. If it stays together and effectively communicates with the public it serves and responds to new challenges and opportunities in the years ahead, it can be supported and celebrated throughout the twenty-first century.

A Call to Action

If you have built castles in the air, your work need not be lost; that is where they should be. Now put the foundations under them.

HENRY DAVID THOREAU

A society preserves that which it treasures. Throughout this book, significant successes emanating from the world-renowned land-grant Morrill Acts of 1862 and 1890 have been noted. So have a plethora of contemporary societal challenges and opportunities. I am especially fond of a brief passage by famed American orator William Jennings Bryan: "Destiny is not a matter of chance; it is a matter of choice; it is not a thing to be waited for; it is a thing to be achieved."

The United States of America is known worldwide as a land of immigrants and a land of abundance. Abundance in natural resources, yes. But even more important, a nation blessed with an abundance of ambitious, courageous people. Those with pervasive individualism and a frontier spirit. People who accept challenge and are grateful for new opportunities to improve others' lot in life as well as their own. This spirit is still thriving in the hearts and minds and backs of the people of this great Republic. Now as we prepare to enter the twenty-first century, it is reasonable to expect that the dreams of the American people, coupled with the time-tested land-grant concept, will call on determined citizens to demonstrate once again that ordinary people do extraordinary things for their country and fellow countrymen and -women, thereby reflecting the philosophy of Antoine de Saint-Exupery, who wrote in *The Wisdom of the Sands:* "As for the future, your task is not to foresee, but to enable."

The goals and challenges outlined in this book should be viewed as the beginning of a process of taking charge and reclaiming the lost heritage of land-grant institutions. All individuals and groups who have a stake in this— and this includes virtually every citizen—are encouraged to review and expand upon the goals and objectives presented. Let us agree that a strong, responsive, and responsible land-grant college and university system can be a

259

fundamental component of the continued growth and prosperity of the United States.

Embracing the challenges set forth here will accelerate our nation's movement along a promising pathway toward greater global competitiveness, health, and prosperity. So let us enter into a compact—a Jeffersonian compact—that calls on the best of everyone in an enthusiastic, renewed commitment to reclaim our lost heritage—to revitalize land-grant institutions—and to get and keep in close touch with this nation's citizenry in order to determine how to better serve the various publics to whom these institutions should be accountable and responsible. This would be in keeping with the following words of R. J. Mall:

> The greater the challenge, the more glorious the triumph. What we obtain easily, we esteem lightly. It is conquering the struggle that gives value to the objective sought. Never give up. Think positive. Major additional significant achievements in land-grant colleges and universities, and great happiness and rewards, are in store for determined, resourceful people.

Over the mantle of the dining hall fireplace at Earlham College in Richmond, Indiana, are inscribed the following words: "They gathered the sticks, kindled the fire, and left it burning." With reference to the challenges facing land-grant colleges and universities as they prepare themselves for significant service in the twenty-first century, let us paraphrase these words: *They gathered the land-grant institutional leaders and proponents—those committed to improved service to their various publics—those committed to higher levels of excellence, productivity, and efficiency; they reviewed the needs and opportunities at hand; and they worked together—sharing ideas and fostering a spirit of cooperation among all stakeholders—to improve teaching, research, and public service. And, for these commitments and contributions, they were remembered in history as those whose vision and collective efforts resulted in a better society for all.*

Index

261